Labor's Mind

The Working Class in American History

Editorial Advisors

A list of books in the series appears at the end of this book.

Labor's Mind

A History of Working-Class Intellectual Life

TOBIAS HIGBIE

UNIVERSITY OF ILLINOIS PRESS
Urbana, Chicago, and Springfield

1 2 3 4 5 C P 5 4 3 2 1
This book is printed on acid-free paper.

Library of Congress Cataloging-in-Publication Data
Names: Higbie, Frank Tobias, author.
Title: Labor's mind : a history of working-class intellectual life / Tobias Higbie.
Description: Urbana : University of Illinois Press, [2019] | Series: The working class in American history | Includes bibliographical references and index.
Identifiers: LCCN 2018029189| ISBN 9780252042263 (hardcover : alk. paper) | ISBN 9780252084027 (pbk. : alk. paper)
Subjects: LCSH: Working class—United States—Intellectual life. | Working class—Education—United States. | Labor movement—United States—History—20th century. | United States—Intellectual life—20th century.
Classification: LCC HD8072 .H65 2019 | DDC 305.5/620973—dc23
LC record available at https://lccn.loc.gov/2018029189

E-book ISBN 978-0-252-05109-8

For my children

There are many roads to freedom

Contents

Acknowledgments

The city of Chicago is responsible, in many ways, for this book. Early in my career, I had the great fortune to work at the Newberry Library, where the papers of the Dill Pickle Club, Jack Conroy, and the Charles H. Kerr Publishing Company sparked my curiosity about the city's working-class public sphere—as did the dramatic street protests around the time of the second Gulf War. The result was an exhibition, *Outspoken: Chicago's Free Speech Tradition*, co-curated with Peter Alter of the Chicago Historical Society and assisted by Jennifer Koslow (now at Florida State University) and Ginger Shulick Porcella (now at the Tucson Museum of Contemporary Art). Over the years, others at the Newberry have continued to support the project in various ways, especially Jim Grossman (now at the American Historical Association), Paul Gehle, Martha Briggs, Doug Knox, and Liesl Olsen. The late Franklin Rosemont, radical historian, collector, and publisher, deserves credit for keeping this history of Chicago bohemia alive, maintaining the Kerr Publishing Company, and preserving a rich collection of radical pamphlets and ephemera.

My own engagement with the contemporary labor movement has been another touchstone for this project. The decade-long campaign to win collective bargaining rights for graduate employees at the University of Illinois was my first introduction to social movement education and the beginning of an ongoing conversation about practical democracy among comrades who are now old friends. Later I worked at the University of Illinois Labor Education Program, where I encountered remarkable worker-students in the United Steelworkers of America summer institutes, the International Brotherhood of Electrical Workers apprenticeship school, and in other settings. I especially want to thank my Illinois colleagues Joe Berry, Helena Worthen, Ed Hertenstein, and Bob Bruno. Stories I heard from two veterans of the labor movement didn't make it into the book, but on reflection they inspired much of my research. The late Les Orear, long-time champion of the Illinois Labor History Society, recounted his experiences as a student at the University of Wisconsin, and as an organizer of packinghouse workers during the Great Depression. Ed Sadlowski, former head of the United Steelworkers in Chicago, told me about his youthful love of story magazines and about a worker in the U.S. Steel plant who introduced him to the work of James T. Farrell. Observing firsthand the vibrant program of the UCLA Labor Center and the Institute for Research on Labor and Employment has been another inspiration for this project, and I especially want to thank Kent Wong, Gaspar Rivera Salgado, Janna Shadduck-Hernandez, and Victor Narro for the amazing work they do to keep alive the best traditions of the labor movement.

No scholarly work leaps fully formed from the head of its author. We share drafts and comments and encourage and redirect one another. This is especially so with long-germinating projects like this one. Years after I moved away from Chicago, I was honored to spend a year back at the Newberry as the Lloyd Lewis Fellow in American History. The outstanding collections enriched my story, and I benefited from the support of outstanding librarians and a community of scholars with their noses to the grindstone. The participants in the Newberry's Labor History Seminar provided critical encouragement, especially Leon Fink, Erik Gellman, James Schmidt, Rosemary Feurer, Elliott Gorn, and many others. Among my class of fellows, I especially want to thank Cristina Stanciu, Cathleen Cahill, and Mary Campbell for their detailed comments. Beyond the Newberry, many others read, commented, and urged me to "finish the damn thing," including Elizabeth Faue, Scott Nelson, Kathryn Oberdeck, Cindy Hahamovitch, Nelson Lichtenstein, Adam Nelson, John Rudolph, Tony Michels, Caroline Merithew, Tim Lacy, Steve Meyer, Ron Schatz, and Emily LaBarbera Twarog. My colleagues in Los Angeles, including John Laslett, Jan Reiff, Karen Brodkin, Jennifer Luff, Kelly Lytle-Hernandez, Vinay Lal, Ellen DuBois, Nile Green, Michael Meranze, and Ruth Milkman have provided invaluable support and feedback on this project. Finally, I want to thank Jim and Jenny Barrett for their support, friendship, and good humor for over twenty-five years. Jim's accessible scholarship and his dedication to his students continue to inspire me. I also want to thank two anonymous readers from the University of Illinois Press for invaluable feedback drafts of the manuscript.

This project has been generously supported by a number of institutions, including the Newberry Library, the University of Illinois Institute for Labor and Industrial Relations, the Iowa State Historical Society, the University of California Labor and Employment Research Fund, the UCLA Institute for Research on Labor and Employment, UCLA History Department, UCLA Academic Senate, and UCLA Center for Digital Humanities. I also want to thank the many archives I visited and their dedicated staff members, including the Walter P. Reuther Library at Wayne State University; the Southern California Library; the Tamiment Library; the Wisconsin State Historical Society; the Labor Archives and Research Center at San Francisco State University; and university archives at the University of Wisconsin, the University of Illinois, the University of Michigan, and the University of California at Berkeley and Los Angeles. Without the long-term investment in these publicly accessible collections, no work of history would be possible. Portions of chapters 1 and 2 originally appeared as "Unschooled but Not Uneducated: Print, Public Speaking, and the Networks of Informal Working-Class Education, 1900–1940," in Adam R. Nelson and John L. Rudolph, eds., *Education and the Culture of Print in Modern America* (Madison: University of Wisconsin Press, 2010). Readers of the journal *Labor* will recognize chapter 5 as a revised version of "Why Do Robots Rebel? The Labor History of a Cultural Icon," *Labor: Studies in Working Class History of the Americas* 10 (Spring 2013). I thank the editors and publishers of these pieces for their permission to build on my earlier works. I also want to thank the small army of editors and library and production staff that helped assemble the final product. At the Newberry, John Powell helped me with images. At the University of Illinois Press, James Engelhardt, Laurie Matheson, and the production staff helped me get over the finish line. Pauline Lewis from UCLA provided invaluable research and editing support for the final product.

When a project is so long in development, births, deaths, and everything in between are the unseen companions of an author's words. My parents, Peter and Frances Higbie, both passed away in the years this book germinated, as did my mother-in-law, Sharon Gaffney. We miss them every day. My children were born near the beginning of this project and now are beginning their run as teenagers. They would like me to write something of interest to them now, preferably fiction. We will see about that. Through it all, my lifelong companion, Loretta Gaffney, has cheered me on to the finish line. Together, we are spanning time.

Introduction

In the depths of the Great Depression, a youthful Ralph Ellison had an unexpected encounter with intelligence and high culture that stuck with him for decades. The recent college graduate and future novelist was supporting his budding literary career on the staff of the New York Writers Project and dabbling in progressive politics. Canvassing Harlem tenement buildings with a petition for some long-forgotten cause, Ellison knocked on each apartment door asking for signatures. As he stood at the door of a basement apartment, he heard the voices of men arguing in accents he thought marked them as unschooled African American migrants from the rural South. Behind the door, "a mystery was unfolding," Ellison remembered, "a mystery so incongruous, outrageous, and surreal that it struck me as a threat to my sense of rational order." The men, cursing and shouting, "were locked in verbal combat over which of two celebrated Metropolitan Opera divas was the superior soprano!"[1]

Gathering his courage, Ellison knocked and then entered a scene fit for a proletarian novel. "In a small, rank-smelling, lamp-lit room, four huge black men sat sprawled around a circular dining-room table, looking toward me with undisguised hostility," he wrote. "The sooty-chimneyed lamp glowed in the center of the bare oak table, casting its yellow light upon four water tumblers and a half-empty pint of whiskey." Leaning against the fireplace were four huge shovels, indicating that the men relaxing at the table had spent their day in one of the nation's worst-paid occupations. One of the men stood and confronted Ellison with words that might have been on the lips of any working person whose home was suddenly breached by a representative of a higher class: "What the hell can we do for *you*?"

Ellison introduced himself and presented his petition. The men dismissed it as pointless but signed anyway as a token of support for their young visitor, a fellow black man who had graduated from college and aspired to a career as a writer. Still baffled by what he had heard, Ellison finally asked, "Where on earth did you gentlemen learn so much about grand opera?" After a round of laughter one man answered, "Hell, son, we learned it down at the Met, that's where. . . . Strip us fellows down and give us some costumes and we make about the finest damn bunch of Egyptians you ever seen. Hell, we been down there wearing leopard skins and carrying spears or waving things like palm leafs and ostrich-tail fans for *years*!"

The laughter that followed dissolved the tension lingering between Ellison and the men, but the social distance remained palpable. In the historical record of industrial America, working people appear predominantly as statistics, frequently as victims, and sometimes as heroes. But working people, especially African American laborers, very rarely appear as aficionados of high culture. Even after forty years, the event was vivid in Ellison's imagination and freighted with meaning. He called it a "hilarious American joke that centered on the incongruities of race, economic status, and culture." The artist, Ellison concluded, must perform with the knowledge that even among these supposedly low audiences, there were those capable of critical understanding. Despite their regional dialect and low station, the coal heavers were not simple rural folk: backward relics out of place in modern New York. Ellison concluded they were "products of both past *and* present; were both coal heavers *and* Met extras; were both workingmen *and* opera buffs."[2] They were fully human and fully modern.

The surprise and sense of cultural dislocation Ralph Ellison felt in that basement apartment reflected the pervasive assumption that workers and intellectuals were not only very different types of people, but also unbridgeable social categories. The champions of proletarian revolution asserted this truism as often as college professors and capitalist newspaper editors. The school of hard knocks was the eternal rival to every university and college. Ironically then, stories of encounters between surprised intellectuals and working people who somehow knew more than was expected of them were common in American letters. The elite New York writer Hutchins Hapgood went to turn-of-the-century Chicago to look for a "human document" of the city's industrial conditions to match those depicted in his study of New York's Jewish Lower East Side, *The Spirit of the Ghetto*, and in his portrait of a criminal life, *The Autobiography of a Thief*. Instead, he found the immigrant labor leader Anton Johannsen, who engaged him in a conversation about Tolstoy, thereby demonstrating his "intellectual vigor, his free, anarchistic habit of mind, and the rough, sweet health of his personality."[3] The two men became friends, and Hapgood was drawn into Johannsen's social scene to a degree he had avoided in his previous ethnographic excursions. "A thousand times," Hapgood wrote of his time among Johannsen and his proletarian friends, "I felt myself to be in the midst of a kind of renaissance of labor."[4]

University of Wisconsin economist Don Lescohier traveled the length of the Great Plains during the summer harvest seasons of 1919, 1920, and 1921, documenting the lives of farmworkers. In one migrant camp he met his intellectual match in the person of an unschooled Irish immigrant named Doyle, who was, Lescohier wrote in his field notes, "one of the brainiest and thoroughly read" workers he had ever met. "I drew him, or rather he drew me, into an economic discussion. This hobo, this bum, this chap *who had never been inside of a school*... knew the classical economists well and quoted readily from Ricardo and Adam Smith." Doyle identified himself as both a Bolshevik and member of the militant Industrial Workers of the World (IWW) and impressed Lescohier with his thorough knowledge of current events. He couldn't agree with Doyle's radical politics, but Lescohier respected his intellect and his commitment to social justice. "The 'Red' is on a higher social level than the unorganized hobo," he concluded.[5]

Another economist, Broadus Mitchell of Johns Hopkins University, might have expected to meet intelligent wage earners when he agreed to teach at the Summer School for Women Workers at Bryn Mawr College in the early 1920s. He and the school's organizer, Hilda Smith, were surprised, however, when students—young women from recently unionized industries—went on strike to demand the African American housecleaning staff be given better living conditions. Among those students may have been Rose Pesotta, who attended the school in 1922. A Ukrainian immigrant, garment worker, and anarchist, she would go on to a long career in the labor movement. Mitchell later said of Pesotta, "Talk with her a few minutes as casually as you may, and strength is poured into you, as when a depleted battery is connected to a generator."[6] Although the gender conventions of the 1940s dictated that Mitchell emphasize Pesotta's emotional intelligence, she knew her Tolstoy as well as or better than many of her male counterparts in the labor movement.

I had my own encounter of this kind in a classroom full of steelworkers back in the summer of 2005. A newly hired assistant professor, I was teaching a class of rank-and-file leaders from steel mills and tire factories in Illinois. While leading my class through an infamous passage of Frederick Taylor's 1911 book, *The Principles of Scientific Management*, I had one of those "aha" moments, a sudden cognitive dissonance that bumped my thinking onto a new, more productive track. Taylor, a factory manager turned management consultant, detailed how he reorganized the work of moving heavy iron "pigs," or ingots, at an iron foundry. His first task was to choose a worker who was eager and compliant, an immigrant laborer he identified only as "Schmidt." Taylor then micromanaged Schmidt's every motion and emotion. He told Schmidt when to work, how to work, and when to rest. Evidently, Schmidt thought Taylor's orders were bizarre, but he considered himself a "first class worker" and did what he was told. By following Taylor's careful plan, Schmidt was able to move forty-seven tons of iron in a day instead of the mere twelve and a half tons he had moved daily before Taylor's intervention. As a reward for this improved efficiency, Taylor increased Schmidt's pay from $1.15 to $1.85 per day.

Having taught this text to undergraduate students several times, I was prepared for my students to identify with Taylor's drive for efficiency and to accept Schmidt's lot uncritically. Perhaps they would object to Taylor's insulting treatment of Schmidt or possibly understand that Schmidt's pride and desire to be considered a "first class worker" made him particularly suitable for Taylor's experiment. I assumed it would take me some time to bring the students to an understanding of the economic inequalities at the heart of Taylor's relationship with Schmidt. Instead, a steelworker in the back row raised his hand and explained with surprising precision that Taylor had extracted a productivity gain of over 250 percent in return for a pay increase of about 60 percent. While I stood mute, the other students nodded in agreement and the rest of my lesson plan went out the window. I listened in as the conversation turned to their own negotiations with foremen on the shop floor and with managers at the bargaining table. It was a humbling lesson for a new professor: my students knew much more than I had assumed. In their own way, they were echoing the coal heaver's reproachful question to Ralph Ellison: "What the hell can we do for *you?*" I began to wonder how often—and with what results—similar interactions had taken place in the past. What I found changed the way I think about the history of industrial society. It also changed how I think about myself as a scholar and a worker in the knowledge factory.

Like a broken record, American intellectuals have been discovering the wisdom of working people for more than a century. This leitmotif of our industrial culture does some interesting work, marking separate spheres of mind as unbridgeable, but somehow beside the point. Intellectuals and workers are two very different types, we are reminded, but the homespun intelligence of the unschooled works to balance the cultural asymmetry. The two sides can go their separate ways in peace. *Labor's Mind* flips this script, finding the imagined divide between workers and intellectuals both tragically real and frequently crossed. At the center of the story are working people with little formal schooling who deployed ideas with vigor and creativity. In this social history of reading, writing, and teaching we can glimpse the conditions that make democratic intellectual life possible, and why those conditions have been so difficult to obtain.

When Ellison encountered his operatic coal heavers, American society was on the cusp of a new way of thinking about literacy, education, and the intellectual capacities of working people. At the turn of the twentieth century, almost nine in ten Americans could read and write, according to the U.S. Census. Of course, literacy was not spread evenly across the nation. Literacy rates among foreign-born workers in the early twentieth century ranged from a low of 48 percent among Portuguese to a high of 99 percent among Swedes. Ninety-six percent of Irish immigrants could read. In 1900 just a little over half of the black population could read and write—the legacy of slavery, segregated schooling, and poverty. By World War II, however, nearly 90 percent of African Americans were literate. These changes reflect a dramatic expansion of public schooling between 1900 and 1940, including a twelvefold increase in high school attendance. Even so, at the start of World War II nearly 60 percent of Americans age twenty-five years or older had an eighth-grade education or less. This percentage was even greater among foreign-born whites and African Americans of this age, with roughly 80 percent of those populations having eight years or less of formal schooling. Only 14 percent of the working-age population had completed four years of high school. For working people who came of age between 1900 and 1940, higher education was a rare privilege indeed. It was typical for working-class kids to leave school by age fifteen, and even as high school attendance rates climbed steadily in the 1920s and 1930s, many of these students mixed school and work as family finances dictated. Higher education lay just beyond the realm of possibility for many smart, ambitious working people, who today would attend college without a second thought.[7]

Massive government investment in education after World War II reversed these figures within three decades. By 1970 more than half of Americans twenty-five and older had finished high school, and another 20 percent had at least some college experience. The portion with an eighth-grade education or less was under one-third. In the course of one lifetime, formal secondary education became a normal experience for young people in the United States. By the turn of the twenty-first century, the United States had become a country of brain workers—at least by the standards of the previous century. Fewer than one in ten Americans age twenty-five or older had no high school experience in 2000. More than 80 percent had completed four years of high school, and more than half had some college experience.[8] Radically transforming the relationship between class and formal knowledge, the expansion of public education democratized many aspects of American culture and enabled new forms of capitalism. As a professor in a public university founded in 1919, I owe my livelihood to this historic transformation.

In a curious twist of history, the celebration of practical experience and the reach of book learning increased in tandem over the course of the early twentieth century. Some of the best-known figures in American history lacked formal schooling. Honest Abe Lincoln, rail splitter and future U.S. president, famously educated himself by reading by firelight after long days of physical labor on his frontier farm. The abolitionist Frederick Douglass, first introduced to reading by the wife of his slave master, secretly honed his skills before fleeing the South. The steel magnate Andrew Carnegie went to work in a mill at the age of thirteen, long before he endowed thousands of local public libraries. Even Henry Ford and Thomas Edison had only the bare minimum of formal education before they launched their legendary careers. Like these famous businessmen, prominent leaders of the labor movement were proudly self-educated. Terence V. Powderly, leader of the largest labor organization of the 1880s, the Knights of Labor, was the eleventh of twelve children born into a poor Irish Catholic family in 1849. He went to work at age thirteen after a few years of unmemorable schooling in the basement of a church. Samuel Gompers, the long-serving leader of the American Federation of Labor (AFL) from 1882 until his death in 1924, went to work at age ten with only a few years of formal education.[9]

For every life lifted into fame, thousands more carried on striving in relative anonymity. Iconic stories of self-improvement encouraged them, but a nagging question faced those who failed to live up to the promise of American meritocracy. Were those who failed simply not smart enough? One individual's failure to live up to the American story of the self-made man was tragic but personal; however, an entire class or race failing to advance posed different questions. Progressives pointed to vast disparities of wealth as the cause of America's troubles and celebrated the contributions of immigrants to a "Trans-National America," as the writer Randolph Bourne did in 1916. Less charitable voices were louder and often more popular. A 1922 best seller by a Harvard-trained historian, for instance, insisted that immigrant workers were racially "unadaptable, inferior, and degenerate elements" who would eventually drag "civilized society" down to their own level.[10] No less a champion of the common man than Henry Ford thought much the same of his factory workers, whether immigrant or not. "Many want to earn a living without thinking," he wrote in 1926, "and for these men a task which demands no brains is a boon." In a similar vein, Frederick Taylor summarized the method of so-called scientific management as a process of so minutely specifying work tasks that "it would be possible to train an intelligent gorilla" to be more efficient than women and men.[11]

Managers and conservative ideologues were not alone in believing that factory work made people less than fully human. Working-class characters in literature and film often found themselves subsumed, or consumed, by the machinery of production. As Upton Sinclair said of the working-class antihero of his 1937 novel, *The Flivver King: A Story of Ford-America*, "So Abner Shutt became a cog in a machine which had been conceived in the brain of Henry Ford . . . and this was something which suited Abner perfectly. His powers of thinking were limited, and those he possessed had never been trained."[12] In the film *Modern Times* (1936), Charlie Chaplin's Little Tramp character is driven to distraction by the repetitive tasks of the assembly line and dragged into the gears of the factory. Unlike so many real-life workers who lost life and limb to industrial accidents, the machine spits Chaplin out physically whole but mentally deranged. The insubordination and uncontrolled libido that manifest after his trip inside the machine drew laughs in part because it lampooned common assumptions about mass production workers. Horace Kallen, a defender of immigrant culture and confidant of progressive labor leaders, blamed the assembly line for the "strange psychoses of industrial society, the crazes, tempers, [and] unrests which its critics dwell on and assign to decay." The reason was a kind of human mechanization. "The machine-tender is integrated with the machine," Kallen wrote in 1925. "His operations are part and parcel of the automatized activities of the machine process."[13] With such words written by an ally of the labor movement, it is hardly surprising that many in the middle and upper classes doubted working people's fitness for citizenship in a modern society. White or black, immigrant or native born, if the assembly line turned workers into virtual machines, or working people could be replaced with "intelligent gorillas," then they would remain permanent outsiders to the body politic.

Taylor's condescending assessment of workers' mental capacities notwithstanding, the first decades of the twentieth century witnessed a worldwide fascination with the question "What's on the worker's mind?" Like the book of that title by management consultant Whiting Williams, much of this interest stemmed from the actions of workers, especially the wave of mass strikes by immigrant factory workers that rose to a crescendo between 1916 and 1922. American observers were mystified by seemingly spontaneous and leaderless strikes of textile and garment workers in the East, meatpackers and steelworkers in the Midwest, and even among the transients who took seasonal railroad, timber, and agricultural jobs in the far-flung West. Europe experienced its own version of this strike wave, culminating in the mass desertion of the Russian army that brought the downfall of the tsar in 1917. The Czech playwright Karel Čapek memorialized the phenomenon in his 1920 play, *R.U.R. (Rossum's Universal Robots)*, imagining workers as a class of automatons who rise up and slaughter their human masters.[14]

This was also an era in which so-called brain work proliferated as bureaucracies in business, education, government, and civil society generated a greater demand for those who could write, figure, and manage flows of information and people. Understanding and managing working-class rebellion became the full-time job of a growing class of researchers, journalists, and organizers. In a variety of ways that seem muddled and contradictory with the wisdom of history, these brain workers struggled to reconcile the era's Tayloristic cultural logic with ample evidence that working-class people had minds of their own. One influential line of interpretation asserted that radical intellectuals were the guiding hand behind the proletarian upsurge. How else to explain the spectacle of untutored laborers quoting Marx and Engels? This was not far from Lenin's assertion that workers were not, on the whole, ready for communism and would need to be led by the vanguard party. Both perspectives accepted Taylor's basic framework: modern efficiency demanded a clear divide between brain work and hand work. Mainstream progressives in the United States rejected these extremes but also understood working-class and immigrant lifeways to be bordering on pathological. Education would lift workers up and discipline their minds in ways that would support democratic participation. Theirs was a modified Taylorism in which workers became raw material passing through a process planned and directed by elites. A smaller group of progressives and radicals, who appear frequently in this book, aimed to cultivate the capacity of working people to develop their own minds and organize their own educational, industrial, and political agendas.

The relationship between this latter group of activists and the working class at large was a subject of contentious debate reflecting different views about the authenticity of working-class radicalism. Commentary on the labor movement, whether scholarly or popular, frequently aimed to distinguish organic expressions of working-class sentiment from those derived from some external influence. Selig Perlman, a former revolutionary who fled Russia and became a professor at the University of Wisconsin, had little patience for radical intellectuals who hoped to steer workers to the left. They were, he wrote, typically unable "to withstand an onrush of overpowering social mysticism" because they imagined the working class as "a 'mass' driven by a 'force' toward a glorious 'ultimate social goal.'" In contrast, Perlman celebrated trade unionists associated with the AFL as the "organic groups" among the workers. Their defining intellectual feature was their practicality: they always "keep in sight the concrete individual, with his very tangible individual interests and aspirations," even as they "enforce, upon their individual members, collectively framed rules" in the form of trade standards.[15]

Despite Perlman's dismissive opinion of the radical left, they, too, identified a split between "organic" working-class thought and that of formally trained intellectuals and sought to ground their work in the particular grievances of individual workers. Radicals often found evidence of class sentiment in the most mundane of workers' experiences and sought to cultivate it. As a manual for "worker correspondents" to the radical press put it, the average worker "is not inarticulate because of lack of words, but because he has been taught by capitalism to look upon the thousand and one tyrannies, inconveniences and hardships inflicted on the workers as of little importance." These everyday indignities—workplace accidents, layoffs, abusive foremen—mattered to individual workers because they structured life's possibilities. Worker correspondents would write about these grievances and connect them to a broader pattern. While this advice came from the communist editor William Dunne, himself the child of immigrant workers, who was forced to drop out of college for financial reasons, the sentiment was shared by many labor partisans across the ideological spectrum. Along with the Marxist left, religious leaders known as labor priests, immigrant journalists, and even progressive settlement house workers shared to some degree the desire to cultivate working-class voices. They sought out and developed "organic intellectuals," to use a phrase that was not known at the time.[16]

In the following chapters, I explore the social world of working-class reading and learning alongside debates in text and image over workers' intellectual capacities. Part I probes a set of paradoxes at the heart of working-class intellectual life in the United States during the early twentieth century. First, although limited in their access to formal schooling beyond the eighth grade, the vast majority of urban working people could read, write, and count. In fact, one could hardly navigate daily life in American cities without basic literacy, much less thrive in the modernizing economy. Noisy and cluttered streets were awash in words and numbers: addresses, price tags, paychecks, discarded newspapers, and advertisements. Decoding this stream of information was key to finding a job and a place to live, noticing whether you had been short-changed by a merchant or employer, avoiding violence at the hands of a rival community, or momentarily escaping everyday boredom through the pages of a novel. Useful and necessary for survival in the industrial city, reading also opened for working-class readers social worlds beyond the everyday. The excitement generated by encountering these new worlds drove many working people on to more reading and more questions. By the early twentieth century, the curious could find what they were looking for in well-stocked public libraries, programs of public lectures, and in the pages of newspapers written in many languages.

I refer to this process as "self-education" and to the participants as "self-taught," but it is important to use these terms with some caution. Although most of their learning took place outside of traditional schools, the so-called self-taught were not solitary hermits.[17] They were deeply entwined in networks of other learners, communities, organizational cultures, and markets for books, newspapers, and pamphlets. Text—and the ideas it transmitted—created, strengthened, and in some cases splintered communities. The drive of coal miners, garment workers, and housemaids toward self-education signaled both their desire for the intellectual fruits of modernity and the great economic and cultural changes that would be required to fulfill those desires. Pamphlets, newspapers, study groups, and street speakers amplified and circulated a vast and contentious dialogue about inequality to audiences that were fragmented by race, sex, skill, nationality, and location. The ethical traditions of progressive Christianity and Judaism motivated and shaped the ideas of many who were active in popular education; however, questions of inequality here on earth were paramount.[18] Many others rejected religious traditions in favor of various forms of radicalism. Struggling trade unions, radical political groups, advocates of equality for immigrants, women, and African Americans—the labor movement broadly defined—were key components of this working-class public sphere.

As I sat in libraries and archives, paging through the newspapers, magazines, and books that circulated through workers' reading groups, union halls, and open forums, I was struck by the pervasive use of drawings, cartoons, and, to a lesser extent, photography. Even crude mimeographed pamphlets often include a cartoon or an illustrated masthead. When you view hundreds of these images, you begin to see patterns, motifs, and echoes suggesting ideas about knowledge, power, and social order. Along with these pictures, texts also create images in our minds, and together these both reflect and structure our expectations about how the world operates and our relationships with others—what the philosopher Charles Taylor identifies as a "social imaginary."[19] The chapters in part II explore this social imaginary through the politics of movement storytelling and the iconography of workers' education. Stories and images structured Americans' expectations about workers and their intellectual horizons. What did intelligence look like, and could people readily imagine working people of all kinds as having intelligence, however they might understand the term? Another key question for labor and radical movements was exactly how individuals became committed to working for fundamental social change. Conversion stories in the labor and radical movements secularized the tradition of inspirational storytelling rooted in American Christianity, but movement storytellers also confronted a changing cultural terrain in the 1920s. Influenced by social science and literary modernism, social movement storytellers between the world wars consistently emphasized lived experience over book learning. In the process, they "modernized" the very concept of working-class experience as the arbiter of authentic understanding and identity.[20]

The educational landscape of the United States has changed radically over the past sixty years as formal education became commonplace, even for those of modest means. The way we talk about intellectuals and ordinary people, however, is much the same as it was in the early twentieth century. For many in the media, the 2016 presidential election ratified the divide between the cool and distant intellectuals and technocrats associated with Hillary Clinton and the ordinary folks who voted on "gut instinct" for the "blue-collar billionaire," Donald Trump. Drawing on hollowed-out social categories inherited from our industrial past, these assertions barely withstand a gentle encounter with reality. Still, they echo through mass and social media. Today relatively few Americans work in the kinds of industrial settings that were common in the early twentieth century, and an unprecedented proportion of wage earners have college degrees. There are more than twice as many graduate teaching assistants as coal miners working today in the United States. About 2.5 million registered nurses care for sick and injured in hospitals and clinics, while only about 160,000 workers staff the much-diminished automobile assembly lines.[21] Despite these changes, the idea that workers and thinkers are distinct kinds of people with opposing interests remains potent in popular culture and politics. Returning to the moments in the early twentieth century when activists, educators, and artists struggled to balance the competing claims of laboring status and formal education, I hope this book will help readers to understand the past and to embrace more productive ways of thinking about social movements and popular education in the present.

PART I

Reading the Marks of Capital

In the closing months of 1922, cartoonist Art Young lampooned the intellectual class with his typically sharp visual wit. The veteran socialist depicted a scrawny, bespectacled "UN ORGANIZED BRAIN WORKER" facing off with a beefy "ORGANIZED MANUAL WORKER." The word "STRIKE" floated behind them, invoking the unprecedented labor strife of the early 1920s. "Bo, you may have more brains than I've got," the laborer tells the intellectual, "but you don't know how to use them."

The image carries two key ideas that remain with us today. First, it presents education as the great divide. The campus and the factory are distinct; professors and the people are two opposing camps in modern society. Second, for all of their mental acuity, intellectuals are impractical, ineffective, and weak. Their knowledge has been gathered in isolation and is of little use to ordinary folk. In contrast, laborers have learned their most important lessons in the "school of hard knocks" and possess a clarity of purpose driven by bitter experience. Young's cartoon was the visual equivalent of a saying attributed to the radical trade unionist Big Bill Haywood: "I don't know much about Marx's *Capital*, but I've got the marks of capital all over me."[1]

An ironic commentary on the presumptions of elite knowledge, Young's image also asserted the cultural value of working-class masculinity and embodied knowledge. But there was something more. In its time, the cartoon face-off portrayed the very real interactions between college-educated and unschooled intellectuals. In the decades before World War II, exchanges like these were common in the vibrant world of urban open

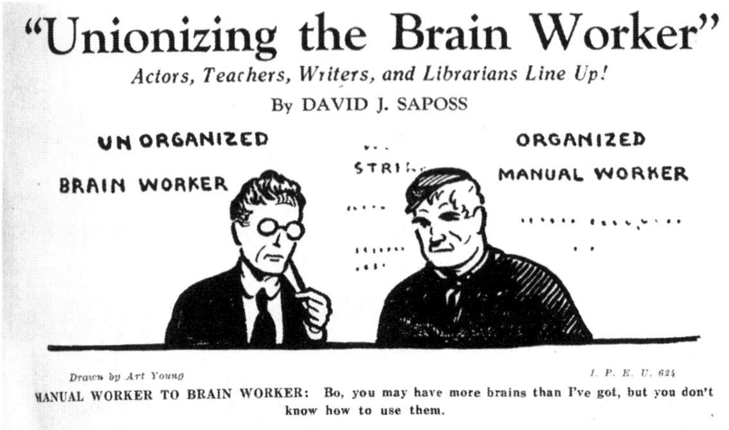

Art Young's 1922 cartoon suggested the gulf between white-collar and blue-collar workers while lampooning so-called brain workers' sense of superiority. Young studied art in Chicago, New York, and Paris and was one of the most widely published radical cartoonists of the early twentieth century. *Labor Age*, December 1922, 1.

forums, settlement houses, and labor colleges designed to train working-class activists. More than a few American social scientists faced critiques like this from workers they studied and whose lives they translated into academic articles, government reports, and sometimes popular books. Real or imagined, interactions like the one portrayed in Young's cartoon sparked debates about the comparative value of experience versus book learning, the line between education and propagandizing, and the nature of authentic social movement leadership.

The first three chapters of *Labor's Mind* explore the social and institutional contexts in which formally trained intellectuals encountered their working-class counterparts. Chapter 1 interrogates the notion of "self-education" through an ethnography of working-class knowledge gained through experience and reading. Despite the pervasive invocation of the "school of hard knocks" as the origin of practical knowledge, I show how many working people found their way to reading and drew inspiration from the printed word. Most working people in the United States were literate, and after the turn of the twentieth century the market for inexpensive texts blossomed. Political radicals and progressives took advantage of new printing technologies to market magazines and books aimed at self-educating workers and farmers in English and a variety of immigrant languages. The socialist *Appeal to Reason* and the Little Blue Books from the Haldeman-Julius Publishing

Company were just two examples of the profitable strategy of embedding marketing within social movement networks.

Like Art Young's unorganized brain worker, professors who encountered working-class intellectuals often found them surprisingly well informed, if sometimes dogmatic in their politics. The radical unionist and future Communist Party leader William Z. Foster was mainly self-educated after a few years of primary school. When he lectured the students of labor economist John R. Commons at the University of Wisconsin, however, he gave what the eminent professor considered "the most scholarly account I have heard of the evolution of Communist doctrine." As historian Timothy Lacy recounts, the Great Books advocate Mortimer Adler led a series of classes at the People's Institute at New York's Cooper Union, where he found his working-class students to be receptive to the works of Shakespeare, Descartes, and other classics. Some were "as good as my Columbia groups," Adler reported, although they were also "intellectually untrained" and "full of prejudices and 'ideas.'"[2] The line between "intellectual" and "worker" became increasingly blurry in these contexts and ever more in need of policing.

Just as readers were never in isolation, authors' words rarely stayed on the printed page. On street corners, in public parks, and in lecture halls in most North American cities, speakers repeated and amplified the printed word. Radicals of every stripe joined preachers, transient salesmen, and assorted entertainers in these raucous public venues. If speakers were not always selling revolution, they nevertheless learned to modulate their pitch to appeal to their overwhelmingly working-class audiences. In this way, the concerns, doubts, and ambitions of workers indelibly stamped the urban public sphere. Chapter 2 explores this world of urban open forums, especially those of the Midwestern industrial metropolis of Chicago. Situated at the crossroads of the nation's vast rail network, Chicago was home to a militant working-class movement eager to hear (and sometime pay for) the words of visiting radicals. Supplementing the outdoor forums, cultural entrepreneurs launched a variety of venues, including the famed Dill Pickle Club, the brainchild of Jack Jones and Ben Reitman. Like other bohemian clubs, the Dill Pickle was an intercultural site that drew audiences with an open appeal to taboo subjects, especially sex and radicalism.

Chapter 3 moves from the everyday intellectual practices of working-class urbanites and the colorful world of the open forums to an exploration of formal programs of "workers' education." Building on experiments in the socialist and women's reform movements, workers' education grew rapidly in the early 1920s. After a string of painful defeats for trade unions from 1921 to 1925, workers' education remained a viable movement practice in part because it took place away from the workplace. Innovative programs, such as those developed at the Brookwood Labor College, seeded a new generation of activists trained and waiting in place as the Congress of Industrial Organizations (CIO) arrived to transform American industries in the late 1930s.

After 1945, universities and unions grew in ways that obscured the pervasive intersections between learning and labor in the prewar years. Postwar universities became sprawling physical plants and bureaucracies as much as they were centers of intellectual encounter. The children of working-class families, who entered higher education in large numbers after the war, did so as students only. University administrators, faculty, and many students assumed that working people would rise out of their class rather than with it. Even if workers were reading, writing, giving speeches, teaching classes, and carrying out research—quintessential scholarly practices—few university-based scholars understood these activities to be legitimately intellectual when done outside of universities. At the same time, the largest industrial unions developed their own education departments that more rigorously aligned curriculum with the institutional goals of their parent unions. This change was not bad in itself; many workers faced with the task of building their new unions clamored for nuts-and-bolts programs. But the change betrayed a fundamental shift in labor's strategic thinking. The workers' education movement of the 1920s and 1930s had also taught practical skills such as parliamentary procedure, managing union treasuries, and labor journalism. Earlier efforts, however, had paired practical skills with broader goals and strategies for seeking power. It was commonplace before the 1940s to see the "labor movement" as a variegated social and organizational network. Worker-students learned to organize their own ethnic, gender, and occupational communities, along with their cooperative enterprises and political associations. Once they had organized these primary groups, they could more effectively act in solidarity with other groups of workers. However, the stability and power of the labor movement after 1945 made this coalitional approach seem less necessary. Individual unions could go it alone, and their educational programs tended to follow suit.

1

"A little avenue to self-mastery"

The Social World of Working-Class Readers

Ed Falkowski felt a pang of remorse as he walked to work at a Pennsylvania coal mine in the fall of 1916, two weeks shy of his fifteenth birthday. Months earlier, in a detailed "self-analysis," the grandson of Polish immigrants had confidently declared himself to be well educated and ready for work. He enjoyed reading books of science, he explained in the neat cursive of a public school student, and "the best novels," including those of Dumas, Hugo, Tolstoy, Poe, and the Polish author Henryk Sienkiewicz. He knew that work was the more practical and manly path, but he felt his resolve weakening as he parted ways with his former schoolmates and, like his father and grandfather before him, went to work in the local mine. As he wrote in his diary that night, "I felt kind of queer today because I missed school. However, the greatest education a young man can get is that gotten by earning his own living, so I see I am attending the High School of Life, and not that of Shenandoah, Pa. And more—a graduate of the H[igh] S[chool] of Life is much more respected than a graduate of H[igh] S[chool] of Shen[andoah]. I am satisfied as far as that part is concerned."[1]

Falkowski's enthusiasm for what he called "industrial education" did not survive its encounter with the monotony and danger of coal-mining work. Reading and fellowship with other readers became a precarious refuge from the darkness—literal and psychological—of his underground labor. He carried books down into the mine to read on his breaks and at night struggled through dense volumes with a dictionary close at hand. On days off he hiked into the hills with friends. They spent hours telling jokes, reading aloud from their favorite books, and holding impromptu debates. Over the next few years, Falkowski and his friends launched a chapter of the Young People's Socialist League, put on plays, and edited a literary journal in their little town. Falkowski nurtured "lofty dreams of literary success," filling journals with handwritten poems, stories, and essays. The final pages and back covers of each volume were filled with long lists of books he had read, "rescued from the slumbers of second-hand bookstalls, borrowed from public libraries, or paid for with sweaty dollars."[2] He sent some writing off to Frank Harris, editor of *Pearson's Magazine*, who wrote back admonishing him not to romanticize the life of a writer. Chastened by his hero's words, Falkowski kept most of this writing to himself. "Would these studies open a little avenue to self-mastery?" he worried in a particularly dark journal entry. "Or would the torrential burdens of each succeeding day wash away the effects of the evening's devotion to my studies?"[3] His plans to finish high school and go to college proved elusive, but ten years after he first went into the mines, his union sponsored him for a two-year term at Brookwood Labor College. There he learned from leading labor intellectuals and forged lifelong friendships with workers from all over the United States. The wide world seemed to spread out before him once more.

The lessons of book learning and everyday life were never as far apart as many would insist. Advances in printing technology, repeated waves of social movement organizing, and the savvy marketing of publishing entrepreneurs combined to place text before the eyes, and minds, of working people. Whether the topic was sports, romance, or revolution, printed texts became the occasion for conversations, and conversations led people to read texts. The cycle of text and talk helped people frame their own experiences. Nevertheless, what Falkowski called the "High School of Life" was jam-packed with lessons for working people. In the streets and on the job they learned about race, gender, and the power of bosses and how each of these discrete factors came together in real-time situations. Coming of age in a society increasingly mediated by commercial images, sounds, and text, many Americans learned that their own experiences could be put to use if they were packaged in just the right ways. When asked how they became conscious of the social and economic world around them, working-class activists often left out the books. As one prominent trade unionist insisted, his radicalism sprang "not from what I read, because I was active in radical circles long before I could read. It came from what I lived."[4]

The "little avenue to self-mastery" that Falkowski sought in reading was a path that many workingwomen and workingmen took in the years before attending high school or college became commonplace. Like Falkowski, Jack Conroy grew up in a Missouri coal camp. He lost his father to a mining accident, but his mother nurtured literary aspirations while she attended to unending rounds of household chores, and Jack memorized the romantic poetry and stories that were her favorites. He edited a "camp paper" of comic strips and sporting news before going off to work for the railroad and later became a leading figure in regionalist proletarian fiction as the editor of the journal *Anvil*. Conroy and Falkowski met in radical circles during the 1930s and corresponded for years, sharing memories of their unlikely intellectual histories.[5] Straddling Victorian and modern approaches to knowledge, the self, and the mind, working-class readers were engaged in a process often referred to as "self-cultivation" and "self-culture." They embraced reading as an effort to capture the "very best" ideas of human society. But their embrace of "civilization" was hardly a ringing endorsement of the culture of their social betters. As the sons and daughters of peasants, farmers, and workers, and as ethnic and racial outsiders, their claims to knowledge challenged the prevailing allocation of brains and brawn.

The High School of Life

In workplaces and homes, on the streets and in the fields, through paid and unpaid labor, working people had to think, craft ideas, and strategize in order to survive. They learned how to work purposefully in order to preserve their strength and to prolong work in order to increase their pay. They learned where to find the least expensive food and clothing, how to sew and mend, how to build their own homes, and how to harvest delicate crops without a bruise. What workers encountered on the streets shaped their perception of the social order and their place in it. As historian David Montgomery wrote, workers' daily encounters with class distinctions visible in modern urban life convinced many that "workers' only hope of securing what they wanted in life was through concerted action." In the best of circumstances they could listen to the wisdom of those who had come before them and offer advice to newcomers. But knowledge did not always bring unity. Working people also learned how to understand, and act upon, divisions of race, ethnicity, and gender.[6]

Industrial managers inflicted the marks of capital with growing sophistication during the early twentieth century, but working people found ways to fight back by drawing on both experience and book learning. Social scientists of the era described a guerilla struggle between workers and their supervisors over the motion of workers' bodies, the scale and timing of wages, and the question of who would be laid off first as work became slack. Managers had their stopwatches, slide rules, and clipboards. Workers' knowledge was lodged in their bodies, their memories, and their social networks. The sheet metal worker Ben Reisman, a Jewish immigrant from eastern Poland, recounted one way that skill and experience gave workers a certain amount of leeway if they were wise enough to take it. Reisman noticed that the bosses announced large rush orders to see how quickly workers could fill them. Afterward, they introduced new piece rates based on the rushed pace, which translated into more work for less pay. So when a rush order came, Reisman was sure to "work very slowly, but in such a way that it not draw any attention." Skillfully pretending to work quickly, he preserved a tolerable pace of work and an adequate income.[7]

Management consultants such as Frederick Taylor and Frank Gilbreth reorganized production to eliminate the power of workers like Ben Reisman, but instead of destroying workers' ability to subvert the tempo of production, they splintered it into the hands of hundreds of machine operators. And while these supposedly unskilled operators remained largely nonunion until the 1940s, they used their fragmented power to claw back time for themselves, to bump up wages, and sometimes just to poke fun at the system. Researcher Stanley Mathewson, working undercover in a factory during the late 1920s, discovered how an experienced punch-press operator could easily foil management's efficiency schemes. When the time-study man approached his work station, one operator made "a very slight alteration in the position of his right thumb" that made his machine jam frequently and lowered his output. When the time-study man went away, the operator went back to flawlessly punching out product.[8] Workers in some plants went so far as to taunt their managers over their ability to restrict production with impunity. Mathewson found the poetry of one machine operator tacked to a factory bulletin board:

HARMONY?

I am working with the feeling
That the company is stealing
Fifty pennies from my pocket every day;
But for every single pennie
They will lose ten times as many
By the speed that I'm producing, I dare say.
For it makes me so disgusted
That my speed shall be adjusted

So that nevermore my brow will drip with sweat;
When they're in an awful hurry
Someone else can worry
Till an increase in my wages do I get.[9]

Just getting a job could be an education in American gender and racial conventions as well as in the value of putting on the right public front to employers and coworkers. Hiring agents in Northern industrial cities, for instance, associated different types of clothing with various lines of laboring work. Newcomers soon learned that they needed a different outfit to be hired out as a railroad worker, a teamster, a lumberjack, or a factory worker. One Russian immigrant learned that American bosses thought she was a Bolshevik because she wore a leather jacket and no makeup. Unable to find a job, she ditched the jacket and "dressed myself in the latest fashion, with lipstick in addition, although it was so hard to use at first that I blushed, felt foolish, and thought myself vulgar. But I got a job."[10] Beyond the factory gates, working people derived "lessons" from all manner of experiences. Stjepan Mesaros recalled that even as a boy of twelve with only a fifth-grade education, he began to understand something of the changes taking place in rural Croatia in the early twentieth century. Although his own village retained traditional communal property rights, a nearby wealthy landowner controlled more than two thousand acres, had the most modern farm machinery, and sold his crops on the export market. In the same years, but on the other side of the world, the young hobo Robert Saunders of Kansas City liked to ride boxcars with the doors open despite being derided as a "scenery bum" by his fellow hoboes. It was the beginning of a lifelong passion for natural science that he would develop through correspondence courses and reading.[11]

The wisdom of experience was a tool but could also be a weapon and a burden. Working people might withhold their knowledge from other workers (newcomers and outsiders especially) out of prejudice, to gain advantage, or just to enjoy a little schadenfreude. Hazing was common, done for both amusement and assessment. As Floyd Dell wrote in his autobiographical novel, *Moon-Calf*, it was the foreman's job to evaluate a new worker's productivity. Workers had different standards. They wanted to know whether a new worker was one of them or "so odd as to be set utterly apart, laughed at behind his back, made the victim of hostile contempt, or, what is worse, shunned and ostracized."[12] Dell passed muster with his coworkers in part because he was another white man. But for those who were "set utterly apart," by virtue of race, gender, or some other status, the knowledge and hostility of coworkers could be put to devastating effect. White workers routinely leveraged their social ties to factory supervisors and union leaders, for instance, to secure good jobs for themselves and to relegate African Americans and new immigrants to the lowest paying and most unpleasant tasks.

The defeats and injustices that were the daily lessons in what Falkowski called the High School of Life could turn working people toward collective action. But workers also learned to keep quiet: to go along and get along, to abandon their dreams as unrealistic, to bow their heads before their social betters, and to stay in their place. Chicagoan Rosella Burke had hoped to finish high school and rise above her working-class roots, but the Great Depression intervened, forcing her to quit school and find a job. "I began to feel chilly inside when I thought of the future," she wrote in a labor college essay. "I knew that once a worker, always a worker."[13] The St. Louis union leader Ernest Calloway said he "grew up hating white people" after witnessing the lynching of a friend in West Virginia. The vision and smell of the crime scene stuck with him like a toxin, limiting his effectiveness as an organizer, he came to believe. "Later I found hatred a waste of time," Calloway concluded. "What you have to deal with are institutions, laws, customs. I have spent 50 years working hatred out of my system."[14]

"My gateway to the world"

Most who claimed to be "self-educated" had some formal schooling, however intermittent or incomplete. They chose the label as a badge of honor in the context of a labor movement that increasingly included formally educated intellectuals.[15] Some of the self-educated grew up on farms and began working as young children. Lewis Evans, leader of the Tobacco Workers International Union, said he "went to work at a tender age" and after eighteen months of formal schooling had "many years in [the] school of hard knocks, with midnight oil, poor light, good books, and a dictionary." For a few, self-education was a statement of dissatisfaction with the conservative curriculum of public schools. Roy Woods, an electrical worker and local workers' education activist from St. Paul, Minnesota, attended a Baptist College, a technical school, and the St. Paul Labor College but considered himself "self-educated in economics and sociology." Among those who identified as "self-educated" were prominent radicals like the German-born Anton Johannsen, a leader of Chicago's woodworkers, and the Russian-born

Pauline Newman, a gifted organizer and leader of the International Ladies Garment Workers Union (ILGWU). Others were well-known conservatives, like the trade union leader John P. Frey, who first went to work at age nine and then "received a little schooling until [the] age of 12."[16]

Whatever amount of schooling they acquired, the self-educated struggled to master text and put it to use. They worked into the night, accompanied by dictionaries and notebooks. They listened to lectures conveying or arguing with the ideas in books, and they talked and talked about ideas until they annoyed their friends and family members. This cycle of text and talk helped to create a public sphere that circulated and amplified ideas about social order and politics. Popular reading, like the American working class generally, was fragmented by race, ethnicity, gender, and ideology. This was true for the topics different workers chose to read as well as the spaces where they did their reading. But the pervasive culture of reading among ordinary people, and the practices and institutions that developed around texts and conversations about texts, created potential for commonality. Through their mutual fascination with ideas, readers might recognize one another across otherwise unbridgeable social divides.

Research on working-class reading patterns in the early twentieth century found mass-circulation magazines and daily newspapers to be the most common reading fare, along with popular adventure and romance novels. Workers read fewer books than middle-class Americans, but they were interested in many of the same topics. For instance, the 1931 American Library Association study *What People Want to Read About* found that workers, farmers, housewives, and teachers all considered topics like "the next war," "self-improvement and happy living," and "laws and legislation" to be the most interesting for reading.[17] Among Milwaukee vocational students, a slim majority of the over three thousand surveyed in 1932 were active users of the public library, usually reading one or two books a month. Milwaukee's young workingmen, like others in the United States, read adventure novels, among them *The Call of the Wild, Treasure Island, Tom Sawyer*, and *All Quiet on the Western Front*. Milwaukee's young women favored their own form of romance and drama, including *Rebecca of Sunnybrook Farm, Little Women*, and *Anne of Green Gables*.[18] Although educators hoped to stimulate book reading (which they called "serious reading"), magazines and newspapers were more popular. The sensational literature of *True Story* and similar story magazines was popular among women and men, as well as *Popular Mechanics* for young men and *Ladies Home Journal* for young women.[19]

Contemporary observers were eager to draw conclusions about what particular texts did to working people and to get the right kinds of books before workers' eyes. But reading had unpredictable results. One labor college student wrote to her former teachers that reading about personal hygiene and physical education helped her avoid ill health, and as a result she was more active in her literary club, and was "appointed editor of our club paper and in that way [I] try to inspire and encourage the value of choosing good books." As Jonathan Rose argues in his study of British autodidacts, escapist literature had its own logic for those trapped in unpleasant neighborhoods and work routines. Working-class memoirists in the United States often noted a similar dynamic. Jewish garment worker Abraham Bisno taught himself to read with inexpensive Yiddish romance stories and newspapers, which, as he recalled in his memoir, "opened my eyes to new worlds." Similarly, as a boy growing up in segregated Mississippi, Richard Wright was transported by the novels of Zane Grey and other popular writers. According to Wright, the stories "enlarged my knowledge of the world more than anything I had encountered so far. To me, with my roundhouse, saloon-door, and river-levee background, they were revolutionary, my gateway to the world."[20] Radicals sometimes decried American workers' weak understanding of Marxist theory, but the socialist author Floyd Dell thought there was "as much truth in the soap-box phrase, 'Labor is the source of all value,' as in the maddening mathematics of Marx." It was Walt Whitman, Dell argued, who wrote the "Socialist's Bible" in his *Leaves of Grass*.[21]

Despite frequent encouragement to read serious books, workers most often read newspapers because they were the most accessible and pervasive form of print in the early twentieth century. On the eve of the First World War there were more than twenty-five hundred daily newspapers in the United States, with a total circulation of more than 28 million.[22] In larger cities, such as New York and Chicago, English-language daily papers competed in part by issuing at different times of the day. Readers cast off their used papers when new editions appeared, creating a great supply of free reading material for the down-and-out, not to mention improvised blankets for those sleeping outdoors. Roughly 90 percent of Milwaukee vocational school students, mainly the children of workers, read newspapers regularly with both men and women who were interested in sports, theater and movies, and crime.[23] In addition to the English-language press, every immigrant group of substantial size had at least one newspaper in its own language. Robert Park's 1922 study, *The Immigrant Press and Its Control*, listed more than thirty language groups with at least one newspaper in New York City alone. In Chicago in 1930 there were twenty-five foreign-language daily newspapers publishing in twelve languages, according to historian Jon Bekken. Beyond the mainstream immigrant press, radicals and labor activists produced a wide array of periodicals ranging from the handwritten "Fist Press" of Finns in Canada to the commercially successful Yiddish-language *Forverts* (Forward).[24] A 1925 directory counted nearly six hundred labor movement periodicals across the United States, including thirty-two socialist papers, twenty-nine communist papers, and fourteen associated with the Industrial Workers of the World.[25]

The simple language of many English-language daily papers that made them accessible to broad audiences also made them a useful resource for immigrants

Clothing workers, on strike, reading newspapers in front of the Art Metal Products Company, Chicago, September 1915. With multiple daily editions, newspapers were the most common reading material for early twentieth-century working people. DN-0065306, *Chicago Daily News* negatives collection, Chicago History Museum.

with limited English language skills. Working as a domestic servant in Michigan, sixteen-year-old Swedish immigrant Mary Anderson learned English by listening to her employers' dinner table conversations and "by reading the morning paper over and over again until finally it occurred to me what the words meant," according to her memoir. Anderson may have been an unusually intelligent domestic servant; she went on to become a union organizer, a Women's Trade Union League activist, and the first director of the Women's Bureau in the U.S. Department of Labor. However, the use of English-language newspapers was common among immigrant workers. For instance, a survey by one New York City Russian-language newspaper found that a quarter of its readers also read English-language papers, many of these readers simply scanning the headlines in English, because "these are easy to understand, and you know all the news."[26]

Newspapers have a deep connection to the formation of nation-states, helping to constitute a shared public sphere and what Benedict Anderson called the "imagined community" of the nation. Immigrant newspapers had a dual role in this respect, supporting a culture of nationhood among groups of immigrants while also crystallizing links between the immigrant community and its new American surroundings. In his study of Polish newspapers in Chicago, for instance, Jon Bekken notes the long-running dispute between Catholic and radical papers, which each claimed to be the voice of Polish culture and viewed the other as a traitor to the Polish people. This debate, and the circulation numbers it stimulated, reflected a growing Polish American reading public.[27] By reading newspapers that were published in the United States but written in their own languages, immigrants reaffirmed their ethnic communal bonds while contributing to the logic of ethnic pluralism that would become a national ideology in the United States during the mid-twentieth century.[28]

In his study of early twentieth-century New York City, Tony Michels places newspapers at the center of a fervent Jewish radicalism that was distinctly American. Yiddish newspapers reported local and European news and were filled with educational articles on science, health, and politics. The socialist *Forverts*, with a circulation of more than two hundred thousand in the 1920s, was the anchor for what Michels calls a "socialist newspaper culture" that included popular dances, excursions, and educational programs promoted by, and promoting, the publication.[29] Although *Forverts* would become one of the most successful left-wing media businesses in the United States, it began as a series of public performances in New York's Rutgers Square during 1897. Completely lacking funds to publish a physical newspaper, the editors gathered donations by hosting "spoken newspapers." Prefiguring similar staged news events that would occur during the New Deal more than three decades later, these performances featured news, editorials, poetry, announcements, and even letters to the editor. According to Michels, "Reading a [Yiddish] newspaper was as much a collective endeavor as an individual one." Many immigrant Jews from Eastern Europe arrived with very limited literacy skills. Few had seen a Yiddish newspaper before arriving in America, and the American papers were written in a local style of Yiddish that was difficult to understand even for some educated readers. As a result, Jewish workers read to each other at home, in public, and in their own self-education societies.[30] The most successful of these, the Arbeter Ring, or Workmen's Circle, grew to be the largest Jewish workers' group in the United States by World War I. Originally organized by rank-and-file socialist workers in New York City, the Arbeter Ring combined education, mutual aid, and recreation, inviting all who were in sympathy with "freedom of thought and aspiration, workers' solidarity, and faithfulness to the interests of their class and its struggle against oppression and exploitation." With thousands of members and a healthy balance sheet, the Arbeter Ring also contributed to many socialist and union-organizing efforts, as well as to left-wing educational initiatives such as the Rand School of Social Science.[31]

For many African Americans contending with the aftermath of slavery and the rise of Jim Crow, literacy implied liberation and personhood. In the pre–Civil War South, reading was taboo for slaves and punishable with violence. As Frederick Douglass's master had warned, teaching the enslaved to read "would forever unfit him to be a slave. He would at once become unmanageable, and of no value to his master."[32] The incomplete work of emancipation and Reconstruction and the advent of the Great Migration stimulated a rich publishing and reading culture among African Americans in both the South and North. As Steven Hahn notes, black Mississippians alone opened nearly 150 newspapers and magazines between 1890 and 1910. In Chicago, Detroit, Cleveland, Pittsburgh, and New York, where African Americans were moving to take jobs in industry, social and literary clubs became sites of discussion about race "uplift," and their members eagerly consumed the newspapers and magazines that spoke to their community's most pressing issues. Working-class autodidacts, like the Caribbean-born Hubert Harrison, became regular contributors to African American news outlets as well as important voices on the race question within the American left and Pan-Africanism.[33] Northern newspapers like the *Chicago Defender* traveled deep into the South bringing news of jobs and the vibrant cultural life of the city, and publications like the NAACP's *Crisis* and the Brotherhood of Sleeping Car Porters' *Messenger* regularly featured book suggestions for readers.[34] As a black trade unionist in Alabama told sociologist Horace Cayton in the 1930s, "Colored people do more reading. They read these different books as the union gives them." This observation was also backed by a white union leader who noted that black members complained right away if they didn't get the copy of the *American Federationist*. The effect was especially profound for those who took on leadership roles in newly created union locals of the 1930s, Cayton found. They maintained the account books and correspondence and grew increasingly assertive on interracial bargaining and grievance committees.[35]

Those American workers who were actively engaged in radical and progressive politics encountered a particularly rich print culture that focused on issues of economic inequality. The Socialist Party, under the leadership of popular trade unionist Eugene V. Debs, was a mass political movement that included moderate reformers (such as those advocating public ownership of water and power) as well as militant industrial unionists and revolutionaries. Trade unionism was also in an upswing during and immediately after the First World War. A booming industrial economy and tentative government support for collective bargaining helped drive union membership above 20 percent of the workforce. Nonconformist and radical ideas circulated freely among precarious workers in North America's far-flung industries, spurred on particularly by the Industrial Workers of the World, a revolutionary union movement founded in Chicago in 1905. Although the IWW, or the "Wobblies" as its members were known, successfully organized wheat harvesters, oil field workers, miners, lumberjacks, and textile workers in the World War I years, they were as much an educational organization as a union. The two weekly English-language newspapers, as well as a number of foreign-language papers either directly affiliated or politically oriented toward the IWW, were full of reports from rank-and-file organizers, commentary on current events, theoretical debates about unionism, and book reviews. Its growth stymied by employer and government repression, the IWW nevertheless influenced the course of unionism by educating thousands of young workers in a practically oriented Marxism that emphasized the power of workers' direct action over politics.[36]

The IWW and the Socialist Party had officially parted ways after 1912, but left-wing socialists remained close to the Wobblies, and in many local struggles the two groups worked together. Radical workers also came together in a variety of anarchist, socialist, and reformist organizations, adding to the effervescent nature of radicalism in American cities during the era. The formation of the Workers (Communist) Party in 1919 heralded the fracturing of this precarious coalition into many warring camps, but connections of sentiment and history remained, especially while admiration for the young Soviet Union was strong in left-wing circles. While factionalism divided the left organizationally, it also stimulated the creation of independent educational and propaganda initiatives available to workers interested in self-education. During the early 1930s, the Communist Party's John Reed Clubs and its network of party-supported schools, bookstores, and publications became important venues for popular education in larger industrial cities. The creative vitality of Communist Party artistic and literary programs has drawn a good deal of scholarly attention, but the Communist Party was rarely the only player on the field. As Michael Denning argues, the Popular Front of the 1930s was the meeting ground of leftists and liberals from a variety of organizational and intellectual positions.[37]

The struggle to build and consolidate trade unions and radical movements supported, and in many ways required, a collective orientation toward texts and reading. Working people came together around labor texts across generations, occupations, ideologies, and to a lesser extent races and ethnicities. Chicago union leader Agnes Nestor treasured an 1881 copy of *History of Labor* that was handed down to her from her father, who had been in the Knights of Labor. She recalled her father frequently reading the book, which also became a resource for their "long talks about labor problems" when she was involved in a strike shortly after joining the workforce at the age of fourteen.[38] New York union leader Rose Schneiderman, who left school after the ninth grade to support her brother and widowed mother, recalled reading aloud to her mother in Yiddish and sharing books with her coworkers.[39] Workplace conversations also frequently centered on what workers were reading. Spanish-speaking cigar makers, for instance, were known to pay one of their coworkers to read aloud from a newspaper or book. Although historian Patricia Cooper doubts that this practice was widespread outside of Cuba and South Florida, she does note that cigar makers had a reputation for political debate and conversation in the shop. As one cigar maker recalled, "They would talk on every subject of the country—what the Congress was doing, everything. . . . They were very well read people."[40] Similarly, tramps and hoboes were said to seek out muckraking literature to employ in heated debates and conversations in lodging houses, work camps, and while traveling in boxcars. As a Chicago bookseller noted, when hoboes could afford to buy books, they would "devour them with keen interest. Hunger seems to quicken the senses, and that may account for their perception in discussing things."[41]

In addition to newspapers and periodicals, early twentieth-century radical publishers produced an array of books and pamphlets aimed at working-class audiences, especially those engaged in self-study. The Charles H. Kerr Publishing Company of Chicago and the weekly newspaper *Appeal to Reason* out of Girard, Kansas, were the most successful of these radical publishers up to World War I, reaching beyond the ranks of the Socialist Party for readership. With popular writers like Eugene Debs and Upton Sinclair, the *Appeal* claimed a peak circulation of 750,000 in 1913. Sales were propelled by thousands of volunteer distributors known as the "Appeal Army," but the newspaper's publisher, Julius Wayland, also developed a thriving mail-order business selling a range of books, not all of them political.[42] Like the *Appeal*, the Kerr Company found its core readers among socialists and the lingering adherents of populism, publishing volumes on social science, literature, and current affairs, including the basic texts of Marxism. Closely associated with left-wing socialism and industrial unionism, Kerr's *International Socialist Review* began as a dry theoretical journal before making the turn toward a wider audience with colorful covers and dramatic articles on union organizing and strikes, often illustrated with photographs taken by rank-and-file activists. World War I and the subsequent "red scare" marked a turning point for left-wing publishing in the United States, helping to create a less explicitly political culture of self-education. In 1918 the postmaster general revoked the first-class mailing privileges of the *International Socialist Review* in response to a series of antiwar articles, leading to the demise of the journal. Factionalism within the left and the costs of legal defense for political prisoners further sapped the company's finances and personnel, and by the 1920s Kerr was a shell of its former self.[43]

Appeal to Reason suffered in a different way from the wartime political climate. In the hands of new editors, the newspaper split with the antiwar position of the Socialist Party, renamed itself the *New Appeal*, and published on a prowar basis. Subscriptions collapsed, allowing one of the editors, Emanuel Haldeman-Julius, to purchase the paper and take it in a new direction. Haldeman-Julius was the self-educated son of an illiterate Russian immigrant bookbinder and the husband of Marcet Haldeman, daughter of a Kansas banker and niece of settlement house reformer Jane Addams. Drawing on the mail order business of the *Appeal*, Haldeman-Julius published a number of different periodicals and book series; his greatest success was the "Little Blue Books," pocket-size, paper-covered volumes that sold for five cents each. An early advertisement in a radical journal emphasized the books' convenient size for surreptitious reading: "Many readers have become so enthused that they make a practice of slipping four or five of these books into a pocket before starting the day's work. They do not bulge the pocket and are not noticeable, yet are always available." Among the nearly one thousand titles in print by 1929 were works of European and American literature and drama (Wilde, Voltaire, Hugo, Emerson, and Poe); popular histories, political tracts, and works of science and religion (including debates on Christianity, introductions to Buddhism, Confucianism, Islam, even a book on yoga); treatises on marriage, sexuality, and birth control; studies of politics, including Tom Paine's *Age of Reason*, various popularizations of socialism and reprints of documents from the German and Russian revolutions; how-to books on gardening, baseball, home ownership, psychoanalysis, hypnosis, and writing one-act plays; and rhyming dictionaries, joke books, and the like. Haldeman-Julius also published brief synopses of various philosophers by Will Durant, which in 1927 were repackaged by Simon and Schuster as *The Story of Philosophy* to great popular acclaim.[44]

For many young workers, reading represented not only a desire for respectability but also a way of achieving it. Many found in self-education a path to less physically taxing work, cleaner living conditions, and higher pay, as well as personal intellectual development. Even radical publishers appealed to workers' desire for the best of culture and linked reading to intellectual independence. For instance, when publishers Albert Boni and Horace Liveright advertised their newly launched Modern Library series in the November 1917 issue of *International Socialist Review*, they appealed to readers' desire to stay on the cutting edge of modern cultural trends. The series included "the best books of recent times in the fields of literature, philosophy, drama, poetry and science," the notice boasted. "The leaders of modern thought have been iconoclasts in their respective fields, and no Socialist can afford to be ignorant of their best expression."[45] Even the classics had lessons for rebels. The Haldeman-Julius Company pushed its edition of Plato's *The Trial and Death of Socrates* as a "valuable book" about state repression of free speech, something that was very much on the minds of socialists during and after World War I.[46]

Commercially successful in their heyday, the Little Blue Books also loomed large in the memories of workers decades later. As Falkowski wrote to his long-time friend Jack Conroy, "The Blue Books were my university curriculum when I worked at the Collieries, for some of the softer jobs I occasionally got enabled me to read a book a day at work—an ideal set-up for the reading and enjoyment of such small lunch-pail editions as came out of Girard, Kansas[,] in those years."[47] When historian Dale Herder placed ads in Michigan newspapers in the early 1970s seeking memories of the Little Blue Books, he received a slew of letters recalling the convenient size of the books—useful for hiding from family members or keeping in pockets and lunch boxes—and their power to debunk political and religious orthodoxy. One self-described "autodidact" wrote, "As a kid . . . I was filled full of religious bunk and dark age superstitions, until it drove me mad. The Little Blue Books brought the first light from out of the darkness for me." A retired railroad worker linked Haldeman-Julius publications to his own political and intellectual awakening in the Socialist Party during the World War I era: "Little Blue Books were my bible, and account, to a great degree, for my education and what I am today, intellectually." A retired office worker recalled reading his older brother's Little Blue Books. "At the age of 13 this exposure to 'Culture' in a Catholic home was a bit jolting," he wrote. "In retrospect, I firmly believe that my brother's supply of Little Blue Books encouraged me to further home study and self-education. Eight years later I 'broke away' from the church—and have never regretted it."[48]

Working people who could maintain a personal library of any size had achieved an important level of financial and personal stability. Given the precarious labor markets of the early twentieth century, which were punctuated by regular bouts of unemployment, many who gathered book collections lost them during hasty moves and periods of homelessness. Others built their libraries in unexpected places, such as lumber camps, as journalist Stewart Holbrook recalled. During the heyday of the IWW, he wrote, "every mail brought a large bundle" of newspapers and pamphlets to the camps. And one could still find in many camps well-thumbed copies of works by Upton Sinclair, Voltaire, and Tom Paine. While the majority killed time with Zane Grey, *Popular Mechanics*, and pornography, Holbrook had found in every camp "at least one man who, all things considered, might well be termed a bibliophile." The cabin of a skilled sawmill worker in British Columbia was crammed with the collected works of Dumas; volumes of Dickens, Brontë, Carlyle, and Darwin; and the *Encyclopedia Britannica*. Whether out of boredom or genuine interest, coworkers in the camp availed themselves of this de facto camp library.[49]

Swedish immigrant John Edwin Peterson, a skilled worker at the Pullman Car Company near Chicago, compiled a library of some three hundred books that his historian grandson later inherited and analyzed. Educated in a Swedish-language parochial school through eighth grade, Peterson went to work at Pullman around 1905. He soon joined the IWW and the Socialist Party and would be a rank-and-file militant in several unionization efforts over the course of his life. His library reflected his organizational attachments and the practical needs of those who lacked formal higher education. Many of his books were multivolume encyclopedias and other reference works. About half of the volumes were nonfiction: current events, social science, history, natural science, and philosophy. Another quarter of the volumes were fiction. The largest number of books dated from his intense engagement with the socialist and IWW movements from 1904 to 1924. With the decline of these movements, particularly the IWW, Peterson's book buying slowed, picking up somewhat in the mid-1930s with the revival of industrial unionism. While Peterson's book buying and his ability to compile a large library was certainly a measure of his participation in the consumer market, it was equally an artifact of his engagement with social movements.[50]

Like John Peterson, the working-class men and women who bought Kerr, Haldeman-Julius, and other radical publications were often on a quest to justify their feeling that all was not right with the world. For instance, Roy S. was a middle-age machinist and a socialist when during the 1930s he began attending Milwaukee's vocational school, where his story was recorded in a student case file. He grew up "in a very poor home without books or magazines" and attended parochial schools where his teachers beat him for asking too many questions. He got a job as a machinist and married, but as he told social workers, "he felt out of place, lost." Looking for answers, he went to the museum, the library, and to lectures and slowly "began to find himself," in the words of his case file. He began reading systematically, first on religion, then economics, politics, and labor issues. Roy S. became a radical and convinced his parents and siblings to follow suit. He was so dedicated to his studies, he chose to remain on relief so that he could attended school five days and two nights a week rather than work.[51]

Many of the self-taught never rose beyond the rank and file and left few records of their engagement with ideas, but some went on to careers in academia, labor, and radical politics. The lives of these exceptional individuals, which are comparatively well documented, help us understand the intellectual possibilities and limits that faced many other ambitious young working people. Sociologist Nels Anderson—the son of a farmer and sometime factory worker—was a migrant worker in his youth and traveled to graduate school at the University of Chicago by hopping a freight train. Labor economist Gordon Watkins, who later became the provost of the University of California, Riverside, worked as a coal miner in his native Wales as a youth, in a machine shop in North Dakota while he attended high school, and as a lumberjack while an undergraduate at the University of Montana.[52] Frank Tannenbaum, who became an influential historian of Latin America, fled his parents' Massachusetts farm for the bohemian life of Greenwich Village, where he worked in restaurants and took night classes at the anarchist Modern School. In the winter of 1913–1914 he led a sit-in of unemployed workers at a Catholic church in New York and landed in jail for a year. Upon his release, he wrote a series of essays on prison conditions for the monthly magazine *The Masses* and shortly after enrolled as a Columbia undergraduate, with his tuition paid by wealthy New York progressives.[53] Similarly, Philip Taft traversed the social divide from laborer to university professor. He grew up in New York City and ran away from home before finishing grade school. He worked as a sailor, a railroad laborer, a grain harvester, a ditchdigger, and a slaughterhouse worker. He joined the IWW before he was fifteen years old and later became an organizer in the wheat belt, writing several articles for the union's national newspaper. In the early 1920s, Taft participated in the legal defense of radicals, finished high school at night, and with the encouragement of progressive lawyers went to the University of Wisconsin. He quickly acquired his undergraduate credentials and then studied under labor economist Selig Perlman, eventually earning a doctorate. By the 1930s he was well known for his scholarly defense of AFL strategic orthodoxy.[54]

These men were the exception, of course. Many more workers who encountered the educational outreach of unions and radicals had no desire for a career in academia. Instead, they sometimes found careers in the labor and radical movements or the state bureaucracies that grew with the New Deal. The experience of Rose Pesotta was typical of Eastern European Jewish immigrants and radicals who played such a key role in the workers' education movement, particularly in the garment unions. Born in 1896 in Derazhnya, a market town in western Ukraine in the Russian Empire, Pesotta received her primary education in traditional Hebrew schools and underground radical groups. She read Russian novelists and English writers in Russian translation. In this way, long before she arrived in the United States, she was familiar with Stowe's *Uncle Tom's Cabin*, Twain's *The Adventures of Huckleberry Finn*, and Longfellow's *The Song of Hiawatha*. In addition to novels, translations of European and American pamphlets and newspapers also circulated within her radical group, bringing news of the world. Pesotta's account of her early reading suggests an international, anti-imperial print culture that linked struggles against empire in Italy and Turkey to struggles against slavery and the campaign for the eight-hour day in the United States to the plight of Jews in the Russian Empire. "When issues of these forbidden papers arrived in Derazhnya," Pesotta wrote, "they were passed around for private reading, and, passing from hand to hand, they became limp as rags and the printed words became so blurred it was no longer possible to read them. The paper was finally disposed of in the river."[55] She compared her hometown to a node on the Underground Railroad that guided escaped slaves to freedom in Canada. Refugees from the tzar's justice would come to Derazhnya on market days, blending in with the crowd and finding their way to sympathetic local homes. Weeks or months later they would disappear as they had arrived, on their way to freedom in Western Europe.[56]

Well versed in radical thought, Pesotta left Russia to escape the prospect of marriage and a life of domestic labor in her hometown. With her sister already established in New York City, Pesotta and her grandmother made the long trip across Europe and the Atlantic, arriving in the United States in 1913. She attended night school to learn English, suffering through the instructor's thinly disguised contempt for her students. In the public library, she found an extensive collection of Russian-language novels. She then read the English translations "with the original fresh in mind. And meanwhile I learned to read the daily press and magazines, and I listened to the pronunciation of Americans and steadily picked up phrases that would be useful in everyday life."[57] But while learning English, Pesotta continued to use Yiddish and Russian in daily conversation among friends and coworkers. Following her sister into the garment trade, she got a job as a shirtwaist maker and joined the ILGWU. Near the conclusion of the second of her two autobiographies, Pesotta wrote that by the end of her first year in the United States, "I had become an American."[58] But there was still much to learn about how to operate in the American scene. Through participating in the educational programs of Local 25 of the ILGWU, Pesotta found her way to the Bryn Mawr Summer School for Women in Industry and afterward to Brookwood Labor College. Relationships with workers and instructors from Brookwood, in particular, would play an ongoing role in Pesotta's career as an organizer. In 1934, after leading a series of high-profile strikes, Pesotta reconnected with "chums of long standing and classmates at Brookwood," who soon after nominated her as a candidate for a vice presidency of the ILGWU, a position she won at the union's next convention.[59]

While Philip Taft rose from the streets to an elite university career and Rose Pesotta challenged the stranglehold of male leaders on her largely female union, Harry Haywood's path to intellectual maturity wound from the packinghouse cities of the Midwest to Moscow and then New York City. Born in Omaha, Nebraska, in 1898, Haywood was part of the only black family in an overwhelmingly Czech immigrant neighborhood. His family got on well with the Czechs but fled to Minneapolis after receiving threats from an Irish street gang. There, Haywood was quickly alienated by his white classmates and quit school in the eighth grade. Like other African Americans who fought in Europe during the First World War, Haywood was impressed by the lack of overt discrimination in France. Shortly after his return to the United States, he found himself in the midst of the bloody Chicago Race Riot of 1919. "At the time," Haywood wrote in his memoir, "the racist deluge simply revealed great gaps in my own education and knowledge." His experience growing up in Omaha seemed to refute the idea that whites and blacks could not live as equals, but he longed to find validation for this experience in the more authoritative voices of published authors. His search began with the nineteenth-century rationalist Robert Ingersoll and from there moved on to Darwin. He read *On the Origin of Species* "armed with a dictionary and . . . knowledge gleaned from Ingersoll's popularizations." He found support for his own atheism in what he considered Darwin's "scientific refutation of religious dogma."[60]

Haywood's personal intellectual development was deeply embedded in his family and organizational connections and reflected the diverse radical milieu of American industrial cities. Like the more famous black communist, novelist Richard Wright, Haywood worked in the Chicago post office, where he met others seeking knowledge and understanding. He and his coworkers formed a short-lived study group but soon felt "the need for a broader political arena of activity." They went to lectures and forums in public parks and bohemian clubs, where they listened to socialists and anarchists, as well as more mainstream progressives like Clarence Darrow. His older brother, already a communist, suggested more advanced reading: Henry Morgan's ethnological volume *Ancient Society*; Gustavus Myers's *History of Great American Fortunes*; John Reed's history of the Bolshevik revolution, *Ten Days That Shook the World*; and Jack London's dystopian vision of American fascism, *The Iron Heel*. By this time Haywood had quit his monotonous job at the post office for one as a cook on the train from Chicago to Los Angeles. His schedule allowed him time to read and interact with other radicals in both cities, and he soon moved on to a steady diet of Marxist classics until he informed his brother that he wanted to join the Communist Party in 1922. Within a few years he was an experienced activist, and in 1925 the party sent him to Moscow to attend the University of the Toilers of the East, where he studied with communists from Asia and Africa. Taking an intellectual path parallel to Philip Taft's, Haywood became an important theorist in the Communist Party, articulating its policy on race in the United States that identified blacks in the South as a subject nation with the right to self-determination.[61]

Haunted by Education

The achievements of these working-class autodidacts were undeniable. They were public intellectuals in the fullest sense, publishing in academic and popular venues, influencing government and social movement policy, and forming deeply engaged communities of like-minded learners. Still, many self-educated working people felt a deep loss from their lack of formal schooling. In a professional world that increasingly relied on credentials rather than experience, and in which they continually interacted with formally educated middle-class intellectuals, working-class intellectuals felt themselves to be outsiders.

Those with literary aspirations, like Falkowski, often worried that their creativity was slipping away as work consumed their time and energy. As Tillie Olsen wrote in her assessment of the fate of many female and working-class authors, "Substantial creative work demands time, and with rare exceptions only full-time workers have achieved it. Where the claims of creation cannot be primary, the results are atrophy; unfinished work; minor effort and accomplishment; silences."[62] Formal education as the gateway to a more leisurely, middle-class existence often weighed on the minds of gifted daughters and sons of the working class who looked back on their lives and wondered how an education might have made things easier. As the communist literary critic Mike Gold wrote to a young correspondent in the early 1960s, "Education haunts me. At the age of 12 I was forced to leave school and work in the hot hell of a New York factory. . . . I was no Lincoln, unfortunately. I was just one of the many who try and fail. But I always wanted an education, and kept trying and failing again and again."[63] Gold had reason to be bitter, despite a long and successful career. An ambitious working-class student, he briefly attended Harvard but had to drop out for lack of funds, and he regularly interacted with those who had been more privileged. Like Gold, Falkowski also was haunted by his lack of formal education. "I have always felt somehow having been cheated from the very start," he wrote at the end of a two-year program in Brookwood Labor College. "I am certain I have long since acquired the full equivalent of a high school education, but it is credits and diplomas rather than the content of one's mind that goes farthest in the world of opportunity."[64] These were among the "hidden injuries of class" that Richard Sennett and Jonathan Cobb described in their sociology of class in Cold War America.[65] Better read at age eighteen than the average college graduate today, Falkowski went on to publish essays in the English- and Polish-language radical press, travel to Europe as a worker-correspondent, live in the Soviet Union, and, back in the United States, work as an instructor at a labor college himself. He did not quite fulfill his loftiest dreams, but his years of self-study had set the stage for a life of adventure beyond the little mining town of Shenandoah.

Despite the evident loneliness of these working-class autodidacts, the paradox of working-class "self-education" lay in the fact that it was a deeply social process. As they read aloud at home and in the workplace, working-class readers fashioned communities out of text and the spoken word. At the center of this world were "class partisans," to use Shelton Stromquist's phrase, people who viewed the Progressive Era social divide from the bottom up.[66] On street corners and in open-forum lectures, speech and text were further intertwined as speakers peppered their talks with references to books and authors and plied the gathered crowds with pamphlets and newspapers. Out of a variety of informal practices and networks, a movement was educating itself. Whether working people read weighty tomes of literature, Marxist economics, or gossip about movie stars and sports heroes, they moved through a world filled with text and talk. They could learn from coworkers, street speakers, libraries, and even advertisements. Organizational and cultural networks connected individual workers to others with similar interests. They traded texts and ideas, argued, and learned how to speak in public. In the next chapter, we see how these public spaces structured the possibilities for free speech and social movement culture.

2

"All sorts of wild, impassioned talk"

Open Forums and the Working-Class Public Sphere

You could hardly miss the talk in the working-class neighborhoods of North American cities during the early twentieth century. Barkers stood in front of theaters, grocery stores, and bars; drivers yelled to, and at, one another; and newsies called out the headlines several times a day. In the parks and on the busy corners of working-class districts, especially on warm summer nights, voices exhorted passersby to come to Jesus, fight capitalism, embrace free love, or demand the single tax. Every large American city hosted at least one center of public speech and debate. Union Square, Washington Square, and Rutgers Square in New York City were in constant use for organized and impromptu protests, as were Pioneer Square in Seattle, Pershing Square and La Plaza in Los Angeles, and Boston Commons, among others. Chicagoans knew their city's two most prominent open-air speaking forums as "the Bugs," reflecting a common association between heterodox ideas and insanity. Washington Square Park on the city's North Side—known as Bughouse Square—and weekly meetings of the South Side Washington Park Forum—known as the Bug Club—drew the curious, the bored, and the committed to listen, debate, and relay ideas about the emerging social order. The very wildness of speakers' claims and the variety of topics addressed captured the imagination of many young people, judging from their vivid memories recorded decades later. The poet Kenneth Rexroth, who spent his weekends as a teenager at Bughouse Square, described the park as a venue for "every variety of radical sect, lunatic religion, and crackpot health panacea." Studs Terkel, whose family ran a residential hotel in the neighborhood, recalled,

"There was a great deal of 'bull' at Bughouse Square. There was a great deal of all sorts of wild, impassioned talk and conversation of all variety, from all strata of our thought, and to me, at least, as a young boy it was a very colorful and very rich area."[1]

These were just the most visible manifestations of a working-class public sphere: a broad field of social interaction and communication that linked the causes of unions, radicals, and working-class communities. Like the broader American public sphere, which was driven by large metropolitan daily newspapers and, increasingly, by radio and film after World War I, the working-class public sphere circulated ideas through text, talk, and imagery. Unlike the mainstream public sphere, the spaces and practices of the working-class public sphere were fundamentally shaped by the concerns and accents of working people.[2] The timbre of this conversation reflected both utopian aspirations for working-class emancipation and the less high-minded pressures of organizational rivalry and ideological schism. But whoever did the talking, in venues that ranged from immigrant fraternal societies to settlement houses, political rallies, and bohemian social clubs, the accent was on working people and their problems. Whether advocating for the labor movement, vegetarianism, Christianity, ethnic nationalism, or one of the myriad tendencies of the political left, successful speakers and writers took great care to hold the attention of their working-class audiences.

Where free speech flourished, and when it faded away, depended very much on the shape of the city itself. On hot summer nights, working-class residents living in transient hotels and furnished-room apartments flowed into the streets and parks to enjoy the cool air. Lacking other forms of entertainment, they were happy to take in the circus-like atmosphere of the parks or pause to listen to street-corner speakers. During the cold winters in Northern cities, the meeting halls of unions, settlement houses, ethnic associations, public libraries, and bars offered a warm place to pass the dark evenings in sociable conversation. Moments of political crisis activated these same spaces for more directed purposes. Word of protest meetings, marches, and rallies circulated quickly through neighborhoods in part because residents were familiar with all the regular gathering sites.

After World War II, these same spaces were among the first targets for urban redevelopment. As highways and high-rise apartments displaced older neighborhoods and their residents, radical activists who had powered the circulation of ideas also found the city and the nation to be increasingly hostile to their speech and very existence. In these years the working-class public sphere retreated to safe havens and shifted to new locations—neighborhood bars, private homes, college campuses, and church basements. Bughouse Square and other public spaces for speech and gathering lost their vital connections to social movements and communities. Some of the old guard continued to make speeches from soapboxes, sustained financially by tour bus operators who catered to the curiosity of tourists. Others embraced the new locations and drew a direct connection with their antecedents. By the last decades of the twentieth century, memories of Chicago's open forum heyday became part of the battle over gentrification, both a resource to resist the commercial revision of urban space and a cultural adornment for young city dwellers. Returning to the early twentieth century reminds us that what we now celebrate as "free speech" was more than a marketplace of ideas. Generated through social and organizational practices that rang with decidedly proletarian accents, the working-class public sphere challenged the cultural domination of elites while bending the broader culture toward the needs of the many.

Speech, Space, and Labor's Contentious Networks

Public lectures and open forums were the easiest point of access to informal education and heterodox ideas. Just as the streets of industrial cities were awash in text, so the air was filled with talk. The public parks, street corners, and lecture forums of modernizing American cities were theatrical spaces where ideas about power were circulated, contested, and amplified.[3] The spirit and tone of the open-air forums spilled out onto busy street corners as speakers addressed passersby from boxes and stepladders, lifting their voices above the crowded sidewalks. In this way, political speech created sites of sonic and social focus within the urban cacophony that disoriented and excited newcomers and longtime residents alike. The photographer Gordon Parks, unemployed and broke in Harlem in the spring of 1933, captured the city's clashing sound, text, and imagery in a passage of his 1965 autobiography, *A Choice of Weapons*. Parks described Harlem as a stream of sensations: the sounds of jazz clubs, preachers, news vendors, and street speakers blending with the sensational headlines and disappointing "help wanted" notices of the city's newspapers:

> *the duke's latest hit come in listen the mooche come on in brother it don't cost you nothing* and the african methodist episcopal church and chick webb at the savoy *What a friend we have in Jesus! Halt halt halt or I'll shoot* POLICE BRUTALITY CONTINUES IN HARLEM! BOY MURDERED! NEGRO GROUPS SET FOR PROTEST! *Get your paper here read all about it brother read all about*

> *it* . . . ads ads ads white waiter wanted ads ads ads white plumber needed ads ads ads white nurse wanted ads ads ads white bartender needed . . . ads ads ads negro maid that can cook sew clean and care for two-month-old baby. *Get your Amsterdam news your Pittsburgh courier your Chicago defender here read your black papers get the truth.*[4]

For newcomers like Parks, who were broke and disoriented by the city, the informal mood of open forums offered a welcoming respite. Typically located in or near neighborhoods that served new arrivals, street-corner and park forums were often spaces of contact between men and women from a variety of racial, ethnic, and religious communities. They were neutral turf for contending radical groups, competing unions, street gangs, and religious groups, as well as convenient meeting places and sites of reunion for those who shared political perspectives but lived in dispersed neighborhoods. Above all, they were free. For workers scraping by on a few cents a day, mocked by the unattainable commerce that surrounded them, this was no small benefit.

Harlem's open forum, which was located in front of the 135th Street branch of the New York Public Library, proved an attraction for the future civil rights leader Ella Baker. She arrived in New York in 1927 as a recent college graduate and quickly found her way to the Young Women's Christian Association (YWCA) and the Harlem branch of the library, which was a thriving intellectual center with an integrated staff, a world-class collection, and regular lecture programs. As librarian Ernestine Rose noted of the emerging black political debate in 1921, "Some of the most intelligent questions I have ever heard have been asked after the lectures at our Thursday night forum, devoted to social and racial problems. So much for Mr. Madison Grant's assertion, 'Negroes never become socialists.'"[5] A regular at the library, Baker helped to start a Negro History Club that sponsored lectures and debates on the busy corner in front of the library and in a nearby park. As she recalled, "If you hadn't stood on the corner of 135th and 7th Avenue [protesting and debating] . . . you weren't with it." As historian Barbara Ransby notes, Baker took some of the lessons she learned in Harlem back South when she returned to fight segregation there.[6] In Chicago's Bronzeville neighborhood, the George Cleveland Hall branch of the Chicago Public Library served a similar role for the migrant community. Under the direction of librarian Vivian Harsh, the branch library not only developed a rich collection of materials on African American history and culture but also provided a lecture forum and clubs that supported writers such as Richard Wright and Gwendolyn Brooks.[7]

Arriving in Los Angeles in the late summer of 1931, immigrant garment worker Rose Pesotta was drawn to the city's lively public squares. Strolling in the old city plaza with fellow garment workers and listening to speakers debate the topics of the day, she could see in this infamous open shop town an echo of New York and even her Ukrainian hometown. The neighborhood around La Plaza had long welcomed workers, immigrants, and radicals—although recently it had been the subject of a romantic architectural makeover designed to make it more welcoming to tourists and middle-class residents. The Flores Magón brothers lived there during their exile in the United States, and muralist David Siqueiros painted his controversial *America Tropical* on the outside wall of the nearby Italian Hall the year after Pesotta's arrival. Residents in neighborhoods around the square spoke Chinese, Spanish, Italian, and Yiddish as well as English. A few blocks to the south was the more modern Pershing Square, a center of English-language

Rose Pesotta and her union sisters confront a policeman during a Los Angeles ILGWU strike. Pesotta first came to Los Angeles in 1931 and was welcomed by a group of labor college graduates who went on to organize a labor college program with the University of California. Golden Anniversary of the Los Angeles Central Labor Council (1951), UCLA Library.

street speaking. Like the humming city parks and squares in other industrial cities across North America, La Plaza and Pershing Square were centers of public speechifying that attracted diverse audiences and near constant police harassment. But Pesotta did not think the talk was particularly effective. She wrote to her mentor A. J. Muste of the Brookwood Labor College, "This burg really needs some honest-to-goodness place where people could get a fair education." The radical forums, she wrote, attracted the same small group of militants who made a lot of noise, but took no actions: "a big cloud but very little rain," she concluded.[8]

The familiar social forms, sounds, and personal networks that surrounded free speech venues served an orienting role, especially for transients who moved in and out of the cities as economics demanded. Especially in summer months, soapbox speakers in parks became part of a wider social scene. While radicals hoped to convert their audiences, it was more common for listeners to stop only for an entertaining moment and then move on. Seasonal workers who spent the summer months on the Great Plains and returned to Chicago, Kansas City, and Minneapolis in the fall found their way to these neighborhoods to reconnect with old friends on the streets, in bars, union halls, and cheap flophouses. The poet Keene Wallis captured the social geography of these returns in a long free verse that follows the odyssey of a wheat harvest worker from farm to city. The poem traces the sights and sounds that marked successive ethnic and economic zones of the city—the songs of a black church, the "giddy tunes" of Mexican food vendors, the calls of prostitutes, a Salvation Army band, and finally a group of Wobblies "on the curbstone singing low."[9]

Every major city had its open forums, but Chicago's central location, its important role in publishing, and its political history make the city especially useful for understanding the working-class public sphere of the early twentieth century. The central city of the booming American Midwest, turn-of-the-century Chicago was home to some of the country's most profitable, and most virulently antiunion, employers. As a distributive center for the entire western United States, Chicago's influence lay not only in its products but also in its people and the ideas they eagerly consumed and shared. The intellectual life of the city benefited from its position in the rail system as much as it did from its soon-to-be-prominent universities. Speakers traveling across the country by train had to spend some time in Chicago as they switched train lines. While in town they could give a talk and raise a little money for their cause.

Chicago also played a special role in the folklore of early twentieth-century American radicalism. The city's dramatic industrial history added narrative weight to the presence of numerous union headquarters. The 1886 bombing and police riot in Haymarket Square amid citywide demonstrations for the eight-hour workday led to a show trial and execution of four men associated with the city's radical labor movement. Less than a decade later, federal troops occupied the city to crush a nationwide job action by railroad workers against the Pullman Car Company. The Industrial Workers of the World was founded in Chicago in 1905 and maintained its national headquarters and printing presses there. The city had a strong Socialist Party presence, and in 1919 left-wing socialists chose Chicago as the place to launch the American Communist Party. In 1925 there were seventy-two newspapers and magazines publishing on labor topics in Chicago, many in languages other than English.[10] Only New York City outpaced Chicago as a center of activism and social movement publishing.

Whether on street corners or in parks, open-air speaking followed a predictable pattern of practice, even if the content was unorthodox or radical. These events were observed by the undercover sociologist Nels Anderson, who took notes on the speakers at a busy Chicago intersection during the early 1920s. The six active speakers worked together to attract and hold a crowd, each limiting his talk so that the others could have a turn. After their performance, each speaker walked through the audience briefly, either selling or giving away pamphlets and newspapers. "Regardless of how much they differ in their schemes of reforming the world," Anderson wrote in his field notes, "they are seldom personal in their opposition to each other. Soap-boxers behave toward each other when not on the box, much as lawyers do when they are out of the courtroom, and even while on the box they consider each other's interests."[11] In this way the shared interest of speakers in drawing and maintaining the attention of working-class audiences tended to create a regular format for public speechifying.

Similarly, the expectations and interests of working-class audiences shaped the form and content of the educational programs developed by middle-class reformers, immigrant community leaders, and self-conscious radicals. Settlement houses like Hull House and the Chicago Commons learned quickly that forms of education that were familiar to their upper-class patrons would not fly with workers. But neither could reformers tolerate the pugnacious discourse of the streets. Settlement forums aimed to gently guide the class-conscious rhetoric of organizers onto what they considered to be more constructive terrain. "Over-cautious people sometimes raise the question whether the unrestricted freedom of expression . . . is safe," wrote Graham Taylor of the Chicago Commons regarding the tone of speech at the settlement's popular "Free Floor" meetings.

No doubt speaking to anxious donors, Taylor argued, "Nothing else would be safe. No boiler was kept from explosion by sitting on the safety valve."[12] A 1921 report on adult education at the Chicago Commons noted, "Lectures and routine teaching of abstract ideals will not suffice" in the effort to "make good citizens of our foreign-born neighbors." Music was a good bet, although the author recommended avoiding American patriotic tunes. It was better to give talks in Italian that were "intended to interpret America to the New-comer"; for instance, favorably comparing Italian and American holidays.[13] By the 1930s much of the programming was in English, but it still reflected the concerns of the neighborhood's overwhelmingly working-class residents. In the depths of the Great Depression, the Chicago Commons hosted meetings of the city's unemployed councils and put on plays about unemployment, European fascism, and unionization.[14]

From the mid-1920s, reform and religious groups in Chicago sponsored a financially successful lecture circuit known as the Chicago Forum. Created in the wake of Chicago's 1919 racial violence and the rise of the Ku Klux Klan, the Chicago Forum Council aimed "to promote understanding and good will by bringing people of different groups into friendly association with each other for discussion of problems related to the public welfare."[15] The idea caught on, and by the late 1920s, Chicago's forum scene included self-identified "forum hounds," enthusiasts who spent much of their leisure time attending different lectures and discussions.[16] In the Cold War years, the Chicago Forum adopted an explicit prohibition on "propaganda," but controversy was key to its early success. Debates between intellectuals with opposing ideas were among the most popular events, typically pitting progressives against conservatives. Socialists like Norman Thomas and Scott Nearing were frequent speakers who were sometimes paired with religious leaders. In March 1929 NAACP leader W.E.B. Du Bois debated the racialist author and fellow Harvard PhD Lothrop Stoddard. An overflowing interracial audience of five thousand peacefully watched as Du Bois argued the affirmative on the question "Shall the Negro Be Encouraged to Seek Cultural Equality?"[17] At the height of New Deal social programming between 1935 and 1938, this system of public affairs programming went national with Works Progress Administration funding and coordination, model programs in Denver and Des Moines, and federal funds to train popular educators.[18]

Immigrant communities sponsored their own rich educational life through both outdoor and indoor forums, promoting literacy and maintaining intellectual ties to their home countries while also negotiating their place in American society. Many newspapers with smaller circulations were linked to organizations such as ethnic fraternal associations, unions, or political parties. Their pages promoted and documented the accomplishments, activities, and conflicts of the groups and created a rich symbiosis between print culture and the public sphere. The debate among immigrants about how best to adjust to the American setting was richly documented by a New Deal translation project, the Chicago Foreign Language Press Survey, which is now available online to the public.[19] For instance, the Danish paper *Revyen* reported on a discussion hosted by the Danish Young Peoples Society on "What are the most important interests of Danes entering the U.S.A.?" The main speaker emphasized learning English and adopting American ideals. Participants from the floor objected, insisting that new arrivals should "first of all, join their respective trade unions and the Socialist Party." The heated debate was extended an hour past the allotted time by unanimous vote of the audience, the paper reported.[20] Even as immigrants became more grounded in the American scene, they could maintain community ties through ethnic forums, much as immigrants today settle into American society in part by organizing hometown societies, soccer clubs, and trade unions.[21] For instance, Lithuanian forums in Chicago debated social issues such as women's suffrage and "Women's Sexual Life." Similarly, Czech-speaking free thinkers chartered a new forum in 1922 with the aims of organizing lectures, publishing pamphlets and books in Czech, and making "the most intimate contacts with other American rationalists." They named their group after American orator Robert Ingersoll, whose writing was a staple of left-wing print culture like the Haldeman-Julius Little Blue Books. By 1937 there was also a rationalist club for English-speaking Czechs known as the Thomas Paine Club.[22]

A few forums were more social than educational, associated with the bohemian subculture that brought together artists, writers, musicians, and working-class activists. In Chicago the best documented of these bohemian clubs was the Dill Pickle Club, located across the street from Bughouse Square in the city's Towertown neighborhood. A mix of open forum, dance hall, tavern, and art studio, the club was the brainchild of Jack Jones, a Canadian-born miner and former organizer for the Western Federation of Miners and the IWW. Jones worked closely with Dr. Ben Reitman to craft the programming at the Dill Pickle. Reitman, who had been Emma Goldman's political and romantic partner, was an able promoter who had previously organized a nearby "Hobo College," a series of educational venues for migrants wintering in Chicago. Reitman and Jones had a knack for attracting audiences of workers, academics, and underworld characters. The lectures and debates on birth control, free love, homosexuality, and other topics began as organic expressions of the heterodox bohemian community but over time developed into an entrepreneurial brand of cultural spectacle.

Created by working-class cultural entrepreneurs Jack Jones and Ben Reitman, Chicago's Dill Pickle Club was a mixing place for radicals, journalists, and progressive academics. The Canadian-born Jones was an iron miner before he settled in Chicago. Reitman spent much of his youth as a hobo and later became a physician who cared for Chicago's outcasts. A poster advertising an "Anti-war Dance" (c. 1917) suggests the mix of politics and socializing that was common in bohemia clubs. Courtesy Newberry Library, Chicago (Dill Pickle Club Records).

The journalist Samuel Putnam, who became friends with several leaders of the IWW in Chicago, recalled that the Dill Pickle Club in its Prohibition-era peak was "a sort of no man's land for radicals—many of them the tired variety—bedraggled bohemians, newspaper men, West Side gunmen, Wobblies, university savants, co-eds and their swains, and the limousined gentry from the neighboring Gold Coast. . . . It was fun to listen to the world-famed physicist gravely debating his specialty with a boxcar bum who had wandered in." Among the well-known Chicago personalities that frequented the club in its early years—and helped to cement its reputation—were Carl Sandburg, Sherwood Anderson, and Ben Hecht. In the late 1920s, however, the club "entered upon its period of inflation," and bohemianism was more of a show.[23] The 1928 travel book *Chicago in Seven Days* featured the Dill Pickle Club as "Bohemia in all its glory!" The author, a Chicago journalist, guided a fictional visitor through the city's daytime and nighttime sights. Described as "a product of the Corn Belt," his visitor was not impressed by the Pickle, with its modern art, a jazz band, and "swaying couples—long-haired men and short-haired women" on the dance floor.[24] Though chided for contrived heterodoxy, the Dill Pickle had once been a real draw for a diverse group of young radicals and artists.

The Dill Pickle Club and other open forums prompted reactions ranging from high praise to complete disdain. A letter to the editor of the *Chicago Tribune* during the summer of 1921 favorably contrasted the plebian Bug Club to its more elite neighbor, the University of Chicago, with its intimidating "medieval towers." The Bug Club, according to the writer, was "a glorious institution and the man with a craving for knowledge who works all day and cannot afford a university education, if he but listens with an open mind, knowing what to discard as bull (for naturally some of it is) and what to digest, will certainly assimilate a wealth of knowledge in a short summer term." Critics found much to fault. The Chicago Park Commission complained that Bug Club meetings were "irreligious, blasphemous, ribald, and revolutionary," as well as being likely to offend the casual passerby.[25] Critics found much to fault. A writer for the *Chicago Defender* described the audience of a 1923 debate on religion as proletarian, dirty, and dogmatic. "They were the kind of white people who do hard, mechanical work," he wrote. "They had grime in their skin and under their finger nails." Worst of all, they unmercifully heckled Ben Reitman, who argued for the values of religion against the atheistic John Loughman.[26] A 1938 visit to Washington Square Park by a University of Chicago researcher captured the mixture of profanity, radicalism, and its motley audience. A soapbox speaker delivered a profanity-laced speech on "negro's rights." The audience included "wild-eyed, fanatical, drooling at the mouth nuts," hotel and restaurant workers, unemployed white-collar workers, aging hoboes, assorted radicals, college students, prostitutes, and homosexual men.[27]

Much like college campuses today, the bohemian clubs mingled social and intellectual life. As historians Chap Heap and Kevin Mumford have shown, the clubs and their associated open forums became zones of sexual exploration for young homosexual and heterosexual urbanites. Chicago's Towertown neighborhood was home to the short-lived Society for Human Rights, an early homophile group founded by Henry Gerber in 1923.[28] Unmarried young women played a key role in the open forum scene as proprietors of coffee shops, speakers and entertainers, and customers and audience members. As historian Joanne Meyerowitz explains, the "furnished room" districts of Chicago and other cities made it easier for young people to live away from their families and to establish their own homes, even if only on a temporary basis. These novel household forms supported young workers' participation in precarious and seasonal labor markets, particularly in Chicago, which was the home turf of the continent's most transient labor force.[29] Critics of the open forums pointed to speakers' profanity, the down-and-out character of audiences, and the forums' role as a venue for sexual encounters. According to one unflattering account, open forums were little more than a pickup opportunity for "bums," "oldish maidens," and homosexuals. "With the aid of a lecture by an unaware professor . . . a smutty one-act 'play' or two, some alleged music, and dim lighted dance floors," forum participants were getting the "thrill of their lives."[30]

Whatever the assessments of outsiders, those who organized forums and spoke from soapboxes and on street corners imagined themselves engaged in an educational mission. Speakers at Bughouse Square used the Newberry Library, at the time a wide-open public reference library, to gather information for their talks or to refute the points of other speakers. Jack Jones spent his days in the Newberry researching an elaborate plan for a postrevolutionary industrial order. Surviving advertisements from the Dill Pickle Club attest to the audience's thirst for knowledge, cursory familiarity with social science, and an equal interest in politics and sex. One series of events known as "Ben Reitman's Social Clinic," for instance, included topics such as "How to Get the Most Out of Life and Love," "Do Perverts Menace Society?" and "Is Industrial, Social, and Sexual Progress Conducive to Human Happiness? (With Living Models)." Jimmie Sheridan, an apprentice electrician who was first drawn to Chicago's Bughouse Square by a nighttime vigil protesting the execution of convicted anarchists Nicola Sacco and Bartolomeo Vanzetti in 1927, became a regular speaker during the 1930s. "Most of us talkers weren't well educated and we wanted to learn," Sheridan told a reporter in 1971. "People didn't have access to so much media like they do today, and through the open forum we learned a lot."[31] Or as Slim Brundage noted in 1967, "The thing today, you see, the kids have outlets that we didn't have. We went and stood on the street corner and listened, you know, to somebody, and got up and said our own peace. Well, where are the kids going now? To college! College wasn't available to us."[32]

Speakers on street corners, in public parks, and in lecture forums spoke to those like Brundage who scratched out a living on wages, lived in cramped apartments, and had few other options for entertainment. Although it became common later in the twentieth century to describe these public speech forums as a marketplace of ideas, the partisans of radical parties, trade unionism, community organizations, labor colleges, consumer cooperatives, and even liberal reform could not fail to see themselves in an organizational context. They traded ideas eagerly, but the overwhelming power of corporations and the state suggested that warfare was a more apt metaphor than free market. Like any battle, contestants were arrayed in organizations that identified leaders, followers, and modes of participation.

Even those with weak ties to organizations had inherited outlooks from a pervasive associational culture that would wither away after World War II. As sociologist Theda Skocpol has argued, organizations like the Masons and the Elks enrolled American men of many classes, creating networks and training generations in the social technology of managing membership organizations. Rooted in the breadwinner democracy of the nineteenth century, the largest organizations were for men only, and frequently only for white men. African American men in the South established all-black Odd Fellows and Masonic lodges in large numbers in the late nineteenth century, as well as churches and local benevolent societies. Women, too, were part of this associational culture through church and reform groups, reading clubs, the YWCA, and, eventually, predominantly female unions like the ILGWU.[33] Labor and radical organizations benefited from this widespread knowledge of organizational life, mobilizing existing social networks and the social capital of their members. Among prominent labor and progressive leaders of the 1920s, for instance, the Masons and Elks were the third and fourth most common organizational affiliations behind the American Federation of Labor and the Socialist Party. For women trade unionists, the YWCA and the Women's Trade Union League would serve as important training groups.[34] Associational life had a diffuse impact, introducing millions to the useful arts of group life: respecting rules of order, managing treasuries, and taking leadership. Radical Americans repurposed these skills to manage their reading groups, socialist clubs, and unions. Others brought organizing traditions with them from the revolutionary movements of Europe, Latin America, and Asia. Affinity groups—often narrowly based on friendships, hometowns, and ideological niches—drew on these varied organizational traditions as they flowed into larger left-wing organizations like the Socialist Party.

The outpouring of speech and writing that accompanied the rise of cities like Chicago was diverse in its political orientation, form, and content. But much of it was offensive to the people whose hands held the levers of political and economic power. As legal scholar Geoffrey Stone puts it, in the early twentieth century "civil liberties were intended for respectable, law-abiding citizens," not for radicals, immigrants, and workers.[35] During the first two decades of the twentieth century, the IWW, sometimes in coalition with the Socialist Party, launched a series of dramatic "free speech fights." Often in smaller industrial cities such as Spokane, Washington; Missoula, Montana; San Diego, California; and Sioux City, Iowa, these public confrontations began when police, at the behest of local employers, prevented organizers from speaking to crowds on street corners and in public parks. One speaker after another mounted a box to read the text of the Declaration of Independence or the U.S. Constitution. When police arrested each speaker in turn and delivered them to the local jail, activists demanded a trial, clogging the jail and courts until local officials relented. In some cases, free speech fights won a modicum of tolerance for organizers. In other cases, the results were less pleasant. During the San Diego fight in 1912, for instance, local vigilantes kidnapped and tortured the radical organizer Ben Reitman before putting him on a train heading out of town.[36] Starting in 1912, the IWW led militant organizing drives among mass-production workers, miners, lumberjacks, and harvest hands, even in the face of intense employer hostility and organized antiradical violence. When the United States entered World War I in 1917, the federal government arrested hundreds of IWW members, placing the top leadership in federal prison for lengthy sentences. By 1918 Eugene Debs himself was in jail, accused of hindering the draft. In the years that followed the war, federal, local, and employer agents continued the assault while militants tried to regroup. Hundreds of radical leaders were deported without trial, and employers colluded with local law enforcement to undermine strikes in the rail, steel, and meatpacking industries.[37]

Legal struggles that followed the IWW and Socialist Party free speech campaigns laid the groundwork for a liberal jurisprudence on speech in two ways. First, the public spectacle of men and women being hauled off to jail for the crime of reading the Constitution aloud on city streets frequently achieved its goal of delegitimizing (although not eliminating) police repression of organizers. Like the Movement for Black Lives, which generated a public discussion of police violence and antiblack racism in the 2010s, IWW free speech fights a century earlier forced those on the sidelines to take sides. The legal defense work that followed mass arrests eventually gave birth to the American Civil Liberties Union in early 1920.[38] Second, the activist lawyers who sprang into action to defend Wobblies, socialists, and later communists, would slowly build the case against the commonplace regulation of speech by local police through vagrancy laws. As legal scholar Risa Goluboff argues, lawyers defending soapbox speakers began to see similar patterns in police regulation of African American communities, unmarried women, gay men and lesbians, as well as protesters. In a succession of cases, it became clear that municipal vagrancy laws were a tool that police used with wide, and frequently arbitrary, discretion. The U.S. Supreme Court struck down overbroad vagrancy ordinances in 1972.[39] In the process, "free speech" became a more abstract concept divorced from the organizational networks and politics that occasioned the original cases.

Fifty years earlier, however, the court was much less sympathetic to political dissent and social transgression. When weighing the rights of radicals and the authority of a wartime federal government, the Supreme Court stood firmly for repression. Affirming the conviction of the nation's most prominent socialist, Eugene Debs, the court clearly supported the right of the state to defend itself against the speech of its radical critics. However, in the minority opinion of a second case, *Abrams v. United States*, Justice Oliver Wendell Holmes set down a marker for later liberal jurists to follow. The case involved a group of radicals—three anarchists and a socialist—who distributed pamphlets in Yiddish and English calling on various left-wing organizations to oppose the U.S. intervention in the Soviet Union and "save the Workers' Republic of Russia." The court majority upheld the defendants' conviction under the Espionage Act of 1917 for interfering with the war effort. Holmes argued that fears of subversion, in this case, were overblown by wartime hysteria. In time, he argued, Americans would get past the heated passions of the war years and realize that "the ultimate good desired is better reached by free trade in ideas—that the best test of truth is the power of the thought to get itself accepted in the competition of the market."[40] As historian David Rabban argues, this reflected Holmes's low opinion of the defendants' political potential.[41] As Holmes put it, this "silly leaflet" did not present "any immediate danger that its opinions would not hinder the success of the government arms or have any appreciable tendency to do so."[42] The Abrams petitioners were free to express their opinions, Holmes seemed to suggest, because they were no threat, in contrast to Debs, who remained in jail on similarly flimsy charges.

Holmes's invocation of the "free trade in ideas" was the beginning of a shift from the outright censorship of speech to its regulation in ways that would make it safe and even constitutive of the modern state, according to the geographer Don Mitchell. Holmes, Brandeis, and their followers imagined a separation in time and space between published statements and utterances on the one hand, and their desired outcomes on the other hand.[43] In the temporal gap that separated speech from potential action, ideas competed on the basis of their merits alone, shorn of their political and organizational context. The space between speech and its effects was, in Holmes's term, a "marketplace" where different ideas competed for influence. Although this was compelling jurisprudence, it makes for bad history. Like Debs and other radicals whose cases came before the Supreme Court, the radicals who brought the *Abrams* case to the Court were not so much trading in ideas as operating in a field of contentious intellectual engagement structured by complex organizational, spatial, and ideological networks. These networks were social and mental structures that drew people into activism, and activists into specific political debates and organizational contexts. Not surprisingly, activists disagreed on every conceivable aspect of strategy and tactics. The ideas were important—indeed, vitally important to the activists of the time—but organizations structured the individuals' capacity to act in real time and real spaces and gave actions and speech the potential to effect change.[44] The disruption of left-wing organizational life had a real and lasting impact on the tenor of the working-class public sphere and the possibilities for social change.

Conservative trade unionists, who were skilled and ruthless organizational infighters, gleefully aided the federal suppression of their radical antagonists. Led by the self-taught, ex-Marxist cigar maker Samuel Gompers, AFL leaders were vociferous and effective anticommunists who, according to historian Jennifer Luff, carefully calibrated their antiradicalism to avoid supporting outright government repression while at the same time feeding the FBI information on their enemies. Riding atop a decentralized network of independent organizations, the AFL's national officers had comparatively little power on their own. They not only leveraged the bully pulpit of their national standing and their connections with government agencies but also were quick to ally with any union officials fighting radical activists within the ranks.[45]

Repression and the schisms it engendered doomed the chances for national political power for the socialists. The left fractured into a variety of contentious sects that would regroup only after the global calamity of the Great Depression. Counterintuitively, however, the proliferation of smaller groups maintained a distributed anticapitalist conversation that prepared the ground for this later revival. Nurtured in a culture of disputation at the local level, where rowdy meetings and street speakers vied for the support of the rank and file, the socialist impulse fostered the intellectual capacities of thousands of working people who would pioneer new forms of social movement organizing. Disputes over strategy and ideology demanded argument. Each new faction started a newspaper and engaged a set of writers, readers, and a network of distributors. Editors scoured rival papers and prepared their own caustic responses, feeding the circulation of ideas and newsprint. Divided organizationally, activists were connected by personal histories of solidarity and rivalry. The splits and disagreements were real, but contentious relationships are sometimes the most engaging and intense. Each schism or new alliance produced more text and talk to be circulated in the working-class public sphere. The overlapping imperatives of solidarity and organizational competition meant that every kind of activist fully understood the need to influence public debate and rank-and-file sentiment. It's no surprise that one of the main spoils of leadership within a union or political party was to name the editor of the official newspaper.

Activists living through the intense stress of organizational rivalry would not have been so sanguine about the productive nature of schism. Some partisans fought to the bitter end, poisoning personal relationships and planting seeds of vengeance that would take decades to germinate. Others dropped out, their creative energies lost to the movement. In this context, reading circles, street-corner forums, and lecture programs took on added significance as spaces with the potential to mediate the sharp tensions between warring camps. They attracted activists who were largely outside the power structures of trade unionism and radical politics: women, immigrants, African Americans, and young people. They created networks of ideas, people, and practices that informed grassroots action within and outside of organizations. Like families and friendship groups, these networks did not always divide neatly along party lines, and they frequently facilitated communication across the silos of organization and ideology. In this way, they were part of a labor movement that has remained obscured by our historical imagination.

Interpreting the End of Free Speech

The spectacle and community that developed around open forums indelibly marked the modern city and how it is remembered. Key texts in the Chicago School of Sociology drew upon the social matrix of working-class Chicago and were in turn used by soapbox speakers and activists to support their causes. Social life, sociology, and storytelling came full circle when authors such as James T. Farrell, Richard Wright, and Frank Marshall Davis evoked the world of the open forums in novels and poems.[46] By the 1960s, however, the wild cadences of Bughouse Square and other free speech venues had disappeared from most American cities. Observers disagreed on what caused the decline: McCarthyism, suburbanization, television, and the rise of mass higher education were each blamed as the likely cause. Bughouse Square "became quaint in the end," Studs Terkel said of the 1950s, "when the so-called stars were paid by the sightseeing buses to perform. Then you knew it was over."[47] In fact, this kind of tourism was already well established by the late 1920s when guidebooks highlighted Towertown's bohemian clubs. Sociology, journalism, activism, and voyeurism intersected in the promotion of themed tours during the Great Depression. Hard up for money, Ben Reitman offered tours of Chicago's "slummy" areas for small-town society ladies. The city sponsored "Chicago Tours for Chicagoans" to stimulate visits to restaurants. And in a more organized and mindful fashion, the Fellowship of Reconciliation sponsored educational tours on a variety of themes, including crime, sexuality, and radicalism.[48]

Public speaking at Bughouse Square lost its vitality, but the bohemian community in Chicago persisted for another twenty years, especially in the nearby Old Town neighborhood, which attracted a mix of working- and middle-class youth with low-rent apartments, coffeehouses, and bars. Slim Brundage was a crucial participant in this process of cultural transmission. Once a bouncer at the Dill Pickle Club, Brundage ran the "College of Complexes," a weekly lecture forum that met in bars and cafes for almost twenty years. Part tavern, part misfits club, the college hosted lectures and debates on civil rights, Eastern religions, foreign policy, drugs, and sexuality, among other things. Brundage hosted an integrated audience and showcased voices of the right as well as the left, although his sympathies were clearly with the latter. For instance, he invited Chicago white supremacist Joseph Beauharnais to speak on the topic "Does Integration Mean Mongrelization?" during the same month a Southern divinity student explained why "A Rebel Churchman Rebels against Segregation."[49]

The flamboyant characters who frequented the College of Complexes inspired fascination and romance for many younger attendees. In his early twenties, Gordon Poole wandered into the college by accident after work in a downtown wholesale house, an experience that changed the direction of his life. As he recalled, "The College was full of stimuli for a young man, psychologically weighed down upon by McCarthyism, who considered himself a conservative and, of course, given his conditioning, anti-communist. The conversation in that saloon, the people I met, the example of Brundage, turned my head around." He later went by ship to Europe and ended up in Italy, where he had his "next awakening," embracing the country's "open, pluralistic, permissive, intellectually stimulating culture" and casting off the "leaden headpiece of McCarthyism."[50] Brundage and the College of

1963?

THE

Curriculum

Meetings start at 9:00 P.M.

OFFICIAL NEUROSIS OF THE COLLEGE OF COMPLEXES

Minors admitted if accompanied by their Grandchildren

862 N. State St. Month of June

Sat. 1st - QUIZ PROGRAM. Everyone participates. Scotch to Winner.

Wed. 5th - "UGLIEST MAN" Contest. Girls enter their boy friends Both sexes vote. $5.00 in funny munny.

Fri. 7th - "McCarthyism Still Haunts the Army". Donald Page Moore, staff counsel for the American Civil Liberties Union, reports on the "Red" panic among the brass hats.

Sat. 8th - "The Art of Loving". A debate about famed psychologist Eric Fromm's book on whether LOVE, or TRANQUILIZERS are the answer to human problems. "Love", Mrs. Winifred Wallander—"Tranquilizers", Catherine Baird.

Wed. 12th - SKETCH NIGHT. $5.00 in funny munny to winner.

Fri. 14th - "A Rebel Churchman Rebels against Segregation" Rev. Bill Hinely, University of Chicago divinity student from Savannah, Ga., tells where religious leaders are lax in practicing what's preached.

Sat. 15th - AGE REGRESSION THROUGH HYPNOSIS. A demonstration by Alfred Manaster, M.A. in Psychology.

Wed. 19th - $5.00 in funny munny for the best suggestion on HOW TO IMPROVE THE COLLEGE.

Fri. 21st - "Who's Creating the Crisis in the Middle East?" A debate between Syrian-born Husni Haddad and visiting Israeli student, Uri Drimer; both at U. of C.

Sat. 22nd - Shirley Stremple, Star Lady Wrestler, from the stables of Fred Kohler. "Are men really the stronger sex?"

Wed. 26th - POETRY NIGHT. $5.00 in funny munny for the best reading.

Fri. 28th - "Does Integration Mean Mongrelization?". Joe Beauharnais, head of the well-known White Circle League and outspoken white supremacist, thinks it does.

Sat. 29th - Leon York, Graphologist will headshrink you by your handwriting.

Once the bouncer at the Dill Pickle Club, Slim Brundage served as a bridge between the bohemians of the 1920s and the beatniks of the 1950s. His College of Complexes was part tavern and part lecture hall, welcoming an eclectic parade of unorthodox speakers. This program of events, titled the "Curriculum" to signal his educational mission, includes speakers on the left and the right. Courtesy Newberry Library, Chicago (Slim Brundage Papers).

Complexes served as a tenuous bridge between the working-class bohemianism of the Dill Pickle and the IWW and the emerging youth radicalism of the 1960s. Franklin Rosemont, the son of an activist union typographer, encountered the college in his teens. He and his wife, Penelope, gravitated toward surrealism in their cultural activism. They later helped rescue the Charles H. Kerr Publishing Company from bankruptcy, and revived it by selling reprints of radical texts and recovered snippets from Chicago's bohemian heyday.[51]

But even the College of Complexes lost its fizzle as college campuses became new sites for youth protest and the black freedom movement took center stage on the left. As Brundage told Studs Terkel in a 1967 radio interview, "I discovered there wasn't a revolution going anywhere in the United States that wasn't starting in a church basement."[52] For a generation of free thinkers and Marxists raised on the militant atheism of Robert Ingersoll and the IWW, the emergence of church-based movements for social justice generated real cognitive dissonance. Brundage, Terkel, and others, of course, were inspired by and celebrated the social movements of the 1960s, but the shift to new activist environments dislodged the tight relationship between urban spaces like Bughouse Square and the movement for working-class liberation.

The built environment of the city, which had been such a powerful force in creating the open forum culture, had also been fundamentally altered by the mid-1960s. Interstate highways cut through the heart of working-class neighborhoods on the Near West Side of Chicago, breaking an organic link with the public spaces farther east. The privately funded Sandburg Village development replaced blocks of older apartments with condominiums priced to attract professional middle-class residents with no connection to the plebian traditions of Bughouse Square.[53] Elements of the old bohemian culture persisted, however, especially the welcoming attitude toward gay men and lesbians. A salacious 1950 travel guide titled *Chicago: Confidential!* described Towertown as a faded bohemia "where the avant-garde reads effusions of its confusions to other would-be's" and the haunt of "that mélange of middle-sexed jobs which nature started but never finished." Strip clubs, bars, and pornographic movie houses were common, and prostitutes of all kinds were easy to find, the author noted with a wink.[54] The South Side neighborhoods around Washington Park's Bug Club witnessed a similar residential division as large public housing projects rose to the park's north and the university enclave of Hyde Park resisted integration. At the same time, Chicago's industries declined rapidly as meatpacking and steel production moved out and rail transportation entered a steep decline.

Between 1980 and 2000, gentrification pushed out the last seedy remnants of Chicago's bohemian Towertown, and the legacy of Bughouse Square as a free speech center became a point of contention between developers and progressive memory-keepers. In the 1970s community activists and students tried to revive public speaking in the park to no avail, and the neighborhood's reputation as a center for prostitution became a target of developers, homeowners, and the Newberry Library, who hoped to upgrade the park.[55] In 1976 the Newberry sponsored a July Fourth "reopening" of Washington Square Park with a patriotic program that included a reading of the Declaration of Independence.[56] The event became annual in the 1980s, taking on more progressive tones with the support and advice of Studs Terkel and Len Dupres, who had been the lawyer for the Steelworkers Organizing Committee during the 1930s. But the annual event only underscores the containment of the utopian dreams that speakers once shouted from their soapboxes. Changes to the streetscapes made under Mayor Richard M. Daley, including the proliferation of black iron fences, were designed to make the city more hospitable to white professional homeowners. In 1998 the city built a fence around the park with funds donated by a real estate developer. Studs Terkel considered it a betrayal of memory and a symbol of enclosure. "Bughouse Square always represented open space," Terkel told his audience at the annual Bughouse Square Debates. "Open space means open talk." He asked the audience, "Why do we come here on this August day every year? It's to keep green a memory. Because our memories are being cut down bit by bit. Our amenities are being cut down bit by bit."[57]

Today Chicago's radical past hovers somewhere between commodification and inspiration. Predictably, the bohemian subculture typified by the Dill Pickle Club finds the easiest purchase in contemporary commentary as an ancestor of the urban "hipster" demographic, while the iconography of radicalism, shorn of its organizational heft, features in the branding of microbreweries, cafes, and restaurants.[58] In more hopeful ways, the public memory of Chicago's radical past provides opportunities and inspiration for very real contemporary social movements. The installation of Mary Brogger's 2004 "Haymarket Memorial" near the site of the 1886 bombing and police riot, for instance, was the culmination of a decades-long campaign led by former packinghouse union leader Les Orear and the Illinois Labor History Society. Although some criticized it as excessively mild, and even a betrayal of the Chicago anarchists' memory, the monument created a new focal point for progressive activists, one that is ripe with historical meaning. Progressive groups in the city, along with the Chicago Federation of Labor, made the most of the opportunity by routing the 2006 May Day march for immigrant rights through Haymarket Square, connecting the history of immigrant workers past and present.[59]

New social movements are reviving the wild speech of Bughouse Square, although the park itself is hopelessly gentrified. Organizations and loose affinity groups associated with Occupy Wall Street, immigrant youth and environmental justice movements, and the Movement for Black Lives converge on urban spaces for rallies, banner drops, building occupations, and "die-ins" to protest police brutality, economic inequality, and social exclusion. The surprising scale of the January 2017 Women's March, the spontaneity of demonstrations against the Muslim travel ban, and the spread of school walkouts against gun violence all point to a revitalized activist public sphere. The chatter on social media, shared imagery and text, and the globally recognizable linkages created by "hashtags" are far beyond what activists of the early twentieth century experienced. But in their approach to space, power, and conflict, the new movements echo the everyday speechifying of the working-class public sphere as well as the more dramatic moments of the Wobblies' free speech fights. As we will see in the next chapter, open forums were only one part of a wider educational landscape for organized workers in the early twentieth century. Along with them, activists built an increasingly elaborate program of movement education that trained organizers and built human networks in support of social change.

3

"To see and hear things that have always been there"

Labor's Pedagogy of the Organized

John Brophy believed in the power of ideas. A coal miner since the age of twelve, he rose through the ranks of the United Mine Workers of America (UMWA) to lead one of its key districts in the anthracite coalfields of eastern North America. Inspired by his Catholic faith and what he had seen the miners do in Pennsylvania, he rejected both materialism as explanation and force as strategy. "There are people who think that ideas are of little avail," he told a national conference of trade unionists and educators in April 1921. The wars, revolutions, and counterrevolutions unfolding across the globe convinced some people that force and violence were the only effective tactics. But Brophy told them, "My experience in Central Pennsylvania has convinced me that ideas *are* a power." Over three decades of organizing, the miners of his district had established the eight-hour workday, banished the company store from their communities, and raised income significantly. In the union, "organization and ideas were joined," creating "a consciousness and desire for a better life" among the miners and their families. Together, organization and ideas "have instilled into them a consciousness of the power of numbers. They have made them aware of the fact that they are working in an essential industry, and that because the miner is doing necessary work he is entitled to the best the industry can afford."[1]

To take this final step would require a revolution in the ownership of the industry and the purposes of its management: nationalization and workers' control. The power that could bring about this change would be moral rather than physical: "Not force, not violence, but the Idea is power," Brophy told his audience. An ambitious educational program, voted in by union members, was the engine of this change. Designed to support activists dispersed in semirural settlements, the "Miners' Program" developed in the union's central Pennsylvania unit would also produce "pamphlets and leaflets" and support the labor press to "excite discussion of the question in all its different phases." Organized classes would both "advance the general intelligence of the workers" and develop "the future leaders, the tacticians, [and] the philosophers" of the movement, who would, Brophy hoped, "solve the problems of nationalization."[2] At first Brophy's vision yielded results. Educational events in isolated mining towns increased support for the union, countered employer propaganda, and in one case led to the election of a Labor Party judge, but the postwar open-shop drive soon scuttled hopes for mine nationalization. Moreover, Brophy's organizing efforts brought him into conflict with the UMWA's powerful president, John L. Lewis. After Brophy's unsuccessful bid for the union's presidency in 1926, Lewis expelled Brophy on charges of collaborating with communists.[3]

Brophy's influence was deeply felt in the labor movement and across American industrial society, even without the nationalization of the coal industry. His vision of unionism as a moral power, shared and amplified by activists such as Fannia Cohn and A. Philip Randolph, would come to fruition in Labor's upsurge of the 1930s. The vehicle for developing this moral power was a program of *workers' education*: the cultivation of social movement skills and consciousness among working-class adults. During difficult times of political reaction, trade union retrenchment, and ideological schism, workers' education was the glue that held together a divided and often-defeated union movement at the grass roots. Labor colleges forged networks of like-minded militants and distributed the tools that could effectively contest economic inequality. They also linked trade unions to a wider pool of activism and cultural capital among journalists, writers, and academics. In the process, they built a more secure perch from which working-class activists could effectively engage the public sphere. The main impulse of the movement was toward the development of local activists who would become self-directing nodes in a social movement network. Key to the activation of this network was the seemingly simple task of seeing reality for what it was. As the garment worker Sadie Goodman put it, for the worker who attends a labor college, "the world begins to stretch out. You begin to see and hear things that have always been there, but to which you have been deaf, dumb and blind."[4]

Recognizing that solidarity is less a social condition than a social process, historians have identified education as a key site of social movement formation. Studies of radical activism among groups as disparate as garment workers in New York, sharecroppers in Arkansas, and voting rights activists across the South demonstrate how vital educational efforts were to the process of solidarity making. Multiethnic and biracial organizations overcame the inertia of social division by cultivating deeper understanding of social conditions and articulating a believable, and actionable, path toward change.[5] This process affirmed for working people the idea that "what happen[s] to me is important," as one educator put it, or as a radical organizing manual advised, "nothing that happens to the worker is unimportant." Traditional education and everyday working life taught most workers that their concerns were not worthy of consideration, that their insights were wrong, and that they should leave the important jobs to smarter people. This toxic mix of disempowerment and hopelessness sapped the labor movement's capacity to act. Structures of oppression and the roads to freedom were hidden in the record of every worker's life. The activist educator's job was to help worker-students find the analytical threads in the fabric of their own life histories.

Despite this egalitarian ethic, educators recognized the need to transfer expertise and knowledge to working-class students. Some insisted on a kind of workers' catechism: carefully framed sets of questions and answers designed to introduce the new learners to complex topics and lead them to higher knowledge without distraction. Under the guidance of the self-educated immigrant John Keracher, for instance, the reading groups of the Proletarian Party demanded memorization of key Marxist texts and the party's accepted interpretations of those texts as a prerequisite to more advanced study.[6] Another group of activists, largely college-educated and influenced by the work of John Dewey, forged an approach to teaching centered on workers' own experiences. A generation before the Brazilian Paulo Freire made the idea of critical consciousness a globally familiar part of popular education, the common approach in American workers' education was one of consciousness-raising and capacity building. I call this approach the *pedagogy of the organized* not only as a nod to Freire's 1968 book, *Pedagogy of the Oppressed*, but also to draw a distinction: whereas Freire worked mainly with those who were new to reading and to formal organizations, the workers' education movement in the 1920s and 1930s cultivated the capacities of those with basic schooling who were already active in unions, cooperatives, and progressive politics.[7]

After surveying some of the key institutions of workers' education, I turn to the pedagogy of the labor schools, which coalesced around what would later be called "consciousness raising" through worker-to-worker dialogue, the sharing of life stories, and practical group projects such as theatrical productions and newspapers.

Key to this approach was the selection of a diverse student body that would bring together working women and men from different racial, ethnic, and occupational communities. Teaching strategies that had developed in social movement settings or in private universities faced additional challenges as educators sought to deploy them in the handful of public universities that sponsored workers' education programs beginning in the mid-1920s. How would the political commitments of workers' education square with universities that were dominated by conservative faculty but also proclaimed the universalism of liberal education? The fate of these programs mapped one of the limits of inclusion for the modern university.

Reform, Radicalism, and Workers' Education

John Brophy and his colleagues in the UMWA were not unique in linking their political platform to a grassroots educational program. By the early twentieth century, there was a common desire across the industrial world to train ordinary people to be "leaders, tacticians, and philosophers." Employers, national governments, and every variety of political movement developed plans to influence public opinion and spur ordinary people to action. Whether the purpose was to radicalize workers and peasants, train them in modern modes of production, prepare trade union leaders, or to conform workers' thoughts and actions toward consumerism and upward mobility, popular education was a fundamental preoccupation of modernizing societies across the globe in the early twentieth century.[8] What set workers' education apart from many state-sponsored education efforts was its advocates' commitment to building up the localized capacity of a widely distributed social movement. The fruits of this effort would take time to ripen, but by the late 1930s labor college graduates were waiting in place as legal and political changes opened the door for mass unionization.

Radicals, trade unionists, and immigrant community activists pioneered what would become the interwar workers' education movement. By 1910 the laboring communities of industrial cities like New York and Chicago were overwhelmingly comprised of immigrants and the children of immigrants. Educational initiatives blossomed within ethnic groups, each with its own set of intellectual or religious leaders, newspaper editors, and artistic celebrities. Although some ethnic leaders favored separation, others cultivated links with leaders of other communities and with mainstream American politics.[9] In the years before World War I, however, educational efforts were particularly systematic in consciously multiethnic organizations like the Socialist Party and the IWW, and in trade unions like the ILGWU and the Amalgamated Clothing Workers of America (ACWA). Mirroring the growth of formal education, ideological and occupational communities frequently styled their meetings as colleges and institutes. The Socialist Party organized the Rand School of Social Science in New York City in 1906 and began an educational partnership with the ILGWU in New York in 1914. The Rand School continued into the 1930s and changed its name to the Tamiment Institute, the library of which became an important archive for the study of radicalism when it was donated to New York University in the 1960s. In the Midwest, in 1907 Finnish socialists converted a Lutheran seminary in Duluth, Minnesota, into the Work People's College, which affiliated with the IWW in the early 1920s and continued operations until 1941.[10]

An alliance of middle-class women and immigrant garment workers launched another set of labor schools. The Women's Trade Union League (WTUL) in Chicago, for instance, began in 1905 as a program of Jane Addams's Hull House but moved to the offices of the Chicago Federation of Labor in 1908. The WTUL launched a School for Women Labor Leaders in 1914 so that "the younger working women [could] develop into leaders of the highest type, fitted by experience and education to meet situations arising in industry."[11] The YWCA organized "Industrial Clubs" to support the study of economic issues among women factory and domestic workers. Initiated by college-educated Protestant women known as "industrial secretaries," the leadership of these YWCA industrial groups shifted toward working-class women in the 1910s, and the organization began to openly support unionization as well as protective labor laws. Along with this shift in leadership, the YWCA industrial groups articulated a critique of "discrimination against the newcomer in the industrial field" on the basis of gender, ethnicity, and race, although the organization maintained segregated chapters through the 1930s.[12] Educational initiatives within the ILGWU emerged from the demands and activism of young women garment workers, particularly Jewish and Italian immigrants, and their ability to leverage the assistance of the broader progressive reform community, as historians Annelise Orleck, Jennifer Guglielmo, and others have shown. Spearheaded by Fannia Cohn in the ILGWU and Rose Schneiderman in the WTUL, the union's educational programs first took root in the predominantly female Local 25. The union held classes in trade unionism, economics, and English at their own building, known as Unity House, as well as through a partnership with the New York Public Schools.[13]

Although forms varied, most of these early efforts combined education with advocacy and direct services to their target communities. In this sense, many workers' education groups resembled today's "worker centers," which sociologist Janice Fine identifies as "central components of the immigrant community infrastructure [that serve as] gateway organizations that provide information and training in workers' rights, employment, labor and immigration law, legal services, the English language, and many other programs."[14] Like today's worker centers, many early workers' education programs developed within specific ethnic, language, or occupational communities. However, the most vibrant were multiethnic and multiracial organizations that turned to educational and social programming to build solidarity across their divided membership.

The experiments of the prewar years came to fruition in an efflorescence of educational institution building over the next two decades. Between 1918 and 1921, trade unions, radicals, and reformers established at least twenty "colleges" and "institutes" for workers in the United States. Most of these were local efforts like the Cleveland Workers University, the Seattle Workers College, and the St. Paul Labor College.[15] To guide these efforts, activists held a national conference and launched a Workers Education Bureau (WEB) in 1921. Shortly afterward, delegates from the AFL took the more ambitious step of setting up a residential labor college with financial assistance from wealthy liberal donors. Brookwood Labor College, located in the rustic countryside a short train ride from New York City, would go on to prepare hundreds of union activists and play an important role in the development of industrial unionism until it closed in 1937 amid labor's factional split.[16] Also in 1921, the YWCA and the WTUL helped organize the Summer School for Women in Industry on the campus of Bryn Mawr College, which became the model for a similar program at the University of Wisconsin beginning in 1925.[17] In the South radical intellectuals launched Commonwealth College in rural Arkansas in 1923 and Highlander Folk School in Tennessee in 1932.[18]

The Communist Party developed a more systematic approach to popular education that encompassed publishing, print distribution to bookstores, party chapters, cultural clubs, and training schools. In larger cities the party's John Reed Clubs became sites of artistic and cultural activism that aimed to cultivate creative talent among workers. Party chapters often built on preexisting radical educational efforts, but by 1940 the Communist Party boasted a set of full-service workers' schools, best represented by the Jefferson School in New York, the Lincoln School in Chicago, and the California Labor School in San Francisco. These programs aimed to provide a Marxist alternative to formal higher education—as one historian put it, college without the varsity teams. Like the elaborate program of the Chicago Forum we encountered in chapter 2, these party schools were interclass and interracial sites of social mixing where college-educated artists and academics rubbed shoulders with industrial workers.[19]

Even in its heyday, workers' education drew fire from conservative trade unionists who worried it would be a safe harbor for radicals, and from radicals who thought it was ideologically flabby or a distraction from the real work of organizing. The leaders of the AFL launched a secret investigation of Brookwood in 1927 that condemned the school for its radicalism and its support for John Brophy's rank-and-file insurgency in the mineworkers' union. A year later the AFL convention charged that some of the faculty "were so sympathetic toward communism and the communistic philosophy as to raise a doubt regarding their fitness and qualifications to present to students fairly and accurately the principles, policies and philosophy of the Labor movement in our own country."[20] Others thought workers simply were not ready for rigorous education. Reflecting on his attempt to lecture to garment workers, the socialist journalist Benjamin Stolberg concluded dismissively, "Most dressmakers cannot very well follow a discussion of the wage structure of the United States." The progressive writer Horace Kallen thought the focus of workers' education on poetry and drama was "part of the compensatory mechanism by which current industrial society keeps itself relatively in equilibrium and insures itself against too great upsets."[21] For their part, many communists thought the labor schools controlled by the AFL offered workers only weak tea. They participated in these schools, in the words of one group of California party members, in order to expose the "mistakes and the corruption" of AFL leaders and because as communists they held "the interests of the labor movement higher than the convenience of the reformists, perhaps sincere, who controlled the school."[22] Assailed from the right and the left, labor colleges struggled to survive their precarious economic and institutional condition throughout the interwar years.

"There is no one road to freedom"

By design, labor and political party schools trained only a small proportion of workers and were not meant to be providers of mass education. As journalist Arthur Gleason put it in a pamphlet that circulated widely within the labor movement, "There is no one road to freedom. There are roads to freedom. So workers' education will include elementary classes in English, and entertainment for the crowd. But the road for the leaders of the people will be straight and hard. Only a few thousand out of the millions will take it. It is a different, a new way of life to which the worker is being called." The goal was not personal cultivation but rather "the liberation of the working class, individually and collectively."[23] The pedagogical theorists of workers' education were eager to distinguish how their work was different from other forms of education among working adults, immigrants, or college students. They focused on the development of local networks of activists with the skills and resources to build up study groups, cooperatives, political parties, and unions. As Gleason wrote, workers' education was a process by which "grown persons best educate each other" through discussion, reading, and debate. Self-organized groups ranging in size from five to twenty-five "take to themselves a like-minded teacher, who is a good fellow, and together they work regularly and hard." There should be programs of "semi-entertainment with a cultural slant" for those rank-and-file workers who were less inclined to study. But the most vital part of the movement would "give the ambitious minority of the rank and file an intensive education" in small and rigorous classes.[24]

These classes would put the "self-cultivation" of activists to a social purpose, aiming to promote pragmatic participation in democratic groups. In service of these goals, the movement's early pedagogical thinkers sought to specify the inner workings of social movements and the role of individual activists in shaping movement policy. As a result, prosaic skills took on outsized importance in workers' education. Public speaking and parliamentary procedure hardly seem revolutionary. Yet for those who felt silenced by their lack of confidence and knowledge, as well as by their experiences and social standing, the path to power began on a soapbox or in a union meeting. The innocuous-sounding manual *Joining Public Discussion* by Wellesley College rhetoric professor Alfred Sheffield, which was the first entry in the WEB's "Workers Bookshelf" series, is a case in point. "Every man (and woman too) with an ambition for self-betterment should give a thought to his possibilities of influence," wrote Sheffield. Those who master the "art of transmuting . . . experience into influence [become] an asset to every organization which has a stake in seeing right ideas prevail." The mode of influence that promised the most return was not dazzling rhetoric, superior knowledge, or correct dogma, but "the technique of *discussion*." Sheffield urged readers to see each "deliberative meeting as a sort of field of magnetic forces wherein his mind can conspire with the other minds to organize socially advantageous currents. His speaking is ideally influential when it precipitates a general mood to create an understanding."[25] The goal was to guide, not manipulate, discussion. Sheffield envisioned effective group discussions as a consensual process that would "harmonize" different ideas not by leveling them down but through the conscious technique of having key participants hold pragmatic, collective outcomes as the ideal. Beginning with a wide range of partially formulated ideas, discussion groups "follow up the most promising idea" with research and further discussion. These pragmatic tactics aimed to strengthen group solidarity by drawing upon the ideas and sentiments of all participants. Rather than vanquishing the minority, the successful leader uses parliamentary procedure to maintain "crew-mindedness" in meetings in the service of maintaining group solidarity in the long term. The smart leader "remembers that his opponent on to-day's issue may be his ally on to-morrow's—if the debate leaves no personal sore spots."[26] Rather than win particular internal battles at all costs, the goal was to cultivate an ethic of organizational care that would sustain the kinds of relationships necessary to win protracted and difficult fights with hostile employers and governments.

Gleason, Sheffield, and other early advocates of workers' education imagined the peer study group as the basic unit of action. Before long, however, more structured instruction became the norm in the new labor colleges with important implications for the movement's understanding of educational authority. For anyone trained in the pedagogy of American schools and universities, standing before a classroom of working people like Harry Haywood and Rose Pesotta would be a challenging proposition. Ed Falkowski recalled the unpleasant fate of one unprepared college-trained instructor at Brookwood. The youthful professor was foolish enough to assert the validity of the profit system in a workers' class in economics. "The left-wingers of the class challenged this version," leaving the instructor shaken and stammering, although several "conservative" railroad unionists in the class came to the defense of the instructor and the profit system. Casting aside the core assumptions of traditional education—that teachers know and students learn—how would labor schools structure authority in the classroom and by extension in the movement? "Lectures were taboo," recalled one instructor at Wisconsin's School for Workers. "Classroom discussions proceeded by the exchange of ideas and experiences with the teacher acting as leader and counsellor."[27]

In this context, workers' negative memories of formal education became an important experiential touchstone. Many working-class, immigrant, and African American children experienced public schooling as ruling-class and ruling-race indoctrination. In the words of Bethlehem, Pennsylvania, tailor Chris Sproger, the history taught in public schools was "mainly certain events in the lives of conspicuous characters to celebrate their political successes and record their wars. It is given to cultivate good-will toward those now in power. Such educated ignorance leads the mass of the workers to think that the present order of society, with its schemes of things as they are, has been established by some supernatural power and therefore cannot be changed."[28] Or, as Richard Wright said of his emerging desire for personal equality, "I was building up in me a dream which the entire educational system of the South had been rigged to stifle. I was feeling the very thing that the state of Mississippi had spent millions of dollars to make sure that I would never feel."[29]

The patriotic curriculum of Americanization schools, along with the condescending attitude of many instructors, was a frequent complaint among immigrant workers. One complained that immigrants enrolled to "learn English, but instead they were taught how to love the flag." Like Sproger, the youthful New York garment worker and Socialist Party activist Jennie Matyas considered history a particularly powerful ideological formation that public school teachers used to justify existing inequalities. Workers' education would refocus history from the kings, queens, and generals to the slaves and workers. As Matyas told the first national gathering of worker-educators in 1921: "When I read ancient history and was told that Nebuchadnezzer (or whatever that fellow's name was), built the hanging gardens for the mistress he liked, I thought he was a wonderful man, such a chivalrous man, but now when I think of the number of slaves that built those gardens, I want to know what was the price those slaves paid for the caprice of one man and for the caprice of one woman." More than a decade later, and an ocean away, Bertolt Brecht would pose a similar challenge to conventional history in his poem *Questions from a Worker Who Reads*: "Every page a victory. Who cooked the feast for the victors? Every 10 years a great man. Who paid the bill?"[30]

This reaction against public schooling as indoctrination sparked both useful innovations in the pedagogy and, for many, an aversion to cultural habits of the stereotypical intellectual. Trade unionists attending a conference on the qualities of good labor organizers at Brookwood, for instance, registered concern over "whether attempting to train labor organizers in labor classes and colleges might not be harmful, might not make 'intellectuals' of them or dull the edge of their militancy and working-class enthusiasm."[31] Horace Kallen was similarly dubious of intellectuals in the labor movement, concluding that the "pedagogues and 'intellectuals' and journalists who are in 'sympathy' with labor [have] never helped toward an envisagement or generation of the mechanics of successful control" of industry. For him, the real "teachers of labor have been the officials of labor, and the teacher of the officials has been experience."[32]

This view proved as durable as it was impractical to implement. Ernest Schwartztrauber, longtime director of the University of Wisconsin School for Workers, noted that teaching was a skill in itself that was not necessarily developed through union leadership. Nevertheless, even in the 1950s Schwartztrauber wrote, "Trade union leadership is inclined to believe that the best teachers are those who have grown up in the ranks of labor." He agreed that personal experience as a laborer was an invaluable asset for the workers' education instructor: "The fear of unemployment, for example, the sense of insecurity, the feeling of helplessness in the individual whose only possessions are his hands and his skills—these inner experiences cannot be delivered and transmitted [in classrooms]. They come only to workers as workers." As a former high school teacher, however, Schwartztrauber considered teaching its own kind of skill, blending content knowledge with intellectual flexibility in the classroom. He observed that trade union leaders who tried to teach often used the authoritarian teaching methods they had learned in school, methods that repelled the average worker. In practical terms, he wrote, workers' education programs had to find college-educated instructors because there were so few qualified instructors from working-class backgrounds.[33]

As labor leaders sometimes worried that "a little knowledge is a dangerous thing" and might dilute workers' militancy and class identity, the pedagogical context of labor colleges created pressure to construe lived experience as more authentic and productive than book learning. During the 1920s autobiographical writing became a key pedagogical tool in the growing workers' education movement.[34] Diffused through networks of left-wing educators, the imperative to "wake each other up" by sharing personal stories aimed to teach economics to workers through reflection on their own work lives. The rank-and-file workers who authored these life stories tended to emphasize experience over reading, in part because the pedagogy asked them to do so. As Karyn Hollis explains in her study of writing in the curriculum of the Bryn Mawr Summer School for Women in Industry, instructors quickly found that worker-students hated and did poorly on traditional academic essays. As a result, instructors crafted autobiographical writing assignments as a way for students to explain economic concepts through the medium of life experience.[35]

Drawing on the ideas of progressive education, instructors like Amy Hewes of the Bryn Mawr Summer School for Women Workers began her classes in economics by asking students to research their own first jobs. She also taught history "backward," starting from contemporary issues rather than the distant past. "The worker's experience is the only possible foundation for his education. As a student he must, of course, journey from the known to the unknown; he can grasp the new and the strange only as he succeeds in bringing it into relations with what is already in the field of his interest and attention."[36] Ironically, she had come to this approach because workers in her classes had so much knowledge of left sectarian politics that their arguments disrupted class time. "Radicals and conservatives of all shades expound their points of view and each group is occupied with its own intellectual and emotional position.... There was attack and defense of various positions but no free inquiry and at times the general atmosphere provided an effective blockade to any advance of new ideas."[37] Shifting the conversation to personal experience, Hewes and other instructors then helped worker-students mine their own life stories for evidence of economic structure. As one supportive observer noted of the process, "The writing created and vivified for them usually for the first time in their lives the idea that 'what happened to me' is important. It is interesting to others; it is a part of history."[38] Whether it was true that students saw this connection for the first time is a topic I return to in chapter 5; however, in this exercise they undoubtedly saw the power of a well-told personal story for advancing the cause of labor.

The leaders and faculty of labor schools faced a constant balancing act between the expertise of instructors and the desire of students to learn from one another. The Work People's College, for instance, stressed its flexibility to meet student demands. In addition to offering core subjects such as labor history and economics, "if enough want some other subject taught, so far it has been found possible to offer it." Like at other colleges, socializing with peers was a major attraction, even for radicals: "Dances, skating parties, boxing bouts and the like," as well as collaboration with other students, "adds zest to one's studies, furnishes splendid case material for study, and provides an ideal atmosphere for this work."[39] Kenosha, Wisconsin, faculty worker and union activist Harold J. Newton recalled that for many years after his summer in Madison he reread the lectures of his professor Arthur Calhoun. Despite this, he told an interviewer, "You learned as much, in my book, from the students as you did from the instructors because you exchanged experiences of what you had run into and how you had attacked the problems. And you listened to what they had done, and they listened to what you had done, what your proposals were, and it caused you to think, actually, as to what would be the best way to approach the problems that you were going to face . . . you were facing."[40]

Fostering student interactions across ethnic, gender, occupational, and racial divisions was at once a central purpose of residential labor colleges and one of their major outcomes. As labor historians have noted, many industrial workplaces were deeply divided along lines of ethnicity, race, and gender. In steel mills and packinghouses, for instance, the better-paid, skilled jobs tended to go to Scots-, Irish-, and German-American male workers. Dirty, dangerous, and low-paying jobs often went to workers who were new to the industries: Slavs, Italians, and African Americans. The student bodies of labor colleges like Brookwood, Bryn

Mawr, and the Wisconsin School for Workers were racially integrated but overwhelmingly white. The latter two were initially for women only, although the School for Workers began to include men in 1928. An applicant's ethnic and racial background was made known to faculty and administrators through details on application forms. Applicants listed their birthplace, that of their parents, and their first language. In 1927, the year Sadie Goodman attended, about 70 percent of the students at the Wisconsin summer school were children of immigrants.[41]

Officially opposed to racial discrimination, labor colleges created space for dialogue on race relations and defended the rights of black students in the communities beyond the confines of their classrooms. Alice Shoemaker, the coordinator of the Wisconsin summer school and a member of the Fellowship of Reconciliation, arranged for interracial housing beginning in 1927 and carefully recruited African American women through her contacts in the YWCA. School administrators identified African American applicants through letters of recommendation, and the University of Wisconsin flagged their applications with a discreetly penciled "c" for "colored." The numbers of African American students attending these labor colleges remained small, however, and students experienced both honest fellowship with white students and faculty and awkward moments of prejudice in the predominantly white labor colleges. For instance, the application form of Chicago postal worker Robert Avant to the University of Wisconsin School for Workers in 1933 did not flag his race, although his home address and work experience were suggestive. Avant's instructors praised his performance in racial terms, with one noting that he was "perhaps the most engaging and attractive looking negro I have ever known." Following the summer session, Avant wrote to fellow students that he immediately missed them upon returning home. Heaping on the praise, he noted that "living as a family of big children from many different backgrounds and many variable shades of temperaments was a good sociological experiment chuck full [*sic*] of lessons in social mind[ed]ness." Although the statement might be interpreted as either a positive assessment of camaraderie or a subtle indictment of bad behavior, Avant was clearly on good terms with his classmates. He served as the leader of the school's Chicago alumni club in 1934 and 1935 and hosted his fellow students at a fund-raising event at the South Side YWCA.[42]

Unlike Robert Avant, Pauli Murray was already a seasoned activist when she applied to Brookwood in the late 1930s, hoping to learn more about the labor issues that were so central to organizing in New York City's African American community. In her autobiography she recalled the "almost religious fervor" of the students and teachers at Brookwood, which she compared to that of the civil rights and women's movements of later decades. And through her interactions with fellow students, she had a series of revelations about the nature of oppression that would shape her thinking about organizing for many years into the future. "As I became more immersed in workers' education," she wrote, "my conceptions of racial identity and of injustice began to undergo a significant change." As she listened to her white fellow workers "tell their personal stories of being evicted, starved out, beaten, and jailed when they tried to organize a union," she heard "echoes of the black experience." Murray also developed a greater appreciation for the subtle ways "that a system of oppression draws much of its strength from the acquiescence of its victims, who have accepted the dominant image of themselves and are paralyzed by a sense of helplessness." One of her fellow students, a white man from Georgia named "Red," was so disoriented by the presence of an African American that he left the program early. "For the first time," Murray wrote, she "saw clearly how racism could cripple white as well as black people." Unexpectedly, Red's response to her race triggered for Murray an analysis of her own "psychological conditioning" by racism and her need to "prove myself worthy of the rights that white individuals took for granted," which "reduced my capacity for resistance to racial injustice." After Brookwood, Murray returned to New York, where she taught classes for the Brotherhood of Sleeping Car Porters, but reflecting on the national and global political situation of the mid-1930s drew her back to the South. As she wrote in her journal around this time, it was "the duty of Negroes to press for political, economic and educational equality for themselves and for disinherited whites; that it is the responsibility of socially-minded Negro and white Southerners to work out this problem; and that the job of interpretation and leadership falls to those of both races with a knowledge of the problems and an understanding of the tremendous task to be accomplished."[43]

Murray's experience and her strategic takeaway suggested one of the key goals of the workers' education movement. The isolation of individual activists and localized movements had been a major weakness for union drives in the generation before 1920. Labor colleges brought together workers from different social and occupational backgrounds and a number of hometowns and neighborhoods to create human networks that could span these persistent divides. Unlike the expanding system of colleges and universities with their imposing campus buildings, labor colleges and workers' education classes typically operated on shoestring budgets and donated labor. Although this made them much more precarious, it also led them to focus on the human infrastructure that was their chief educational outcome.

In the Shadow of the University

Alongside the trade union and left-wing training schools, a handful of public universities launched workers' education programs during the 1920s. These programs have not captured the imagination of historians as much as Brookwood, Communist Party schools, and the Highlander Folk School, but they played an important role in training leaders of mainstream unions just as those unions were becoming politically and economically powerful in the 1930s and 1940s. Unlike the movement-based schools, workers' education in public universities had to answer to administrators who were suspicious of ties to labor unions, and governing boards dominated by business interests. Most university faculty were uninterested in educating wage workers, some considered workers' education a kind of propaganda that violated their ideals of academic objectivity, and others were ideologically hostile to unions. Constantly under pressure to justify their connections to unions and the character of their student bodies, the leaders of these university programs articulated creative justifications for their programs that presaged the way activist faculty and students of the 1970s framed ethnic and women's studies. These promising experiments never broke into the mainstream of university education and were typically sidelined in specialized colleges or university extension programs. By the 1950s many were renamed "labor education" to signal their focus on collective bargaining. As universities embarked on their massive expansion in the 1950s and 1960s, opening their doors to the children of working-class families, labor education was sequestered on its own narrow path.

The story of university-based workers' education sheds light on the development of both the university and the labor movement. As workers' education became more formalized and stable after World War II, it also became more dominated by male leadership, more tied to trade union bureaucracies, and more averse to radical expression. Leaders of the postwar industrial relations schools embraced this new institutional context. They interpreted the more fluid context of the 1920s, and especially the participation of the YWCA and the Socialist Party, as a handicap imposed by the novelty of the enterprise. In reality, these networks were both the roots of workers' education and its most important outcome. The leaders of university-based labor schools, like those of movement-based schools, drew on their contacts in unions, progressive politics, and women's reform groups to find and evaluate potential students and instructors, and when students finished their course of study, most returned to the institutional contexts that first brought them to the attention of the movement. The personal connections created by the labor college experience spanned the country's geography, helping leaders like A. J. Muste to gather information about emerging industrial conflicts, assess the talents of young organizers, and direct them to job opportunities that would prepare them for later leadership positions. As a YWCA official associated with the University of Wisconsin's School for Workers noted, "I have observed the Middle Western girls who worked at Bryn Mawr literally become 'hot spots' of contagion on their return to their native heath, and who are not only stimulated themselves to grasp more and more of the facts in question, but who really got a sense of social responsibility and became promoters of classes in their local Associations or other social units."[44] Ironically, the "contagion" that traveled along these personal networks even spawned new educational institutions that universities later claimed as their own.

The university faculty who helped to launch these experiments could not have ignored this institutional and movement context. With advice from economists John R. Commons, Don Lescohier, and Selig Perlman, the University of Wisconsin launched its summer session School for Women Workers on the model of Bryn Mawr's program. The governing committee included representatives of the university, the YWCA, and the Wisconsin AFL. A history of the school written by longtime director Ernest Schwartztrauber acknowledged the state's progressive political context and especially the role of the Milwaukee labor movement in the genesis of the school, the role of the YWCA in recruiting students during the early years, and the "untiring effort and devotion" of the long-serving administrator of the program, Alice Shoemaker. By the late 1930s, the school recruited directly from newly formed industrial unions, leading to a predominantly male student body and a more stable financial status for the school. With the YWCA no longer necessary for recruiting and fund-raising, the school abandoned its cross-class reform network. Likewise, the school's ties to socialists were also easy to forget as many erstwhile partisans shifted into the Democratic Party by the late 1930s. Henry Ohl, a Milwaukee printer and one-term socialist state legislator was a key adviser and promoter of the School for Workers, but he left the Socialist Party when it endorsed a CIO rival to his AFL typographical union.[45]

The institutional setting of postwar universities, in particular the emergence of industrial relations as the dominant field of scholarship for those interested in labor issues, encouraged this process of forgetting. Business school faculty specializing in personnel management had created some of the country's first industrial relations programs at the University of Pennsylvania and Princeton in the early 1920s. Funded by philanthropic industrialists, these programs aimed to promote responsible management that would allow for a certain amount of input by workers without seriously challenging the authority of managers and owners. In New York, Republican state senator Irving Ives spearheaded a new program at the upstate campus of Cornell University that largely ignored the elaborate system of union-sponsored workers' education in New York City. In the face of growing labor militancy, Ives and his legislative colleagues sought a program that would teach labor and management representatives side by side in order to develop "mutual and cooperative analysis of the problems common to both groups." The result was a program that included undergraduate education, a research and information service, and an extension program. Although this was a significant public investment in the study of labor economics, conservative patronage was a necessary precondition and thus a limiting factor on the program's ideological range and practical impact. Labor educator Mark Starr thought it premature to focus on the coeducation of labor and management representatives in a traditional college setting when so few workers had college degrees. Starr worried that a commitment to a four-year program would remove budding labor leaders from their constituencies at work and socialize them to the industrial relations bureaucracy rather than the democratic spirit of the union local.[46]

In other universities, conservative faculty proved an effective bulwark against labor economics and public affairs programming as well as workers' education. Faculty were typically more resistant than administrators, who understood the usefulness of cultivating support from organized workers, especially after the surge of unionism during World War II. Administrators at the University of Illinois, for instance, were not openly hostile when the Illinois Federation of Labor called on the university in 1942 to create a new department to "assist the workers in their many complex problems," just as the university had previously done for farmers. Internal reports discovered, however, that there were no faculty on campus who could lead such an initiative, because conservative faculty in the Department of Economics had driven them out. The labor economist Gordon Watkins had resigned from a full professorship at Illinois to join the newly opened University of California at Los Angeles in 1923 after the chair of his department tried to cut his pay. Watkins was no radical, but he had come to academia from the working class. He had worked as a coal miner in Wales in his youth and, after moving to the United States, worked his way through high school and college as a railroad mechanic and a lumberjack before earning a doctorate from the University of Pennsylvania. Two other labor economists who followed Watkins to the University of Illinois were "subject to continuous criticism" by senior faculty, and both eventually quit in favor of government service. In the late 1930s, the department attempted to hire antiunion business consultants to teach labor courses. A liberal faculty member described one as "a man who by his writings and utterances is clearly a Fascist." The entire College of Commerce, he concluded, displayed "a lack of sympathy and a spirit of hostility toward organized labor." Over the foot-dragging of the faculty, and with direct funding from the state legislature, administrators set up the Institute of Labor Relations in 1946 as a free-standing unit. At the behest of business executives, however, administrators changed the name to the Institute of Labor *and Industrial* Relations.[47]

The fate of the Western Summer School for Workers, affiliated with the University of California (UC), suggests both the generative power of labor college networks and the ability of formal institutions to erase the work of ordinary workers. The University of California Extension started its workers' education program in 1921 and won the designation of a "labor controlled" program by virtue of a partnership with the California AFL. With only one staff person for the entire state, the former schoolteacher John Kerchen, the UC program remained unambitious until the early 1930s, when a group of Brookwood alumni created a summer school program in Los Angeles and invited the UC to be a partner. The summer school was the work of Sadie Goodman and a group of garment workers who had migrated to Los Angeles from the East in the 1920s, some for health reasons and others to escape factional fights in the garment unions. Drawing on her ties to labor colleges in the East and Midwest, and to the YWCA and female reform network of Los Angeles, Goodman and her colleagues launched a western version of the labor colleges that had given them such an intellectually stimulating experience.

Born in England to Jewish parents from Russian Poland, Goodman arrived in the United States at the age of fourteen, worked in garment factories in Rochester, New York, and became a rank-and-file organizer for the Amalgamated Clothing Workers of America. Goodman was already well read when she attended the labor schools at Bryn Mawr and Brookwood between 1921 and 1925. Rose Schneiderman of the WTUL wrote in support of Goodman's application to Brookwood, describing her as "a rare personality" and "sincerity itself," although she worried that a two-year absence from Rochester "might estrange her from the group she is serving." After her time at Brookwood, Goodman worked for the ACWA in Philadelphia but did not return to Rochester, as Schneiderman had feared. She moved on to Chicago, where a fellow Brookwood student, Sarah Rozner, helped her get work and plug into the community of women organizing for a greater role in the ACWA. Feeling unwelcomed by the union's male leadership, Goodman enrolled in the University of Wisconsin's summer school, her tuition paid with a donation by the Wisconsin novelist Zona Gale. As she explained to

A. J. Muste in a letter from Madison, she could not take up the leadership role as expected in Rochester due to a factional dispute between Italians and Jews in the local (she sided with the Italians). In Chicago, male union officials thought the "cry for women's rights in our union was a move for official jobs," which made them guard their positions more jealously. "Constant fighting of this type has a demoralizing effect on me both mentally and physically," she told Muste, "that makes me useless and detrimental to the movement."[48] Instead, Goodman enrolled in the Wisconsin summer school in 1927, where "her influence on the girls was instructive and commendable," according to the organizers.[49]

Goodman's organizing skills, and her connections across the labor and women's reform movements, helped to launch what would become a western version the Wisconsin School for Workers. In the fall of 1927 she traveled to Los Angeles for the first of many stays in the booming southwestern city. Along with friends she established a weekly study group at the YWCA in 1928 that sent several of its members to Bryn Mawr over the following years.[50] Then in 1931, Rose Pesotta—an immigrant garment worker, activist in the ILGWU, and graduate of the Bryn Mawr and Brookwood Labor Colleges—arrived in Los Angeles and began sending reports back to her mentor, A. J. Muste, at Brookwood Labor College. Pesotta connected with Goodman and her group, departed for the East in the summer of 1932, and returned the following year to lead a major strike of the city's garment workers.[51] Following Pesotta's sojourn in Los Angeles, Goodman and her comrades worked their networks in the YWCA to recruit instructors, raise money, and secure Occidental College in Los Angeles as the first site for the Western School for Industrial Workers during the summer of 1933. At the suggestion of their partners in the state's Adult Education Department, the organizing committee invited the University of California Extension to cosponsor the summer school.[52] Between 1933 and 1941 the Western Summer School—later known as the Pacific Coast Labor School—trained hundreds of rank-and-file unionists, nominally under the auspices of the University of California Extension. An accounting of alumni activities from the late 1930s had some dramatic highlights. William Morel, student body president for 1935, was "commanding a Spanish loyalist gunboat in the Mediterranean," and Perley Payne from 1937 was also in Spain serving in the loyalist medical service. Many more former students were active as officers in local and regional union bodies, leaders of workers' education programs, editors of union newspapers, and political activists and organizers, among other activities.

The shifting political climate of the late 1930s also weighed on administrators at the University of California, who could not decide whether the Pacific Coast

Labor School was a worthy experiment or a toxic threat to liberal values. While they cosponsored the school through the university's extension division, officials repeatedly told concerned businessmen it had "no organic connection to the university."[53] The 1935 session, held on the Berkeley campus, prompted a backlash from business leaders in the state, who charged the school with promoting communism. The school's director assured UC president Robert Sproul that "out-and-out trouble makers" had been excluded from the student body and that the content of the curriculum was "in every way sound from the viewpoint of university scholarship."[54] However, the director also noted that not all communist students were bad, and "a few have been first rate students." Often they were "taking their first fling at radicalism" and had only read "a few ten-cent communist pamphlets."[55] Despite these reassurances, the program was never again held on a UC campus. The school's leader, George Hedley, explained to Schwartztrauber of Wisconsin that the western school was caught "between a [university] President who wants to be liberal and a Board of Regents which is almost violently reactionary." To ask for more than the "formal blessing" of the university, Hedley wrote, "would seriously jeopardize what we have."[56]

A progressive political wave washed across the state beginning in 1934 as longshoremen struck in San Francisco and Upton Sinclair nearly won the governorship on a pledge to end poverty in California. After the 1938 election a progressive state senator from Los Angeles, Culbert Olson, took the governorship and progressives held power in the state assembly. The following year the university administration faced the prospect of a budget windfall when Democratic legislators introduced a bill to provide $400,000 annually (about $7 million in 2017 dollars) for a statewide program of education for labor leaders and wage earners modeled on the agricultural extension.[57] Although the bill faced resistance from the university extension and business leaders, university administrators could read the writing on the wall.[58] By the spring of 1942, university president Sproul was said to be "taking a personal interest" in the development of the workers' education program and named UCLA labor economists Gordon Watkins and Paul Dodd as UC representatives on the Pacific Coast Labor School governing board.[59] Dodd was an expert on health insurance and the aircraft industry as well as a mediator for the War Labor Board. Sensing an opportunity for institutional growth, he proposed the creation of an Institute of Industrial Relations at UCLA modeled on the programs at Princeton and the University of Pennsylvania, his alma mater.[60] In 1945 the general assembly appropriated $100,000 ($1.35 million in 2017 dollars) for the biennium to establish Institutes of Industrial Relations on the Berkeley and Los Angeles campuses, develop industrial relations courses, and reach workers through extension services. The final appropriation halved the original proposal in order to appease opposition from business-oriented legislators.[61] The institutes were formally launched in 1946 with Paul Dodd directing at UCLA and Dodd's former War Labor Board subordinate Clark Kerr directing at Berkeley.[62] In the words of an early memorandum defining the program's approach, the institutes were to be geared toward the "public interest rather than toward the special interests of either labor or industry."[63]

Claiming the middle ground proved an effective strategy, especially as the United States and the Soviet Union careened into the Cold War. Industrial relations took a dispassionate academic approach to subjects that had fired the imagination of the class partisans who had driven the workers' education movement. This neutral stance was in turn a product of progressive academics' encounters with conservative administrators, university benefactors, and state officials.[64] The University of Michigan's Workers Education Service, for instance, thrived briefly after World War II, sponsoring a wide ranging and apparently popular program of lectures, courses, and films primarily in the auto-industrial districts of southeastern Michigan. Following a complaint from a General Motors executive to the university's president in 1948, however, administrators quickly defunded the program, and despite widespread protest by labor and civil rights groups, the program never regained its former stature.[65] A similar fate met the California Labor School (CLS), although it had a slower demise. Affiliated with the Communist Party, the CLS grew financially successful during and after World War II, making the most of veterans' educational benefits. The school purchased its own building in downtown San Francisco and launched satellite campuses in Oakland and Los Angeles in 1946. In the summer of 1948, CIO unions in Southern California endorsed the L.A. campus and announced that the CLS would provide research services to CIO locals. "An informed membership . . . armed with an understanding of the economic, social and political forces on the current scene, is indispensable these days to the successful struggle of our unions," wrote the CIO's secretary-treasurer. When the federal government turned against the Communist Party in the years that followed, however, the CLS found itself stripped of its eligibility to use veterans' benefits and under a suit from the Internal Revenue Service. Unable to return the veterans' tuition to the federal government, the school shut its doors and sold its building in the early 1950s.[66]

The fate of these programs suggests both the value and the limits of formal institutional standing for labor scholarship and teaching. While the Pacific Coast Labor School did not reappear after the war, the Institute of Industrial Relations (IIR) at UCLA maintained a robust outreach program to unions and management and to adult education programs in Southern California. Programming for unions included union hall lectures and workshops, as well as annual summer institutes for steelworkers, the ILGWU, central labor councils, labor editors, labor educators, and health plan officers. The IIR even placed graduate student research assistants within union research departments.[67] Unlike the IIR's extensive programs for management, however, labor education required special justification to university administrators. For instance, when the institute assisted unions with collectively bargained health plans, it drew heated criticism from local doctors. An internal report justified the program as promoting public health and therefore being "consistent with [the IIR's] public interest orientation." It warned, however, that labor educators must take special care to "maintain objectivity and intellectual integrity" and to communicate to union partners their neutrality in disputes with management. No similar caveats or justifications were required for management programs, which thrived in the 1950s and 1960s.[68] For workers' education to carry on in this new institutional context, its proponents would have to carefully balance their commitment to both workers and the university.

"There isn't one working class"

The ideas that John Brophy identified when he spoke to educators and workers in 1921 remained powerful in the years between the world wars, even if the goals of nationalization and workers' control remained elusive. The mechanism Brophy and others imagined would be the means of achieving these goals—a systematic program of workers' education—had coalesced from a variety of social practices and institutional experiments, many of which were sharply ideological and partisan. In the 1920s many educational activists turned toward less ideological approaches as they sought to recruit and train workers who were not as steeped in existing sectarian positions. Deportation and incarceration robbed labor and radical movements of some of their most advanced activists, as intended by government officials and employers. Intense factional disputes within unions during the 1920s led some activists to drop out of the movement. The declining membership and weakened state of the unions led others to seek more pragmatic approaches to organizing. Ideological pluralism became the norm within labor colleges and workers' discussion groups, reflecting both the dizzying multiplicity of local settings for the movement, and its partisans and the need to draw workers together across these localized solidarities. As Rose Pesotta said at a 1926 Brookwood conference, "To me, Workers' Education is synonymous with the labor movement as a whole. There isn't one working class. There are groups and conflicts, and Workers' Education is divided in the same way."[69] Learning to see commonality across the divides of geography and community was the role of workers' education as a movement and the task of organizers like Pesotta. Where traditional education aims to give students "cultural capital" that will help individuals in a competitive labor market, workers' education aimed to build a collective capacity for action based on the knowledge and experience gained by individual worker-students.

The goal was not to train labor functionaries, although there was a growing need for treasurers, journalists, and even bankers for the movement. Instead, labor colleges aimed to empower individual workers who could animate a far-flung and often weakly connected movement. Alumni clubs in major cities and regular correspondence between alumni in the field and the organizers of labor colleges, such as Muste and Shoemaker, circulated information about local struggles, job opportunities in the movement, and promising new recruits. Muste and other editors published reports from the field in magazines like *Labor Age*, recirculating strategic ideas across the network of readers and organizers.

The loose network created by labor colleges and their graduates created a point of entry for rising activists or reentry for those who left the movement due to factional disputes or failed organizing drives. Like Sadie Goodman, Jennie Matyas was a promising young leader who dropped out of activism during the faction fights of the 1920s. She had been active in the ILGWU and the Socialist Party in New York and had spoken at the first national conference of the Workers Education Bureau. The infamously bitter factional dispute between left and right in the New York ILGWU was too much to bear. As she recalled in a later interview, "To fight a fellow worker was emotionally impossible for me." She traveled the country enrolling for a semester at a time in universities in Illinois, Wisconsin, and Colorado as a kind of educational tourist, eventually settling in San Francisco. When the ILGWU reorganized in the city during the early 1930s, Matyas reconnected with the union, was hired as an organizer, and plugged back into her activist network. She became an adviser to the Pacific Coast Labor School, creating another direct line from the prewar socialist movement to the emerging industrial union movement of the New Deal era.[70]

Labor colleges helped individual activists focus their knowledge and forge effective relationships within the movement that often lasted a lifetime. Like Matyas and Goodman, Sarah Rozner was a rank-and-file participant in the first wave of garment worker strikes. A youthful immigrant from Hungary to Chicago, Rozner recalled that even before her encounter with the labor movement, she "was a rebel against injustice." She was drawn into the labor movement during the 1910 strike at Hart, Shaffner, and Marx that launched the Amalgamated Clothing Workers of America. Her father had told her that "to work when there was a strike was taking the bread out of someone else's mouth, and that was the biggest sin anybody could commit." She began attending lectures and reading radical pamphlets, including those of the anarchist Emma Goldman. Later, when she stood up to one boss and quit, he called her a "little Emma Goldman." The labor movement became Rozner's community and her religion. "I had greater respect for, and derived greater spiritual satisfaction, from the top leadership of our Unions than I ever did from the rabbis," she wrote in a retrospective of her long career. But if Sidney Hillman was her rabbi, Brookwood Labor College was "the place of the development of our souls," she wrote. During her two-year stint she blossomed, surrounded by coal miners, painters, and garment workers, as well as a student body that included Europeans and Asians, and an African American teacher from the South. Brookwood "wasn't a revolutionary thing," she said. "They gave you the ideas to use them the way you wanted, to interpret them the way you wanted. . . . We had communist speakers, anarchist speakers, conservative speakers. Have your choice. Use your own head and draw your own conclusions."[71]

Workers like Ed Falkowski, Sadie Goodman, and Sarah Rozner were already deeply committed to labor, and well read in the literature of social critique before they arrived at Brookwood and other workers' schools. The pedagogy of the organized used by labor colleges developed students' social and economic knowledge, and their skills as organizers. It also fostered introspection and individual judgment, not for individual gain, but to strengthen the collective effort. Students would return to their own social milieu where they were expected to operate effectively within their organizations. Groups of alumni clustered in various industrial towns offered mutual support and camaraderie, but there would be little direct supervision, minimal institutional support, and only voluntary reporting back to the school. By 1940, workers like these were embedded in many of the country's industrial communities. They ascribed to a wide variety of political philosophies, but they were mainly leftists. They longed for the day that powerful unions would tip the balance of power between workers and bosses, and they knew just what to do when they got the opportunity to organize.

PART II

Imagining Critical Consciousness

"It was Lincoln Steffens who commanded me to write this story," Tillie Lerner wrote in a brief preface to her 1934 essay about the San Francisco general strike, "Thousand-Dollar Vagrant." San Francisco police had raided Lerner's apartment, where she and fellow communist organizers were relaxing after a long day's work in support of the longshoremen's strike. The police beat her male companions and hauled them all off to jail on the charge of vagrancy. An unknown to the national audience of the *New Republic*, Lerner commandeered the voice of the muckraking journalist Steffens to frame her work. He had told her, "People don't know how they arrest you, what they say, what happens in court. Tell them. Write it just as you told me about it." Steffens's instructions highlighted the widespread assumption among cultural gatekeepers that the power of workers' stories lay mainly in their unscripted adherence to experience. To become visible in the national public sphere, Lerner had to play the part. She ended the preface in her own voice—"So here it is." But instead of a raw transcript of experience, she launched into a carefully crafted, literary recreation of her arrest, jailing, and trial at the hands of San Francisco authorities that had the flavor of a hard-boiled detective story.[1] A month later Lerner published a second essay about the San Francisco strike in the left literary journal *Partisan Review*. "Do not ask me to write about the strike and the terror," she began as if she were typing a report. Whether she was addressing Steffens, her readers, or her fellow organizers is unclear, but unlike the linear narrative of "Thousand Dollar Vagrant," this essay blended past and present, foregrounding the labor of writing and the mind of the writer as much as the events of the general strike. "I hunch over the typewriter," Lerner explained near the beginning of the piece, and later interrupted the flow to announce "and the typewriter breaks, stops for an instant" before diving into an account of "Bloody Thursday," when San Francisco police shot into a crowd of workers, killing two.[2]

Lerner's insistence that she and her cultural labor be visible within the text of "The Strike," like her strategic use of Lincoln Steffens's voice, demonstrates that she was more than the sum of her experiences. It was also a plea on behalf of thousands of working-class activists who would remain invisible to history, especially those who found their literary and artistic aspirations thwarted by the struggle to survive. "If I could go away for a while, if there were time and quiet," Lerner wrote, as if speaking to herself about the challenges of cultural production, "perhaps I could do it." Poverty, family, and the daily grind enforced silence on many would-be artists and authors, among them Lerner herself. A child of immigrant radicals, she grew up in Omaha, Nebraska, reading radical pamphlets and magazines, the Haldeman-Julius Little Blue Books, and even *Poetry* magazine. Like many working-class young people of her generation, she dropped out of high school in order to work and support her family. Later she moved west to try her hand at writing but spent much of her time working, organizing, and caring for her children. During the 1940s she abandoned a promising novel and would not publish again until 1961, after her youngest child began school. Some forty years after "The Strike," having long since taken her husband's name, Tillie Olsen lamented the way life in America silenced the voices of working people with artistic ambitions. The "mute inglorious Miltons: those whose waking hours are all struggle for existence," she wrote, were consumed by more pressing needs and were unable to imprint themselves on the historical record.[3] She was almost one of them.

The following two chapters turn to the question of how workers became visible as thinking people in modern America. Reading groups, open forums, and workers' education all made visible for working people the social and economic structures that shaped their lives and supported their own assertions that their lives mattered. As garment worker Sadie Goodman said of the effect of education, "You begin to see and hear things that have always been there, but to which you have been deaf, dumb and blind." This sudden visibility and legibility of economic forces mapped the possibilities for collective action. What change might be possible was in turn shaped not only by economic structures or political strategy but also by the way people imagined the minds of working people. The life stories of rebel workers, allegories of political cartoons, photographs of workers reading and learning, and reportage from the front lines of the class struggle framed what kind of working-class consciousness was imaginable, quite apart from what existed or what was desirable.

If everyone seemed to agree that "knowledge is power," few were certain what powerful knowledge looked like or how best to depict working people as knowledgeable and empowered. In an age of industry and machismo it was relatively easy to imagine power as a dynamo, a locomotive, or a muscular man. But the tools of human industry don't in themselves obtain knowledge, and masculine power did not always sit comfortably with traditional symbols of learning. Knowledge might easily be depicted in the form of a schoolhouse or library, or by the spectacles and mortar board of a professor. But these symbols were not necessarily useful for working people, as they could evoke the distant knowledge of the state and those who exerted power against workers' interests. How, then, to depict male coal miners and lumberjacks with extensive personal libraries, or female garment workers with literary ambitions and a mastery of parliamentary procedure?

Particular stories and images can be rich evidence for the historian, and large numbers of them considered together form patterns of expectation and meaning. British historian Raymond Williams defined culture as a "structure of feeling," and we can understand the role of narrative and imagery as creating a structure of seeing and imagining. Nicholas Mirzoeff, a historian of visual culture, points to patterns of visual and psychological representation that link material structures and social practices. The imagery of society's dominant forces, Mirzoeff argues, projects the existing social order as natural, unchanging, and real. The most culturally resonant images derive their power not only from the artist's skills but also from the viewer's expectation of meaning, the texts that accompany the image, and the social and economic practices that bring image and viewer together. Just as social movements organize their economic and human resources, they also present their own image of the social order and assert the validity of their way of seeing things.[4] Like textual narratives and practices of everyday life, the store of visual motifs was a resource for cultural activists who aimed to both describe and change society. Some images and stories worked better than others but not simply because they were better art. In mainstream culture, images that blended workers, knowledge, and power were out of focus, while images that portrayed workers as "good for nothing but work" and intellectuals as something other than workers were crisp and easy on the eyes.

The iconography of class consciousness was part of a much broader field of cultural artifacts that portrayed industrial society and the relative place of workers and managers in the social order. Advertising, film, radio, and popular fiction competed for the attention of working-class audiences. As historian Roland Marchand explains, the artists and writers of modern advertising agencies skillfully shaped messages not only about their clients' products but also about the appropriate role of government, the meaning of community, and the relationship between the past and the future. Much of the drive to fashion a positive image of corporations in the public mind, Marchand argues, came in response to the vibrant anticapitalist media of the early twentieth century. Taking advantage of new technologies that made print less expensive, the radical and labor movement press presented social reality on its own terms. Partisans of the labor movement were early and active participants in the nascent film and radio industries, as were many in the urban immigrant communities. According to historian Steven Ross, films supplied urban workers with visions of victorious unions and evil bosses. While most of these films are now lost, they drew on stock imagery pioneered by the radical press: cartoons, photographs, and stories that presented a familiar set of visualized plots and characters. Of course, even movies and stories without radical intent could stoke workers' desire for greater personal freedom and economic security. This was especially so for the young workers who spent what they could on movies, dime novels, and popular fashions while also energizing the labor movement in a series of spectacular strikes between 1909 and 1916.[5] The iconography of working-class consciousness, in its varied and contradictory forms, signaled that working people were claiming a kind of citizenship in spite of a society that expected them to remain in their station and invisible.

Chapters 4 and 5 explore how writers, artists, cartoonists, and photographers generated images designed to make structures of inequality more visible and legible and to help labor partisans imagine themselves as powerful actors in the world. Chapter 4 explores how radical activists used the "life story" genre to map out for their potential followers the mental pathways to collective power (or so they hoped). Influenced by trends in Marxist thought and a modernist vision of authenticity, radicals crafted their life stories with an emphasis on experience over education. For some this boiled down to a kind of inborn instinct, an innate class feeling that books and life experience sharpened and refined. The world of reading and self-education faded into the background of these life stories, even as their authors grew more deeply embedded in networks of workers' education and cultural production. This, too, was a kind of silencing that reinforced the widespread cultural prejudice that intellectual habits of mind and working-class life were two very separate domains.

The iconography of knowledge-in-the-making worked against cultural hierarchies that found easier purchase in the modern social imaginary. Beginning with the image of the rebel robot, a metaphor for proletarian revolution, chapter 5 analyzes images of working-class reading, schooling, and political activism. Could images of working-class knowledge visually overpower the association of mental acuity with the middle and upper classes and manual labor with lack of intelligence? Labor's partisans certainly hoped so. In this they were part of the modernization of mass subjectivity: a new way of seeing the minds of workers and new ways that working people imagined the horizon of their own human potential. But if the state and the labor movement learned to see the workers' minds in particularly modern ways during the mid-twentieth century, their versions of modernity were not always in sync.[6] Activists sought to make more workers aware of their pivotal role in modern production and to link individual life stories to the social movement collective. Echoing workers' struggle to reclaim their lives from the demands of wage labor, these images asserted the link between social reproduction, reading, and the right to be seen as thinking human beings.

4

Brain Workers in the House of Labor

Life Stories and the Politics of Experience

In the summer of 1922, the radical *Labor Herald* published a series of autobiographies under the title "How I Became a Rebel. A Symposium."[1] In his editor's introduction, the radical trade unionist and future Communist Party leader William Z. Foster noted, "A fundamental part of the general revolutionary program is to make rebels; to develop men and women who have definitely broken with capitalism and who are looking forward to the establishment of a Workers' Society." In the interest of making future rebels, the symposium highlighted the lives of eight prominent radicals to explain "just how, why, and under what circumstances, they became convinced that capitalism had to be done away with." As conversion stories, the autobiographies shared a number of elements: difficulties overcome, enlightenment gained, battles joined. They also stumbled upon a curious tension surrounding the origins of class consciousness: did rebellion spring more from experiences of deprivation and injustice or from reading, reflection, and debate? California machinist William Ross Knudsen attributed his radicalism to study and reflection: "I investigated. I read all the literature I could get. Reading and thinking produced the result—a Red." The veteran Pennsylvania socialist James Maurer, a champion of workers' education, told a very different kind of story: "It was not from what I read, because I was active in radical circles long before I could read. It came from what I lived."[2]

What makes people rebel? The question has preoccupied countless radicals, trade unionists, managers, and internal security personnel. The leaders of the American Revolution answered it in pamphlets and newspapers that appealed to the republican virtue of independent farmers and artisans. Southern planters pondered the origins of slave rebellions and responded by dividing families, meting out personal punishment, and censuring abolitionist propaganda. J. Edgar Hoover built a surveillance empire in order to disrupt the creation of communist cadres, and today national security operatives monitor cell phone metadata, social media, and online games to discover and disrupt the radicalization of Muslim youth, environmental activists, and many others. We celebrate some rebels and arrest others, but the question of how individuals decide to cross the boundaries of acceptable political and social discourse—how they become rebels—remains fascinating as a feature of historical change, a reflection of the human condition, and a way to talk about the tension between individuality and our common fate.

Social movements as diverse as evangelical Christianity, abolitionism, women's liberation, and Occupy Wall Street have deployed life stories as a powerful way to communicate their origins and aims. It may be a truism that one person's truth is another's lie, but one way or another testimonials like these become historical evidence. Historians of working-class social movements have been particularly aware of the role of autobiography in shaping public personas that differ from the historical record. As Mary Jo Maynes notes in her study of European worker-memoirists, didactic life stories "simultaneously recorded and contributed to the construction of class identities" by circulating models of living as a worker within a market society and appropriate ways of rebelling.[3] The published life stories of prominent labor and radical leaders point to how labor's "militant minority" thought about their own coming to consciousness and what kinds of knowledge were useful at a moment when a revolutionary upsurge seemed possible. Between 1914 and 1919, pervasive rank-and-file militancy and nascent interethnic unity raised the question of "workers' control of industry" in a concrete and hopeful way. But the answers came in the form of a series of defeats: the collapse of strikes in the heavy industries, an awful wave of racial violence, the division of the radical movement, and a sustained legal and policing effort that placed many leaders in jail or in exile. American workers did not seem up to the task of winning "industrial democracy," let alone managing industry for their own ends. With the hoped-for revolution fading into an indefinite future, the task of "making rebels" entered new personal and institutional contexts. The defeat of the postwar strike wave displaced large numbers of working-class militants from their jobs and severed their connection to the labor movement at the very moment they had achieved professional status as organizers. Meanwhile, employers' aggressive pursuit of mechanization and scientific management threatened to turn those with jobs into industrial drones. There seemed to be a growing rift in the working-class movement between those who thought about rebellion (intellectuals) and those who experienced the brunt of industrial exploitation but increasingly slid into quiescence (workers)—a split that mimicked the broader Taylorist logic of the era.

Art Young's image of the brain worker and the manual worker cast this division in terms of two bodies representing competing camps. By the 1920s many activists wrestled with competing claims to their own identity. Were salaried editors and organizers still workers? Or were they more like the professors who studied workers? In his 1937 autobiography, for instance, William Foster described his first job at the age of ten as "the first of my 26 years' experience as a worker . . . [that] gave me a broad first-hand knowledge of the workers' life and its hardships."[4] By that logic the end of Foster's time as a worker was 1917, the same year he became a paid organizer for the Stockyards Labor Council. This was not only a feature of Communist Party storytelling but also part of a broader trend echoing scientific management's division between mind and body, the secularization of educational discourse, the rise of the culture concept in anthropology, and the popularity of life stories in mass-market magazines. The public presentation of identity shifted toward experience as the key frame for self-understanding and, through it, social understanding.[5]

Recasting Proletarian Lives

How one became a rebel proved to be a more complicated question than the editors of the *Labor Herald* imagined. It prompted writers and readers to reflect on a set of value judgments that went to the heart of modern interpretations of consciousness and being. What was the legitimate origin of radicalism? Could it come from book learning and still be authentic? Or must its true origin lie in unmediated and preliterate experience? These questions had circulated in the prewar left as well, but they took on new urgency as contending factions struggled for leadership and argued over strategy in the wake of the Bolshevik Revolution. The eight autobiographical sketches in the *Labor Herald* were just a few of the many hundreds of life stories told in the context of early twentieth-century social movements. They were not representative in a strictly sociological sense. All of the authors were Euro-Americans, and all but one were men. Six of the eight grew up in working-class families. Two were well-known journalists from middle-class backgrounds—the kinds of lives that are more typically represented in the historical record. Only one of the eight, William Knudsen, left no extensive life history. For the other five authors who came from working-class families, we have lengthy autobiographies and biographies.

In this last sense the group is markedly unrepresentative of American workers, most of whom lived and died without much publicity. The lives of these activists, however, offer a window into the politics of social movement storytelling. In the pages of the *Labor Herald*'s sister journal, the *Liberator*, an argument about class experience and knowledge unfolded in commentaries from competing leftist thinkers. Individual liberation had been a central plank of the prewar radical movement that was determined to break with both the cultural confines of Victorianism and the economic inequality of capitalism. But for many communists, the Great War and the Bolshevik Revolution had changed everything and required a new, more disciplined approach to politics. This view was by no means dominant on the left. Communists struggled mightily to convince and cajole IWW members and left-wing socialists into the Bolshevik orbit. The nature of the radical mind became part of this debate as communists increasingly identified their movement with unyielding natural forces.

The *Labor Herald*'s collection of life stories began with Eugene Debs, signaling the socialist leader's great stature within the radical movement and the desire of the communists to share in his popular appeal. The leader of dramatic national railroad strikes in the 1880s and 1890s and a five-time Socialist Party candidate for U.S. president, Debs was a beloved figure widely known for his stirring oratory and acid pen. The idea for the series may have been inspired by Debs's own frequent retelling of his conversion to socialism, a train of narrative that stretched back to 1902 at least. Writing from jail in 1922, Debs declared, "There was never a time in my life when I was not with the weak and poor and against the rich and strong who oppressed them. . . . I had my lesson in wage-slavery early in life and never forgot it." Using little more than a sentence to describe his decade-long connection to the conservative Brotherhood of Locomotive Firemen, Debs moved on to his growing interest in industrial unionism. His conversion to socialism, as was well known, came as he sat in jail in the wake of the 1894 Pullman strike. He described it as a spiritual transformation: "My blood boiled as I sat with my associates in the foul, rat-infested jail at Chicago." Marxism appeared as a miraculous light in his dark cell: "Revolutionary literature came through the bars. My blood cooled and my head cleared. The class struggle came into bold relief and I saw clear as the noonday sun."[6]

Debs and his supporters crafted and nurtured this story of dramatic conversion largely in retrospect, changing the story in subtle ways over more than two decades of retelling.[7] Like his *Labor Herald* contribution, Debs's 1902 version, titled "How I Became a Socialist," drew out metaphors of blood, muscle, and spirit and lingered on his jailhouse conversion. This earlier telling began with Debs as a twenty-year-old, newly elected secretary for his Brotherhood of Locomotive Firemen lodge. It was through his job as an organizer for this conservative labor organization that he "was nourished at the Fountain Proletaire. I drank deeply of its waters and every particle of my tissue became saturated with the spirit of the working class."[8] The story of his jailhouse conversion was more detailed in its earlier iteration as well. He listed the titles of books and pamphlets that influenced his thinking, singling out the gift of Marx's *Capital* from Wisconsin socialist Victor Berger. By 1922, however, Berger was on the opposite side of the bitter split in the American left. Whether Debs left out those details or the editors of the *Labor Herald* took their liberties, it was little surprise that Berger disappeared from the narrative.

Like Debs, Elizabeth Gurley Flynn and William Foster had seen the inside of a jail cell. But in their life stories the bridge to radicalism was a family history of Irish nationalism. The only woman contributing to the series, Flynn struck a searching tone in describing her own story. "It is difficult to say how, when or where our rebellious spirits were born!" she began. "Possibly we are but fortunate inheritors of a rich legacy. Undoubtedly countless generations of wild Irish ancestors who fought and fled into the hills and died for Irish freedom, contributed much to mine." Similarly Foster called his father's Irish nationalism "the intellectual meat and drink of our early lives." Both Flynn and Foster moved from this parental legacy to their own youthful observations of inequality around them. Flynn recalled her early horror at seeing victims of industrial accidents and poverty: a woman who had lost her fingers but had to keep working to feed herself, a man crying as police locked him up for vagrancy, the scalp of a young working girl ripped from her head by machinery. "Imperceptibly my thought processes began to question poverty[,] which was obviously the explanation of these tragedies," Flynn wrote. But it was her father's frequent unemployment that brought home the "pinch of poverty" and that "visualized the problem as no amount of abstract reading could have done."[9]

The decisive moments of conversion for Flynn and Foster, however, came not from physical experiences of deprivation, nor from Irish nationalism, but from listening to socialist soapbox speakers. "Whatever prejudice I had been taught to have against Socialism melted away like snow before a summer sun," Foster wrote. "My rebellious spirit saw the broad way to its goal." Flynn's moment of conversion raised the knotty question of what exactly people were converting *to*. She was already an active socialist street speaker when she attended lectures by Eugene Debs and Daniel De Leon speaking on industrial unionism: "Out of the first flush of youthful emotion, I passed into a second stage—based on a firm conviction which

I still hold to, that the union movement is the real and lasting labor movement." Flynn was referring to the *industrial union* movement, the IWW.

Flynn's 1955 autobiography, *Rebel Girl*, fills out the early life story she briefly sketched in the *Labor Herald* in similar terms. Growing up in a working-class, Irish neighborhood in the South Bronx, Flynn was surrounded by critics of power, starting with her parents, who quit the Catholic Church to protest the treatment of a progressive priest. From neighbors she heard of the Molly Maguires and the Haymarket Martyrs. During the 1902 anthracite coal strike, which shut down local public transit, Flynn participated in a school debate and took an affirmative stance on the question of government ownership of coal mines. As a result, she and her siblings "were conditioned in our family to accept socialist thinking long before we came in contact with socialism as an organized movement." Her father was a vocal critic of the Democratic and Republican parties, voting for Debs instead. Her mother gave her a copy of Edward Bellamy's utopian novel *Looking Backward* (1888), which "made a profound impression" on the fourteen-year-old Flynn. A pamphlet left at her family's doorstep led her to a Socialist Party lecture, and Flynn was an immediate convert. "Needless to say," she wrote in her autobiography, "I was a terribly serious child for many years, the oldest of a poor family, sharing the miseries of the parents."[10]

Already a committed radical by seventeen, Flynn's coming-of-age story—her reckoning between social forces and personal aspirations—turned primarily on her struggle to maintain independence and relevance as a young woman and mother within the radical movement. In 1907 she attended an IWW convention in Chicago, where she met Lucy Parsons, widow of the hanged Haymarket martyr Albert Parsons, and took in the gritty and vital scenes of North America's preeminent industrial city. "I loved Chicago and still do," she wrote in her autobiography. "It's a big sprawly town—dirty, dingy, alive, real, no hypocrisy or false frills there; teeming with life much closer to the heart of America than any Eastern city."[11] After returning to her parents' home, she struck up a correspondence with a Wobbly she had met in Chicago, the charismatic, self-taught Canadian radical Jack Jones, who was working as an organizer on the northern Minnesota Iron Range. Jones convinced Flynn to come to Duluth to tour the rough mining locations of northern Minnesota and speak to the miners. What she saw there and what she thought Jones represented captivated her. The mines were great open pits scraped into the forested landscape; the miners, immigrant Finns and Slavs struggling through a bitterly cold winter. The ore freighters that pulled into the Duluth harbor would carry their reddish cargo to Chicago, Cleveland, and beyond, where it became the very steel rails, wheels, and sheet metal that structured the modern age. It was all owned and controlled by the steel magnates who had crushed labor unions and working lives in their quest for profit and control, and Jack Jones was "the organizer who lived and worked there, under conditions of hardship." They were married in January 1908.

Right away things went poorly. Flynn went to Minneapolis for previously scheduled speaking engagements, and Jones was arrested on bombing charges. Flynn's parents, concerned about her precipitous marriage, urged her to come home to New York. In the spring she returned to Duluth, and soon after her father followed to take a job that Jones had found for him on a city construction crew. The two men agitated so much that they were both fired, and the three returned to New York to ride out the summer unemployed and under the resentful eye of Flynn's mother. "She hated poverty and large families and was fearful that my life would become a replica of her own," Flynn wrote of her mother. In the fall Jones hopped a freight train to Chicago, and Flynn followed as soon as she earned enough for a ticket. The two moved into an apartment in the bohemian Towertown neighborhood, sharing their living space with fellow Wobblies, who helped to keep the now pregnant Flynn well fed. Jones worked as a coal shoveler, spending his free time at the Newberry Library researching an elaborate chart that described an imagined postrevolutionary industrial order. Their first child, a boy, was born prematurely and died in infancy. "If he had lived," Flynn wrote, "it might have drawn Jack and me together. Instead, I sought solace in greater activity." A short while later she was pregnant a second time.

Although Jones is known in Chicago history as the cultural provocateur behind the bohemian Dill Pickle Club, he proved traditional in his ideas about family life, demanding Flynn give up her speaking engagements and settle down. Flynn suspected he was jealous of her success as an organizer, and she balked at the traditional role of a mother. She decided to leave him and return to her parents to give birth to their second son, Fred. Jack followed her several months later, but she was adamant in her displeasure, telling her father "he *bores* me!" Later Flynn attributed the insult to the "cruelty of youth," but her parents supported her decision. "A domestic life and possibly a large family had no attractions for me," she concluded. "My mother's aversion to both had undoubtedly affected me profoundly. She was strong for her girls 'being somebody' and 'having a life of their own.'"[12]

Written long after she was out of the fray of organizing, Flynn's reflective autobiography wove together the personal and political in ways that anticipated the soon-to-emerge second wave of feminism. Foster, in contrast, was closer to his role in factional infighting when he wrote two autobiographies that portrayed his affiliation with communism as an outgrowth of instinctual and embodied class identity.

In *From Bryan to Stalin* (1937) he declared, "I early felt the iron of the class struggle sink into my heart." As he had in his 1922 *Labor Herald* contribution, Foster noted the influence of his father's Irish nationalism, but he clarified that he "was instinctively drawn into the American class struggle. . . . I felt rather than knew that I did not have to look to England for the real enemy but must meet him in the United States."[13] The depression and strikes of the 1890s as well as the spectacle of Coxey's Army, in which thousands of the unemployed marched toward the nation's capital to demand public employment, only deepened his "proletarian class instinct." Foster wrote that the defeat of William Jennings Bryan "had for me a big educational effect . . . rapidly developing my native proletarian instinct into genuine class consciousness." Foster recounted how these events led him to read and described some of the many books that influenced his thinking. But the books only served to refine his understanding of socialism.[14] Class instinct was the basis of his turn to radicalism in this telling, not the "rebellious spirit" he celebrated in 1922.

Communists like Foster often pointed to the idea of class instinct as the core of workers' potential for radicalism, but they also identified a central role for the party in shaping and directing radicalism to what they considered to be the correct ends. As a working-class autodidact who rose to the top levels of the Communist Party, Foster's life story was perhaps uniquely reflective of both parts of that process. His second autobiography, *Pages from a Worker's Life* (1939), detailed a number of work experiences as a migrant laborer, lumberjack, sailor, and railroader, among other jobs, as well as Foster's role in a series of early organizing drives. This episodic view of proletarian life in the first decade of the twentieth century, Foster said, "throws light on the forces that made me arrive at my present political opinions."[15] During this time, Foster read constantly and wrote essays and pamphlets as part of his pugnacious activism within leftist circles, but these practices come into view only fleetingly in his autobiography. In 1912, for instance, Foster took a job as a laborer and sometime actor for a traveling theater company in Indiana so that he and his collaborator Earl Ford could spend their free time drafting the pamphlet *Syndicalism*. Drawing from what Foster had learned about radical unionism during a trip to Europe, the forty-seven-page pamphlet—complete with footnotes—marked his split from the IWW and his turn toward radicalizing the AFL. Later, in *Pages from a Worker's Life*, Foster seemed to reflect on his own development through Upton Sinclair's novel about a militant rank-and-filer, *Jimmie Higgins*. The character represented, Foster said, "the type of tireless, devoted, disciplined, self-sacrificing and brave worker" who is "the builder of every union, party, and other working-class body." Through its educational program, the party transforms "his primitive proletarian militancy into burning revolutionary zeal," a process that echoed Foster's assessment of his own development.[16]

Of the *Labor Herald* writers, only William Ross Knudsen lacks for historical attention. Tall, blond, and blue-eyed, the American-born son of Danish and German immigrants grew up on a Northern California farm and went to work as a teenager in a San Jose machine shop after the death of his father. A graduate of the University of California, he first became a delegate to the San Francisco Iron Trades Council during World War I and then an organizer for the International Association of Machinists, leading major strikes in Ohio in 1922. That same year he ran as an opposition candidate for the union's presidency. After his defeat, he traveled to the Soviet Union as an American delegate to the Fourth Congress of the Communist International and Red International of Labor Unions in Moscow. In the following years he ran for mayor of San Francisco on the Socialist Labor Party ticket and lectured at the San Francisco Labor College.[17]

Knudsen described himself as an accidental radical, a schoolboy with "a bourgeois psychology" and a "beautiful crimson necktie" who wandered into the midst of the 1912 San Diego IWW free speech fight. Roughed up and arrested along with actual Wobblies, Knudsen convinced the police captain he was innocent and was released. Curious about the experience, he found his way to the IWW hall and purchased an armload of pamphlets only to be caught up in another police raid. This time he was thrown in a cell with other protesters, who were "talking, arguing, and singing." The police turned a fire hose on the prisoners in an effort to subdue them, and Knudsen was knocked to the ground by the force of the water. "The brutal actions of the police, the confinement with these rebels, and my mental reactions to all this, caused me to have a great interest in learning what it was all about," Knudsen told his readers. But, he said, it was reading and reflection that made him a "Red."

Knudsen was a relatively unknown character, one of a generation of young militants who challenged the established leadership of AFL unions in the years around World War I. In contrast, the Pennsylvania socialist James Maurer was well known. A self-educated machinist, veteran of the Knights of Labor, head of his state's AFL, and a leader of the workers' education movement, in his *Labor Herald* account he wrote of his impoverished childhood, the moral strength of his mother, and his alienation from mainstream institutions. "Less than thirteen months of my life were spent in school," Maurer wrote of his childhood in the industrial town of Reading. "What education I did secure, I got, not on account of the State, but in spite of it." He flatly declared that his rebellion grew "not from what I read, because I was active in radical circles long before I could read. It came from what I lived." Reading radical pamphlets only "added fuel to the fire." Even the Communist Manifesto did no more than help "weld still more closely my inherent rebel spirit."[18]

Years later Maurer also wrote a full-length autobiography, *It Can Be Done* (1938), which included a twist on his earlier insistence that life, rather than reading, had made him a rebel. Ignored by his teachers because he spoke only "Pennsylvania Dutch," Maurer "regarded school as a penal institution."[19] On the streets he brawled with English-speaking kids and watched as the state militia opened fire on workers during the 1877 railroad strike.[20] From that dramatic scene, Maurer pivoted to his surprising discovery, at age sixteen, that he was illiterate. It would prove to be the event he most directly linked to his conversion to unionism and eventually socialism. As an apprentice in a machine shop, Maurer worked alongside a Knights of Labor activist who spoke constantly about "justice and labor's rights, of the need for workers to organize, [and] of their solidarity at the ballot box." Contrary to his life story in the *Labor Herald*, in his longer autobiography Maurer described feeling clueless about the labor movement: "he might as well have talked about trigonometry or the nebular hypothesis for all the impression it made on me at first." Later this coworker gave Maurer a pamphlet and asked to get his assessment. "It was the first time anyone had asked me for an opinion on something in print," Maurer wrote, and that was motivation enough for him to struggle over the text. But he couldn't read it. He turned to his mother's prayer book hoping to find something familiar, but that, too, was indecipherable. "I rushed to the front room to Mother, fairly screaming: 'Why can't I read!'" he cried. The answer was as unsurprising as it was illuminating for Maurer. "We always were poor and instead of going to school you had to go to work," his mother told him. "And, besides, you never seemed to get anything out of school when you did go."[21]

The sudden realization of what reading was all about—why anyone would want to read or attend school—struck him as "an awakening [that was] as sudden as it was violent." His coworker offered to teach him to read, and shortly after, Maurer joined the Knights of Labor, which began his long career in the labor movement.[22] Still, he was not a socialist. That decision came in 1899 as the natural outgrowth of study. Along with his brother and other young populists in his town, he worked his way through the first volume of Marx's *Capital*, "and after a year's study and discussion of Socialism, we decided that we had at last found out where we belonged."[23] Maurer wrote, "It was a little labor pamphlet that switched me off the narrow path of illiteracy to the broad highway of knowledge and light."[24]

What changed in the sixteen years between Maurer's contribution to the "How I Became a Rebel" series and the publication of his autobiography? The process of reflection may have helped Maurer recover the memory of his coming to literacy. More likely, the real story was just too complicated to recount in the brief space allotted by the *Labor Herald*. Like other labor militants, Maurer could point to an early life of poverty and child labor as the source of his working-class outlook. But to write as he did in 1922 that he was an active radical "long before" he could read was more of a tall tale than a life story.

Intellectual Others

The contributors to the *Labor Herald* followed a long tradition of American politicians' appeal to gut instinct and the wisdom of experience. Presidents and business leaders, as well as trade unionists and radicals, extolled the merits of the school of hard knocks. The turn to Bolshevism, however, amplified a tendency among the more sectarian partisans of revolution to fixate on proletarian experience as the arbiter of authentic radicalism. The prewar left had been a broad and loosely affiliated coalition encompassing libertarian anarchists, industrial unionists, a wide spectrum of socialists, and non-socialist progressives. As this coalition shattered and reformed after 1917, those on the far left were particularly eager to establish themselves as a new center of organizational gravity and political authority. They also sought to distance themselves from leftists who lacked proletarian bona fides. The inclusion of Upton Sinclair and Lincoln Steffens in the "How I Became a Rebel" series reflected these competing goals. The muckraking authors were well known to radical readers, but they had no personal tales of difficult work experience to validate their radical critiques. Instead, their stories were about lost ideals. Sinclair, who described in minute detail the stultifying experiences of the fictional immigrant meat-cutter Jurgis Rudkis in *The Jungle*, penned a two-paragraph statement noting simply that he had learned that business and politics did not subscribe to the Christian ideals he had believed in as a youth, "so gradually I became a rebel." Steffens recounted his journalistic exposés of municipal and corporate corruption, which he had initially attributed to the political and moral failings of corrupt individuals. Only later did he begin to view the myriad forms of corruption as the result of a single process and to believe that "the social problem . . . [was] an economic problem, one and the same all over the world; and that the solution is likewise economic.[25] For the *Labor Herald*'s target audience of industrial workers, these tales of intellectual development probably rang hollow.

The final installment in the *Labor Herald* series was also the most polemical, signaling the editors' assessment of the stories that came before it. Like Foster in his later accounts, political cartoonist Robert Minor stridently insisted that class identity lay beyond the realm of thought and book learning. He began his contribution with an industrial metaphor that echoed Debs: "By a childhood of poverty I was molded for life membership in the working class."[26] Although his parents came from prominent Texas families, his father's law practice did not bring in much money, and Minor went to work after only four years of formal schooling. His early work life shaped his sense that art and beauty stood in opposition to profit. As a fourteen-year-old working in a sign painting shop, he came to see "the conflict between young workers' instinct for beauty and the need of the shop to drive for money." As an apprentice carpenter, he "contracted the peculiar pride of the craftsman" and the solidarity of trade unionists. Through the intervention of relatives, he secured an office job for a railroad company, but he soon quit and became a hobo because, as he said, he "was already branded with a different iron." He went on the road again and after a few lucky breaks landed a job as a cartoonist for a St. Louis newspaper.

Minor came to radical politics through anarchism and the IWW. The trial of Bill Haywood, he said, "came to disturb me—to awaken all of the old-time dreams—the call of my class." The jailing of socialist union organizer Tom Mooney in San Francisco utterly convinced him the system was rigged and made him a "rebel." As with many other radical intellectuals, however, pondering the meaning of the Bolshevik Revolution was the seminal event for Minor. He concluded his *Labor Herald* contribution with a jab at those who resisted the inevitable turn to Bolshevism; times had changed and "being a rebel just generally" was no longer enough. George Washington was a rebel in 1776, but he wouldn't be one in 1920, Minor wrote. "Emma Goldman was a revolutionist in July, 1914," he said, "but today she doesn't mean anything."[27]

Robert Minor no doubt hoped his pugnacious essay would contribute to sorting out which former radical allies would be on the right side of history now that history had decisively shifted in a new direction. Working-class experience became a powerful rhetorical device in this process, signaling an alignment with the policy of the Russian party and marginalizing the voices of middle-class intellectuals associated with more conservative strains of socialism as well as anarchists like Goldman. There was also a brewing fight among the partisans of Bolshevism, something Minor and his colleagues relished. This struggle was much more apparent in the pages of the *Labor Herald*'s companion journal, the *Liberator*. While the *Labor Herald* focused on trade union strategy, the *Liberator* was a literary and theoretical journal—a kind of head and hand division of labor. The two journals also reflected geographic and demographic poles within the party. In New York the *Liberator* was the successor to the celebrated champion of prewar bohemian magazine *The Masses*. Driven out of business by federal prosecution, the radical intellectuals Max and Crystal Eastman, John Reed, Floyd Dell, Art Young, and others regrouped in 1918 under a new title and continued to publish politically charged poetry, prose, and commentary.

Minor had recounted the story of his intellectual journey from anarchism to Leninism in the *Liberator* in the fall of 1920. In the wake of the Bolshevik Revolution, he perceived that the working class was shifting like the tides toward revolution. "It was plain that the Russian revolution had set this current in motion, and that its form was pre-determined somewhere in the origin of the race. It was as pure a natural phenomenon as the breathing of the human lungs." Minor struggled, however, to accept the Bolshevik belief in the dictatorship of the proletariat—not only the dissolution of liberal democratic forms but also the enforcement of ideological discipline in order to carry the revolution through its early stages. Since the "natural law" of the laboring masses could not be wrong, he decided he needed to change his thinking. To reconcile these competing thoughts, he read and reread Marx but had his breakthrough upon reading Lenin's *The State and Revolution*. The book struck him as "an event of my life. I read it four times," he recounted in the *Liberator*.[28] This set in motion a train of reading, rereading, and reassessment of his relationship to the labor, anarchist, and socialist wings of the working-class movement. According to Minor's party-sponsored biography, "The new ideas seemed to stretch the fabric of his mind, carry him winged across intellectual obstacles, [and] mental roadblocks."[29]

Around the time the *Labor Herald* published its "How I Became a Rebel" series, the *Liberator* was entering a newly energetic phase with financial support from the communist movement. Under the joint editorial leadership of Mike Gold and Claude McKay, two rising literary heavyweights, the journal was at the center of what literary historian William Maxwell describes as an exceptional chapter in leftist literary production and community building between white and black radicals in New York.[30] The son of Jewish immigrants, Gold was born Itzok Granich on New York's Lower East Side and went to work at age twelve due to his family's poverty.[31] An ardent communist, Gold would increasingly clash with McKay and the magazine's contributing editors, especially Floyd Dell. McKay was a Jamaican poet who came to the United States to study agricultural science at Kansas State College. He soon dropped out and became "a vagabond with a purpose . . . to find expression in writing," as he put it in his 1937 memoir, *A Long*

Way from Home. He broke onto the American literary scene in the *Liberator* with his poem protesting the racial violence of 1919, "If We Must Die," which he first read to his fellow African American cooks and waiters on a railway dining car.[32] But the two editors did not get along. Gold praised McKay's prose but judged him as a "tropical poet" in the end: insufficiently radical and overly involved with what he called "Negro patriotism." McKay thought Gold's literary tastes were too strongly influenced by politics. According to McKay, Gold "preferred sentimentality above intellectuality in estimating proletarian writing and writers."[33]

Gold and Minor allied themselves with another group of leftists who firmly planted their red flags in the country's factory districts. The *Labor Herald* was the organ of the Trade Union Educational League (TUEL), William Z. Foster's loose grouping of trade union militants whose aim was to transform the AFL from within. Like Foster, many of the TUELers were self-educated or had very little formal schooling. They frequently attacked their New York rivals in the Communist Party as "petit-bourgeois and intellectuals" or as "the City College boys." Their rivals returned the favor, dubbing the Fosterites "half-educated workers" who lacked decorum and used bluster and profanity to cover for inadequate training.[34] Gold occupied a complicated position between these two groups. Like the Fosterites, he had quit school at age twelve in order to work. In his autobiographical novel, *Jews without Money*, Gold voiced the pain of his thwarted education: "I had always loved books; I was mad about books; I wanted passionately to go to high school and college. Since I couldn't, I meant to despise all that nonsense."[35] But Gold had gone to college. He attended Harvard briefly before dropping out for lack of funds, and later he took classes at New York's City College.[36]

While Foster and the TUELers fought over trade union strategy, Gold, Minor, and other leftist intellectuals struggled to proletarianize American letters. Promoting working-class authors on the one hand and attacking the literary establishment on the other, the pages of the *Liberator* were a preview of a "literary class war" that would become more visible in the 1930s.[37] Behind the scenes, editors and associate editors clashed over both style and substance, often broadcasting their disagreements in the pages of the magazine. Tightly wrapped around these disputes over literary quality was a debate about the class position of radical intellectuals. Were writers and editors, even those born into the working class, still workers? Or had they become middle class by virtue of their salaries and royalties, which insulated them from the caprice of the wage system? Over the spring and summer of 1922, Gold and Dell waged a running battle over these issues, lighting up the pages of the *Liberator* with clever zingers that left lasting scars and making the fuzzy lines between artist and wage worker seem as distinct as night and day.

In his 1920 "Psycho-Analytic Confession," Floyd Dell imagined a conversation with his unconscious mind about the hard work of revolution. His colleague William Gropper drew Dell's unconscious as a large and menacing figure who dreamed of the life of leisure and wealth. *Liberator* (April 1920).

Like Gold, Floyd Dell was a child of the working classes, although he had recently found considerable financial success from sales of his autobiographical novels *Moon-Calf* (1920) and *Briary Bush* (1921). The son of a frequently unemployed butcher and a schoolteacher, Dell grew up in towns along the Mississippi River. He went to work in a candy factory as a teenager and later in a print shop in Davenport, Iowa. Socialist politics led him to journalism. He soon moved on to Chicago, where he was part of the city's literary boom, and then moved again to New York City to join the thriving bohemian community and to work as an editor for *The Masses*.[38] As the left embraced the idea of a vanguard party, Dell stuck with the libertarian culture of the prewar left and added a dose of psychoanalysis. In a 1920 article framed as a conversation with his own unconscious mind, for instance, Dell expressed the concerns of many libertarian leftists about the drive for productive efficiency under the new Soviet state. "Now as long as the Co-operative Commonwealth was a long way off, and we could imagine it to be anything we liked, my Unconscious was all for it," he wrote. "But as it comes nearer, and we can see its initial stages in all their realistic detail, my Unconscious begins to protest. Communism begins to look too much like work."[39] Titled "A Psycho-Analytic Confession," the article was accompanied by a set of cartoons drawn by the artist William Gropper that captured Dell's split personality as an embodied class divide. The separate physical forms of the brain worker and manual worker appear as Dell's conscious and unconscious mind, respectively. Dell the brain worker, slightly built, sits with arms crossed near a pile of books and papers while his hulking unconscious self mimics the stereotypical body type of an industrial worker. This was a double commentary with a heavy dose of Freud. Dell's ego displaced his desire for a life of leisure onto his proletarian unconscious. But ego and id were implicitly linked in their rebellion against the Communist Party, which played the role of superego. Dell's "psycho-analytic confession" played for laughs, but the question of workers' willingness to labor for the revolution was a serious one, especially as the repression of the postwar years made the costs of rebellion ever more apparent. The early 1920s were also the years Dell became financially successful and moved to a comfortable country home on the Hudson River.

For his part, Gold was experiencing the harried life of a working editor and traveling the country to report on strikes. In his March 1922 column, Gold juxtaposed mocking descriptions of himself as a leisure-class intellectual with interrupting phone calls, meetings, deadlines, and annoying office mates. If this was leisure, why did he have less time to read and write? Gold then segued into a critique of the typical American intellectual who longed for "a spiritual aristocracy in America, that will hold itself aloof from the sordid life of the nation and create a great, free, cosmic Art and Culture, antiseptic and above the battle."[40] In the May 1922 issue, Gold reported on a trip to a Pennsylvania coal miners' strike. In the article, he wrote that he preferred spending his time away from the magazine's New York offices and mingling with rank-and-file militants. "In New York one gets the illusion that the class struggle is an intellectual concept that one can argue about, take or let alone," he wrote, ignoring the fact that he himself was a lifelong New Yorker. But among the coal miners of Western Pennsylvania, he argued, class struggle "is a living reality, and one can no more dodge it than one can escape from the weather. The miners' union is part of the trees and the hills, the sky and the air of this landscape." Rebel workers, not New York bohemians, were building the new American civilization: "It would be a brave culture, a heroic culture for strong men and women, a culture near to the sources of life. It would move along in beauty under the stars, it would laugh and sing."[41]

Gold's revolutionary ardor struck a number of his colleagues on the left as simplistic, misplaced, and potentially dangerous. When a group of leftists, including Debs, signed a letter condemning the execution of dissident socialists by the Soviet government, Gold lambasted the petitioners as mere "Jesus-Thinkers" who "mistake their own longings for the movement of humanity" and displace objectivity with self-serving "ethics." For his part, Gold wanted "Victory—not purity" and was willing to support the bloody work needed to win. Upon reading this, Upton Sinclair responded rather gently: "From what I know of Michael Gold, I suspect that if he had the job of shooting a score or two of Socialists who didn't agree with him about his dictatorship, he might also find himself feeling very much upset about it."[42] Floyd Dell was less forgiving and responded by taking aim at a target that was closer to Gold's heart. "Comrade Mike," Dell wrote in the June 1922 issue of the *Liberator*, "I think really cherishes the romantic delusion that he belongs to the working class. But the fact is that Comrade Mike is a literary man, an intellectual, and a member of the salaried middle class." Even if salaried intellectuals were paid less than manual workers, Dell insisted, they were of a different class. He believed that he personally had ceased to be a proletarian on the day he became a journalist as a young man in Davenport, Iowa. Reprising his "psycho-analytic confession," Dell argued that hard work was not all it was cracked up to be. "If it were as glorious to work twelve hours a day as Comrade Mike appears to think, there would be no need of a revolutionary movement in this country," Dell chided. "And if the proletarians before whose working ability Comrade Mike has been rhetorically abashing himself in awe and worship were half as anxious for leisure as Mike and I are, there would be a revolution next week."

Dell believed that he and his coeditors were not simply freed from manual toil; rather, they were freed up for a particular purpose: to serve the working-class movement. Not particularly suited to the work of organizing, bookish and artistic types could "put in words or pictures, persuasively or eloquently, the thoughts of the workers. We can be in some sense their spokesmen." The change workers most wanted, according to Dell, was less work and more leisure, and in this regard, at least, they shared interests with artists and writers.[43] The dispute between Dell and Gold, however, hinged not only on different approaches to art and revolution but also on their competing interpretations of the class position of intellectuals, as well as their own experiences as intellectual workers. Stuck between proletarians and bourgeoisie, often working within bureaucratic institutions, radical intellectuals struggled to make sense of where they fit into the emerging story of modern class relations. Gold was still very much the working editor, while Dell was enjoying the more relaxed lifestyle made possible by his literary success. Neither had the words to adequately describe their new, complicated class position.

Life Stories "in regulation style"

Like the well-known leaders who explained how they became rebels in 1922, and the editors who curated and argued over those narratives, rank-and-file partisans of the labor and radical movements told stories about the origins of their activism. Unlike those of their famous leaders, most of these stories have remained relatively invisible to historians. Many were printed in the pages of obscure newspapers or hidden in private journals and the administrative papers of labor colleges. Firsthand accounts of working-class experience had long been a staple of labor movement journalism, and during the 1920s they also became a key pedagogical tool for workers' education. The result was fewer life stories focused on the cultivation of personal intellect and character than had been common in the late nineteenth century. When labor college faculty compiled nearly eighty personal narratives into the book *I Am a Woman Worker* (1936), for instance, they created a rich catalog of otherwise invisible experiences. The book offered fascinating insights into daily life inside factories; relations among workers, supervisors, and bosses; and the struggles of unionists in the years before the Wagner Act made the promotion of collective bargaining a national policy. But none of these accounts mention reading in more than a passing manner. The newspapers, pamphlets, libraries, and street speakers who filled the working-class public sphere remain hidden in the shadows while work, and the search for work, took center stage.[44]

Labor college students were no less avid readers than other working-class activists. The invisibility of reading and open political debate in their life narratives derived mainly from the institutional imperative of the labor schools, their leaders, and their sponsors. We can glean a more nuanced view of these young workers' engagement with reading from the application forms and essays they submitted to gain admission to labor schools. Here they often struggled to balance the competing requirements to prove their intellectual preparation, on the one hand, and their status as bona fide industrial workers on the other. Application forms asked potential students to list books they had recently read and enjoyed and required a short essay on work experience. The result was sometimes two very different portraits of an applicant's life. George McCray, a former Pullman porter from Chicago, studiously avoided the topic of reading in his work experience essay for the University of Wisconsin's School for Workers, yet his application listed Booker T. Washington,

Karl Marx, and George Bernard Shaw among his favorite authors. After completing his summer program, he joined a teacher education program at the University of Chicago.[45] In other cases, applicants' work experience essays highlighted school, reading, and politics in addition to work. Kansas City autoworker John Alspaugh listed over thirty-five books he had recently read, mainly popular literature and social science, on his application to the Wisconsin school. His handwritten "History of Working Experience" started with a job hauling trash from the apartment building where his family lived when he was nine years old and ended with a job in the paint department of the Fisher Body auto plant. But there was more to life than work, and Alspaugh also wrote that his father bought him a musical instrument and books. "This interest in reading," he wrote in an aside, "offers me my greatest pleasure but of late my reading time is very limited."[46]

Longer autobiographies written by labor college students during their studies often called attention to competing claims on their authors' interior consciousness. They plotted the interplay of embodied experience, reflection, and the messages of the commercial and working-class public spheres. Kansas City typographer Elsie Faxon, another student at the Wisconsin School for Workers, wove together work experience and commentary on class, gender, and family. "With due respect for the efforts of conscientious, industrious, adored parents to 'do for' their four kiddies," Faxon began her essay, "I wanted to get away from home, partly to escape the rigors and limitations of the poverty of the home and partly to remove the burden of a mouth too many to feed from a father's all too slender purse."[47] Upon her mother's death, she and her siblings were sent to live with "an old aunt and her husband who had attained to the comfortable status of the middle class" as hotel operators. There she got her first work experiences as a result of "labor trouble" among the staff. Waiting tables became her "port-in-the-storm" occupation, an unpleasant but reliable stopgap between jobs in factories and print shops. She worked her way into the editorship of a country newspaper, what she called "the preliminary apprenticeship so vital to a woman to push on in a man's field in the city," and then moved on to the print shop of the *Kansas City Star*.[48] Practically invisible in Faxon's detailed narrative was her extensive engagement with reading and formal education. Although she started working at age nine, she managed to complete high school and attend junior college and university extension courses between jobs. Her application form listed over twenty books that she had read recently, including the *Rubaiyat*, *The Legend of Sleepy Hollow*, *Up from Slavery*, writings by Emerson and Thoreau, and Jane Addams's *Twenty Years at Hull House*, among others. Even when typing out this list, she suggested the stories behind her reading. She had been fired for reading an Edna Ferber short story on the job, she wrote in her application. She had read "everything about Eva La Galliene," presumably the actress Eva Le Gallienne, founder of the Civic Repertory Theatre, translator of modernist plays. Clearly, Elsie Faxon identified with Ferber and Le Gallienne, two independent women in a literary world dominated by men, and she wanted her future instructors to know it.[49]

Others deployed the language of literary modernism to shape their own public narratives, reflecting the "ethnic modernism" of immigrant writers and proletarian fiction.[50] Rosella Burke was a twenty-one-year-old Chicago necktie factory worker when she applied to Brookwood in 1934. A communist and a child of Russian immigrants, she explained that she was unable to get references from her AFL union because it was "controlled by a racketeering organizer who took no chances of having 'Reds' as officials." She identified Jack Conroy's *The Disinherited* among the books she had recently enjoyed and hoped to learn something about labor history, economics, writing, and organizing techniques at Brookwood, "for in order to be a *real* organizer you must know not only how to talk but also what you're talking about."[51] Burke's handwritten autobiography began, as many such documents did, with an apologetic nod to her own lack of training as a writer and the seeming unimportance of her life events. "Not being much of an author and not having either an inventive mind or an exciting history I will perforce begin this story in regulation style and continue the same way throughout."[52] Despite this, she plotted a dramatic story driven by the tension between her interior state of mind and the social conditions and events that transpired in her life. In this way her writing echoed the practices of any modern novel or short story, even if she wrote in telegraphic form. Her father, failing in a series of small commercial ventures that exhausted his wife's inheritance, moved the family from Dayton, Ohio, to Chicago, where the older children could find jobs to support the household. Barely grasping the implications of the move, the twelve-year-old Burke continued with her schooling in Chicago while her older siblings went to work. When the Depression hit and poverty returned to the family's daily life, she began to understand what this would mean for her: "My dreams and aspirations faded a little. I began to feel chilly inside when I thought of the future." When she quit school, she wrote, "I was finally class conscious. I didn't know what to do or how to do it but I knew that once a worker, always a worker." To fill her idle days, she began reading and "following current events." An anti-eviction protest that led to the death of two black workers "started me thinking," she wrote. "Here were people trying to do something to better themselves," as she had hoped to do through education. But she remained on the sidelines: "I still wanted to struggle for myself alone. When they had made a better world I'd help them enjoy it, I thought." When she, her sister, and their mother were arrested during a bread boycott, she "decided to stop pussy-footing around and really do something so I joined the Young Communist League, the only organization I thought that was actually doing anything beside talking."[53]

Other labor college students openly toyed with their readers' expectations about the origins of class consciousness. Like Rosella Burke, Brookwood student Ben Calderon opened his life story with a classic invocation of innocence and ignorance. "I didn't know 'anything about nothing' until I left high school . . . to go to work," he wrote in his autobiographical narrative "Concerning Ben." This proved to be a narrative feint, as Calderon spent relatively little ink on work per se and wrote of his developing intellectual life in ways that wove together work with the public sphere of print, speech, and performance. A Theatre Guild play left him "aflame and stirred to consciousness of international oppression and misery far beyond the ghetto of N.Y.C." His "real education" began while he was working in a dress shop, where his boss warned the workers against union thugs. "Altho ignorant of reality and green as a young sapling I felt instinctively it wasn't true . . . [and] when the union committee entered our shop and electrified our workers I was stirred as in the theatre." He joined the ILGWU and, "seduced" by an organizer's speech, entered the circles of prominent left-wing activists. There, he said, "I got my education" through "radical philosophy and the workers press which I read avidly."[54] His next lesson would move on to the "immigrant discovers America" genre. He left New York City to see what he imagined was the "real" America beyond the Hudson River. In Fort Wayne, Indiana, his theoretical sophistication caught the attention of the more apolitical leaders of a local unemployed council. "I felt very enthusiastic with this environment," Calderon wrote. "I was in contact with ~~100%~~ American workers and they were looking to me for guidance and leadership." He organized a Free Tom Mooney committee and went to African American churches to speak about the Scottsboro case, in which nine young black men were falsely accused of raping two white women in Alabama. When he returned to New York, he felt confident enough to take a more active role in the union. Coming to consciousness and coming of age were woven together with his baptism in American culture.[55]

For his part, Ed Falkowski was not particularly enamored with the popularity of autobiography in the late 1930s. After his time at Brookwood, Falkowski spent seven years in Europe. He worked in coal mines and steel mills in Germany and Poland and then settled in the Soviet Union, where he married a Soviet woman, Rose Prokofiev, and wrote for the English-language *Moscow Times*. His published work from this time stuck closely to the conventions of proletarian reportage; he expressed his personal thoughts only in private journals and correspondence with friends. In 1937 he decided his talents were needed back at home and, leaving his wife and infant child in Moscow, he made his way to the United States. During his voyage home, Falkowski typed out a journal entry complaining about the "persistent habit of introspection" that produced so many autobiographies, romances, and political thrillers. "It is an ominous sign of the short-lived expectations of our younger generation," he wrote, perhaps reflecting on his own youthful habit of journal writing, "that the younger the man, the more urgent his conviction that the world awaits the revelation of his moods and pensées [thoughts] in books that had formerly been deemed the fruit of venerable age."[56] His journey from Moscow to Leningrad, to London, Paris, New York, and finally Toledo, Ohio, traced a geographic counterrevolution. Confronted with the opinions of traveling American and English businessmen, he felt an intense attachment to the people he left behind and the flawed new society they were building. "A Soviet boat en route to foreign parts retains its soviet character incorruptibly," he wrote. "The crew speaks little English; there is easy mingling among passengers . . . crew and passengers mix easily; there are rules against tipping; the crew and staff are polite without manifesting the slightest trace of servility." Disoriented by commercial orientation of all conversation in the capitalist world, Falkowski felt "a sense of plunging, of pitching headlong into space" as if he were traveling into the unknown rather than returning home.[57]

Falkowski may have expected to return to Moscow, but the war intervened and he did not see Rose or his son for over thirty years. Sensing that he did not intend to return, Rose remarried in 1945. Although he had been away only seven years, Falkowski now felt himself something of an immigrant to America. In 1947 he published an autobiographical essay that framed the life worlds of three generations of Falkowski men. His grandfather knew only the difficult life of a Polish peasant in the Russian countryside, "unaware of history, his universe defined in fireside legend." He fled to America after a local landowner claimed the village land, backed up by the power of tsarist law. His father, who had also been born in Russia, faced the difficulties of a new country and hard labor in Pennsylvania's mines, but he also found joy in his family and a tight-knit mining community. The American generation, especially "those sensitive enough to appreciate the rich expanses of activity" potentially open to them in the United States, had its own kind of struggle. Echoing his teenage journal entries, he wrote that his generation had been sent "off to jobs when they should still have been in school or college"; they would live with the understanding of what was "lost to them." Living as an American in Europe, however, Falkowski gained a new appreciation for the United States. In the Polish mining districts, "the air was heavy with a sense of overhanging doom," and "the common man still dreamed of one day going to America!" The heroic proletarian narrative so popular in the 1930s found little purchase in the postwar years. The growing culture of political reaction in the United States would make it impossible to publish those kinds of stories. Falkowski offered his readers a more reassuring story of Americanization and modernity. He closed his essay by placing himself where his grandfather and father had once stood: on the deck of a ship drawing closer to America, his "one home."[58]

Individuality in Collective Terms

How people became rebels of one kind or another was a complicated process blending experience, reflection, and contingent moments of opportunity. How they would describe their coming to consciousness—which events would be seen and which receded into the background—was often guided by institutional imperatives and ideological commitments. Good storytelling is at the heart of all effective persuasion, and most social movement leaders learn to weave their own life story into a compelling narrative about their cause. Like improvisational musicians, they learn to vary rhythms, accent notes, and volume. They change their stories a bit depending on the audience and the world that surrounds the moment of telling, but the core of the story remains the same. As political strategist Marshall Ganz argues, telling personal stories nested within the stories of movements (he calls them the "story of self" and the "story of us") is a social technology that enables leaders to motivate others to overcome inertia and fear. Through careful modeling of effective storytelling, activists train one another to circulate and amplify the movement's messages.[59] Working-class storytellers of the interwar years could hardly escape the modernist impulse of the era that elevated the ordinary and the everyday as the most real and meaningful.[60] This new cultural context posed challenges and opportunities for radical movements and for the self-educated. The process of reading oneself into an educated state could seem like a put-on in a world that was learning to associate the unconscious with the authentic. These modern ways of knowing and telling shaped the archives historians use to explain the past and, in the process, shaped our understanding of working-class life, the origins of social movements, and the possibilities for democratic culture.

Despite the impulse to elevate experience over education, reading was a consuming and life-defining passion for many activists, young and old, often because their life experiences were so traumatic. As the Filipino American author Carlos Bulosan wrote in an essay titled "My Education," harsh experiences at work, periods of unemployment, and pervasive discrimination against Filipinos during the 1930s made him "sick with despair" and "paralyzed with fear." He overcame this paralysis and isolation not in the swell of a dramatic strike or confrontation with police but by "reading in public libraries." Melville and Poe introduced him to the "humiliations and defeats, [and the] hopes and high moments of success" of those who suffered the "narrowness" of American culture. Hemingway and Faulkner disappointed him, but Louis Adamic and Richard Wright seemed to offer a way to find roots in a rootless America.[61] In his autobiographical novel, *American Hunger*, Richard Wright wrote that the folktales and pulp novels that fascinated him as a young boy seemed to change reality: "the look of things altered, and the world became peopled with magical presences."[62] The words, like incantations, had a power beyond the page, redefining the limits of the possible for readers and listeners; and it was clear to Wright from a young age that those with power over him—whether it be his religious grandparents, or the white supremacist leaders of Mississippi—feared what those words might inspire in those without power.

Learning to mobilize the power of words was the task of literary artists like Wright and Bulosan, but also of ordinary activists. Storytellers working in the labor and radical mode balanced the need to be an example for others while not elevating themselves above their comrades. In his 1948 autobiography, IWW leader Ralph Chaplin noted that his own life story "would be unimportant were it not for the fact that the same thing happened to a great many others—then and since then."[63] Garment worker Jennie Matyas made just this point when she told an interviewer, "The only reason I'm interested in telling any of this story is because it lacks uniqueness. If I thought it were unique, then I would consider it particularly private and nobody's affair."[64] We might take these self-effacing denials with a grain of salt since they are, as a rule, followed by lengthy and detailed life histories, but they also point to a very real taboo against puffery at the expense of comrades who might be unable to claim similar glory for themselves.[65] Invoking their typicality, activists' claimed a collective subjectivity. The imperative to rise *with* your class or race rather than *out of* it was both sincere and in need of constant reiteration.

5

Icons of Ignorance and Enlightenment

The Visual Culture of Critical Consciousness

Pennsylvania coal miner Edward Falkowski watched as his fellow workers stormed the factory office. Years of slave-like working conditions, monotonous food, and lives cut short by industrial accidents had stirred little action in the past, but now the workers were on the verge of crushing those who tormented them daily. Something had changed in the way they saw the world and one another. They sensed their collective power and would no longer waste their lives in toil for someone else's profit. By force of numbers they overcame the last resistance and killed their former bosses, sparing only the one they considered a fellow worker. Standing over the lifeless bodies of the factory managers, flanked by his comrades, their leader addressed the victorious crowd from a high window in Marxian tones: "Robots of the world! The power of man has fallen! A new world has arisen: the rule of Robots!"[1]

Falkowski was no murderer, of course. He and his comrades at Brookwood Labor College were merely acting out the climactic scene of Karel Čapek's 1920 play, *R.U.R.* (*Rossum's Universal Robots*), for a visiting group of educators. Performed hundreds of times on stages across the industrial world in the 1920s and 1930s, the play introduced the term "robot" and the narrative of robotic revolution now commonplace in science fiction. In the world of the play, the Rossum Corporation produces highly efficient artificial workers that neither tire from hard labor nor flinch at the prospect of deadly workplace injuries. These "Robots" quickly replace human workers in factories and armies across the world. But the fabulous creatures have one important flaw: lacking a sense of self-preservation, they regularly fall into the gears of factory machinery and are crushed beyond repair. To rectify this problem, a company scientist gives the Robots the ability to feel pain. This seemingly benign intervention leads to a sudden awakening of class consciousness among the automatons. They organize an international union for Robots, turn on their erstwhile masters, and slaughter humanity.

The idea of a robot rebellion added an exciting narrative element to a richly imagined conversation about industrial modernity and the political awakening of working-class populations. In the process, robots in various forms became a convenient way to talk about the participation of workers in political life, similar to the "memes" that spread over social media today. Voices on both the right and left argued that mass production work irrevocably changed the minds and bodies of working people. Repetitive tasks, the sensory cacophony of modern factories, and the insipid quality of popular culture conspired, many believed, to sap workers of their critical mental faculties. Weakened by their environment and culture, industrial workers seemed to lack the fundamental quality of democratic subjects: a critical and independent will. Others read the play in a different way. Believing the typical worker to be unfit for citizenship by virtue of heredity but well suited to the mindless repetition of machine tending, some conservatives viewed the Robots' violent rebellion as the inevitable outcome of politics without elite leadership.

The question of workers' mental fitness was also on the minds of progressive labor activists. Working-class self-educators were personally familiar with the uneven terrain of political consciousness among wage earners. They could point to family members and mentors who had helped them develop a critical consciousness, but as organizers they recognized the need to widen and deepen the reach of the worldviews they had come to embrace. By the 1920s, as modern psychological concepts became widespread, the temptation to diagnose the mentality of entire classes of people became common. As A. J. Muste of Brookwood Labor College put it in 1928, "The whole psychology of American workers today is wrong from the labor standpoint. They are mentally sick, twisted, tied up. They need to be psychoanalyzed, we might say, need to have their own thoughts and feelings laid bare before their own eyes."[2]

In this chapter I explore the images of working-class ignorance and enlightenment circulating within the progressive labor movement and beyond. These images drew on, and in turn influenced, a wider stock of images circulating in newspapers, magazines, and early film. Cartoons and drawings had long been part of political communication in the United States. Images worked in tandem with textual descriptions to deliver more impactful reading experiences, as editors of popular media were well aware. Some artists and editors, like those with the hugely popular nineteenth-century journal *Frank Leslie's Illustrated*, went for a variety of realism that compressed events into a narrative form, as historian Joshua Brown argues. Others, like the socialist Art Young, took a more overtly allegorical approach, depicting capitalists as grotesquely rotund, tuxedo-wearing villains. This social movement iconography set out expectations of what workers looked like, who represented or opposed their interests, and how workers ought to go about improving their lot. As historian Elizabeth Faue argues, labor movement imagery most frequently drew on a masculinist tradition, portraying the character of Labor as a burly individual man and rendering women's direct and indirect support for the movement invisible.[3] Women often appeared as symbols of education next to men, the aspirants to enlightenment. The cartooning and photography associated with workers' education juggled competing representational goals. Artists sought to represent laboring men engaged in study, an activity more closely associated with women and middle-class men, without portraying their male subjects as feminized. One visual solution was to portray self-education as a kind of heroic activity. Another strategy was to link practical knowledge and book learning through images that evoked craft pride or camaraderie. As with other forms of advertising and popular art, artists often used sex appeal as an attention-grabbing tool. Images of attractive men and women drew the reader's eye and created a positive association between enlightenment, desirable bodies, and the movement.

The Robots of *R.U.R.* introduced the world to the compelling story of robotic self-consciousness, later glossed as the "singularity." Once set loose in the world, however, the story and its imagery were free to be attached to a confusing range of social ills, technological innovations, and political villains. What started as an analogy for workers' revolution became a symbol of factory automation, recorded music replacing human musicians, and the acquiescence of conservative unionists to employer power, among other things. Uniting these and other social ills Americans associated with the robot was the perception that modernity denied working people the fullness of their humanity. The iconography of workers' education imagined the reversal of this process in various ways. Images of workers reading or longing for knowledge evoked the reproductive subplot of *R.U.R.* In the play the Robots face the slow death of their kind because they are unable to reproduce without a formula that their human masters had destroyed before their own demise. Their fate was not unlike that of wageworkers, labor's partisans argued. Deprived of the good things in life by their low wages and long hours of labor, it was feared that working people were becoming little more than machines.

Machine Consciousness

When A. J. Muste assailed unorganized workers as "mentally sick, twisted, [and] tied up," he was following a long line of polemic against workers who fell short of radicals' expectations. These were the "blockheads" lampooned by the IWW's Ernest Riebe in his weekly comic strip in the union's national newspaper, *Industrial Pioneer*. The eponymous character—his head a literal wooden block—was the quintessence of American individualism and patriotism. Each comic strip presented a new lesson about the harsh realities of workers' lives: the venality of employment agencies, managerial efforts to divide workers along racial and ethnic lines, the futility of charity, and so on. The final panel of each strip saw Mr. Block getting a crack over his head, sometimes at the hand of his angry wife, Mrs. Block, who exhibited a great deal more class consciousness than her husband.[4] The physical debasement Mr. Block suffered, his social humiliation at the hands of employers and his wife, and his ever hopeful American patriotism were all of a piece. Thought, action, and social consequence came together within the corners of his wooden head, which, in at least one case, Riebe depicted as split open by the wedge of Wobbly propaganda.[5]

Like Mr. Block, the Robots of Čapek's *R.U.R.* were oblivious to their condition of hyper-exploitation and willing to destroy themselves in service to their masters. Their rebellion was a surprise to all, begging the questions of why and how they had become conscious of their condition and united in action against their erstwhile masters. The play itself suggested contradictory answers, and reviewers disagreed as to whether the Robots' rebellion was part of their budding humanity or a symbol of their monstrosity. The Robots had worked for years without complaint, literally grinding themselves down to scrap. They had been indifferent to the arguments of radicals who had wanted to make them equal with human beings. However, things changed when a corporate scientist enhanced a few of the Robots, giving them the ability to experience pain so that they would protect themselves from injury. Shortly after, some Robots threw down their tools, gnashed their teeth, and refused to labor, a condition of rebelliousness the humans attributed to heightened sensitivity and named "Robot's cramp." In the play's final act, however, the rebel leader—a Robot who developed the cramp after working in the library—offered a different explanation: "Slaughter and domination are necessary if you would be human beings. Read history."[6]

Opinions about the origins of *R.U.R.*'s theatrical robot rebellion tracked real-world notions about the relative impact of experience, education, and radical leadership on working-class behavior and politics. One reviewer suggested the

VERY PLAIN LESSON TAUGHT TO THE LUMBER WORKERS BY I. W. W. STICKERS

Ernest Riebe's cartoon character Mr. Block lampooned antiunion workers who, like Karel Čapek's Robots, willingly gave their lives to capital. A popular feature of IWW newspapers, Mr. Block inspired a song by Joe Hill and organizing materials such as this sticker, which depicts unorganized lumberjacks who accepted substandard bunkhouse conditions as blockheads. *Industrial Pioneer*, April 1926, 12.

uprising was a drunken revolt reflecting humanity's own shortcomings: "inebriated by the virulent hootch of civilization . . . they have acquired through propinquity and the help of a radical biologist, the hatred, irritability and selfishness of human beings."[7] A *New York Times* reader in Brooklyn opined that the play was not an indictment of mechanization per se but rather of philanthropic reforms aimed at uplifting workers. According to this reader, workers, like the Robots, lacked reason and intelligence and were confused by these reforms. In the factory, the worker is told not to think for himself, "while on the other hand, we build for him YMCAs, libraries, community houses, and endeavor to instill in him a desire for better things." The Russian revolution, he concluded, is a prime example of how "a little knowledge is dangerous."[8] A sympathetic review of the play noted that it showed "how utterly helpless are the workmen when they have killed off The Intelligentsia. It would be very interesting to see what an American dramatist might do with this play, were he to frankly substitute the Reds for the Robots."[9] Another review found the Robots "an effective symbol of an increasing section of our population, subject to the relentless discipline of a society dominated by machinery, a proletariat threatening to engulf by the mere force of numbers the finer values of civilization."[10] But the idea that the Robots could not reproduce themselves seemed an inauthentic plot device to this reviewer. After all, "the menace of our new machine-made proletariat lies precisely in its sinister multiplication, in its gratification of the instinct, as Mr. Shaw has expressed it, for producing fresh supplies of men."[11] Echoing these themes, the drama critic for the *New York Times* wrote of *R.U.R.*, "The true enemy of civilization is not the machine, but the mechanized human being—dwarfed in intelligence, stunted in sympathy, swayed by the only idea one can ever derive from the seamy side of the industrial fabric, the idea of soulless mastery, sheer physical power."[12]

As a cultural symbol, the robot encapsulated concerns that factory work was changing the minds, bodies, and habits of working people, and not for the better. The liberal writer Horace Kallen noted in his polemical book *Education, the Machine, and the Worker* (1925) that industrial machinery caused the "strange psychoses of industrial society, the crazes, tempers, [and] unrests which its critics dwell on and assign to decay."[13] A French writer came to a similar conclusion. While working on the assembly line at Ford's giant River Rouge plant, Hyacinthe Dubreuil found that the noise of production "was sufficiently continuous to weigh on the brain." As a result, he wandered from the factory to the movie houses of Detroit or fell into fitful sleep soon after his shift. Like Abner Shutt, the protagonist of Upton Sinclair's satirical novel of auto-industrial society, *The Flivver King*, or Charlie Chaplin in the film *Modern Times*, workers ended the day with a full belly and an empty head or suffered involuntary muscle spasms that mirrored the automatic motions of the assembly line. "I could not have been persuaded to go to a lecture instead," Dubreuil noted. "I even found during this entire time that my taste for reading diminished considerably."[14]

Kallen noted a more fundamental problem of industrial selfhood. The machine, he argued, was the physical union of employer power and worker dependence, subsuming the worker's individual identity into the private purposes of production. Although he never used the word "robot," his description left little doubt about what happened to workers when the shift bell rang: "The machine-tender is integrated with the machine. His operations are part and parcel of the automatized activities of the machine process. He offers his strength and skill in the labor market with this in view. And when he offers them, it is in fact his person, in which they are incarnate, and of which they are energies and habits, that he offers."[15] Workers were one with the machine, in other words, because they lacked the social and economic power to be otherwise. In exchange for a wage, the industrial employer expected a worker's total presence, body and mind. But the modern worker had defeated this expectation through a psychological sleight of hand. "In the biography of any industrial worker," Kallen wrote, "his job is early set over against his life, his vocation against his personality, a living against living. His personality is split and the halves are opposed."[16] The automatic motions of the assembly line permitted many workers to cultivate a dreamy detachment of mind, sequestering their own thoughts from the power of the boss. Likewise, the power of the boss over the tools of production, Kallen noted, tended to strip away the sentimental attachment between a particular worker and a particular job. The "unexpectedly extensive absence of the worker's mind from the conditions of his work" caused high labor turnover, accidents, and loss of profits, Kallen argued.[17] This was in the nature of an "emotional substrate" that existed whether or not workers openly engaged in strikes and other recognized forms of "class struggle."[18] In other words, real workers had something akin to "Robot's cramp."

This conceptual association between industrial workers and robots was matched by a visual similarity. In the early run of Čapek's play, the staging, wardrobe, and advertisement of the play suggested interchangeability between humans and Robots. As a plot synopsis printed with the English translation of the script described, "Robot is a Czech word meaning 'worker.'" The Robots of *R.U.R.* were "living automats, without souls, desires or feelings. They are high powered laborers, good for nothing but work."[19] In an early scene, the play's female lead is unable to distinguish between Robots and humans, leading to a few laugh lines. On stage, clothing, haircuts, and physical build distinguished the human and Robot characters. In the New York and Chicago productions, for instance, Robots all wore the same uniform (black pants and a gray top) and sported angular haircuts, while human characters wore business suits and dresses. A poster advertising the Theatre Guild's 1922 New York performances made no visual reference to automatons, perhaps because audiences would not yet have understood the reference. Instead, clinched fists and forearms stretched into an angular urban streetscape drawn in black and red, perhaps intended to invoke the colors of anarchy.[20]

By the early 1930s, the idea of the robot had spread far beyond the context of Čapek's play or its critical reception. It lost much of its association with working-class rebellion and became a symbol of the negative impact of machinery, technology, and capitalist power.[21] Technological developments in the 1920s, particularly forms of remote control, suggested new—mostly electrical—ways to blend robot and human forms. Each new image was a commentary on human workers and their capacity to resist employer power. A 1926 cartoon in *Labor Age* lampooned the leaders of company unions by showing their heads connected by wires to a control box labeled "Talk" and "Stop." A manager standing by the box warned, "Anyone saying wage increase, I pull the switch." Another cartoon, originally published in *Life* magazine in 1927, more directly drew on this image of workers as robots. Commenting on the switch to the five-day workweek at Ford's River Rouge plant, "An Industry Epoch" depicted Ford workers as wind-up dolls having their springs and gears replaced to match the new production schedule. A cabinet for parts in the workshop includes drawers for mood, temperament, taste, and opinions.[22]

When Westinghouse developed the "Televox," a voice-activated remote switching device, the *New York Times* heralded it as an "Electrical Man." Referencing the *Times*'s report, *Labor Age* invoked "Karl Čapek's dream of robotry," noting

Machinists in the "Regulating Dep't" install new moods, temperament, taste, and opinions in wind-up mechanical workers. Lampooning Ford's management style and the massive retooling that accompanied the switch from the Model T to the Model A in 1927, a cartoonist for *Life* magazine evoked the notion that mass production work turned workers into machines. *Life*, January 13, 1927, 14.

that these workers "will be a docile lot, without the need for such uncertain trimmings as company unions, labor spies, and stock-ownership."[23] The journal of the electrical workers union presented a mock interview with "Mr. Televox" accompanied by a crudely drawn image of a mechanical man. Among other cheeky observations about the electrical switching device, the interview has Mr. Televox declaring that his inability to think for himself "will save me from ever getting persecuted for originating a new idea."[24]

In this manner, conversations about technology and productivity echoed nineteenth-century debates about the independence and political virtue of wageworkers, the notion of "wage slavery," and, somewhat more obliquely, racial slavery.[25] The connection between slavery, machinery, and the idea of the robot appeared, for instance, in a General Electric advertisement headlined "Slaves" that featured a drawing of a dark-skinned man carrying a heavy burden. The text noted that electrical motors "are America's slaves. Through their service American workers do more, earn more, and produce quality goods at lower costs than anywhere else in the world."[26] Suggesting a cosmopolitan interpretation, the ad copy quoted Oscar Wilde's contentions that "civilization requires slaves" and that "the slavery of the machine" was the foundation of modern life. The General Electric ad evoked a range of thinly veiled oppositions: manual labor, slavery, and blackness on the one hand, and modernity, leisure, and whiteness on the other. Machines freed modern citizens from the drudgery of manual labor, but machine production seemed to bind some to a work discipline that robbed them of independence and, ultimately, humanity. As the advertising agency that created and placed the spot probably understood, the membership of the International Brotherhood of Electrical Workers (IBEW) was almost exclusively white and male; thus, they were likely to read the text and images as a confirmation that their craft skill set them apart from unskilled industrial workers who toiled like both machines and slaves.

Whether writers deployed it as a negative symbol of unemployment and cheapened culture or as a positive symbol of technological innovation and progress, by the 1930s the robot was decidedly mechanical rather than organic. As the *New York Times* noted in 1933, the story of the robot originally had symbolized men reduced "to the status of machines. But we now use Robot to designate machines raised almost to the level of humanity."[27] By the early years of the Great Depression, the "worker as robot" no longer loomed as a collective threat to civilization. In its place was the robot as a symbol of automation run amok. Robotic machines towered over masses of unemployed workers, swept the unemployed into the

By the late 1920s, most images of robots were distinctly mechanical, although the automatons of Karel Čapek's play had been organic. This image from a trade union publication, titled "Caught by the sweep of the machine," depicts factory automation as a humanoid machine sweeping the unemployed into the dustbin of history. *Labor Age* February 1930.

dustbin of history, and symbolized the problem of overproduction and underconsumption. A machine tool corporation advertised its wares with the headline "For Sale: Mechanical Man Power" over an image of a gear-driven robot body. In another instance, a prominent statue at the 1933 World's Fair featured an oversize robot figure seeming to push smaller human figures into the future.[28] Unions and radicals frequently deployed the mechanical-man robot as a symbol of technological unemployment. In 1931 the American Federation of Musicians sponsored a publicity campaign condemning the introduction of recorded music to movie theaters, saying the "Robot and his sponsors should be rebuked" for replacing real culture with "canned music."[29] The mechanization of the robot's body achieved a separation from, and sublimation of, the specter that had haunted Čapek's play and the minds of many of its viewers in the early 1920s: critically conscious and organized workers. Now the danger was machinery.

Social Reproduction and Critical Consciousness

When Kallen, Dubreuil, and other observers highlighted the physical and mental deprivations of actual assembly-line work, they echoed an important subplot of Čapek's play: the link between sexuality, critical consciousness, and the survival of humankind. Unlike some later science fiction robots, Čapek's automatons were asexual. While there were male and female Robots, the automatons' corporate creators withheld from their progeny the capacity to reproduce. Only the factory could create new life. During the play it becomes clear that human women also no longer bear children, perhaps because Robots have made additional humans unnecessary. Near the climax of *R.U.R.*'s second act, one of the last humans destroys the formula for making new Robots. Facing extinction, the victorious rebels spend the play's final act struggling in vain to recreate the formula and themselves. In the play's implausible ending (frequently panned by reviewers), two of the enhanced Robots discover their mutual love and attraction. Their love becomes the new secret formula, generating the capacity to reproduce and ensuring the future of the robotic race, a new kind of humanity.[30]

The themes of social and sexual reproduction linked the robot to a broader field of conversation and image making among labor activists about political economy, family, and the creative power of rebellion. Seeing the Robots' allegorical rebellion in positive terms, for instance, trade unionist Victor Olander made the plot of *R.U.R.* a central aspect of his speeches to labor union conventions during the late 1920s. A Norwegian immigrant with only a fourth-grade education, Olander had been a sailor on the Great Lakes before his long stint as an official of both the sailors union and the Illinois Federation of Labor.[31] Mechanization, Olander declared, was "destroying the workers by thousands in the sense that it is preventing them from developing the creative powers that are the distinguishing mark of men as differing from beasts." The failure of unions to organize unskilled workers, he argued, allowed for "a sort of robot growing up in our industrial life, great hordes of unskilled workers with whom we have but little contact and who are moving restlessly from factory to factory."[32] The problem was not machines alone, Olander argued, but one of "use and control" of machines, an observation that echoed a wider progressive critique of mechanization.[33]

The profitability of robots pointed to a key question: who would bear the costs of creating and sustaining workers? Compared to mass-produced robots, human workers were exceedingly complicated and expensive. The production of just one American worker, as Olander told it, involved the migration of two strangers from distant shores, their happy meeting here in the United States, falling in love, marriage, and pregnancy. A newborn child was useless as a worker and removed the mother from the labor force. Only after years of school and an apprenticeship was the child finally available as a worker. Employers paid for these costs indirectly through wages. By driving down wages and creating a class of contingent workers, Olander argued, employers were shedding the cost of social reproduction. This created a class of "robots" in the sense that employers paid only bare survival wages and not enough for workers to live a fully human life, one that covered the costs of family, childhood, and education. *R.U.R.*'s saccharine ending appealed to trade unionists like Olander because it overturned the logic of robotic reproduction. Two Robots—one male and one female—realized their mutual love and were thereby able to reproduce. Čapek's implausible ending rejected the market logic of social reproduction and returned workers to an Edenic landscape ready to be repopulated the old-fashioned way. By destroying the formula for producing Robots, the play affirmed a humanized reproduction with all its patriarchal baggage.

Setting aside the literary quality of this finale, about which even Čapek had his doubts, the story of the Robot based the continuation of human sexual and social reproduction on the emergence of workers' critical, rebellious consciousness. If not for their enhanced perception and rebellious spirit, the play suggested, Robots would have remained sterile. The iconography of the progressive labor movement often worked similar thematic material from different directions. Many cartoons juxtaposed the liberation of enlightened workers with the debasement of those who remained in the metaphorical darkness. Others mobilized sex appeal (and less often sexual danger) to associate the desire for higher learning with these most centrally motivating human emotions. Drawing on their training as commercial illustrators, many artists portrayed the desire for education through the longing gaze of workers upon some distant object. They also portrayed the challenges of workers' education with images of male-female couples or domestic scenes that suggested heterosexual households. Even those artists with little formal training used these visual cues. Not surprisingly, unions with a predominantly male membership portrayed the desire for education differently from those with a large female membership. Both the electricians union and the IWW favored images of individual male readers, while the iconography of the ILGWU more frequently depicted reading as a sociable practice.

One of the most common themes in movement cartooning was the imagery of distance between the difficult past or present and a better future, which symbolized workers' longing and desire for change. It also conveyed an awareness that workers struggled against the odds and that along with the hopefulness of movement rhetoric, dark memories hung over many workers' lives. This was especially the case for images drawn by nonprofessionals, who often referenced personal experiences in their cartoons. For instance, John F. Anderson's 1924

Drawn by J. F. Anderson for LABOR AGE

OUT OF THE DARKNESS—INTO THE LIGHT

The Workers Education Bureau, in female form, leads a young workingman away from the brutal world of hunger and child labor. The artist, machinist John F. Anderson, came to the United States from Sweden at age ten and went to work shortly afterward. The self-taught artist had only a few months of formal schooling. *Labor Age*, April 1924, 14.

cartoon in *Labor Age*, "Out of the Darkness—Into the Light," showed a bestial, caveman-like figure with "HUNGER" inscribed on his belly and a club labeled "WORK" pulling a young boy away from an idyllic country schoolhouse. In the second panel the boy, now an adult wearing workers' overalls, walks hand in hand on the way to a "Workers College" with a female figure wearing a sash labeled "Workers Education Bureau of America" and holding aloft a torch lighting the words "Knowledge Will Make You Free." Informed by Anderson's life experience, the cartoon was a commentary on child labor and a gloss on the racial and gender politics of economic deprivation. Born in Stockholm, Sweden, in 1878, Anderson's family migrated to the western United States when he was about ten years old. He went to work shortly afterward, attending grammar school for less than a year while he worked. He apprenticed as a machinist and worked for railroads around St. Louis, where he became active in the International Association of Machinists (IAM). Eventually he rose to the vice presidency and narrowly lost a bitterly contested election for the union's top slot. Although Anderson had obviously overcome his lack of formal schooling through self-study, the "Workers College" he imagined was somewhere in the future. Enlightenment was a process with an as yet unrealized destination. The child and the adult in the cartoon seem to be on the same road but heading in opposite directions. The cartoon also suggests that the road toward workers' education rebalances male workers toward heterosexuality (albeit with a mythological woman). In the first panel, a bestial HUNGER hauls the boy in the opposite direction, down toward a darkness that implies sexual danger and debasement. As historian Daniel Bender argues, images that juxtaposed deprivation and progress were part of a racial discourse linked to evolutionary thinking and racial hierarchy. The backwardness wrought by HUNGER and WORK was at once primitive and nonwhite.[34]

A similar message about struggling to rise above a troubling and (potentially) bestial life is visible in a 1925 cartoon titled "And the First Great Step is Education," which appeared in the *Industrial Pioneer*, the monthly English-language journal of the IWW. Conceived at a moment of great hope for the radical labor movement, the *Industrial Pioneer* was filled with educational articles, commentary on culture and politics, book reviews, original cartoons, plays, short stories, and poems that the editors hoped would "spread the doctrines of Revolutionary Industrial Unionism."[35] Reflecting the movement's participatory approach to organizing, IWW newspapers and magazines routinely published member-created reports from the field, as well as cartoons, songs, and fiction. As Franklin Rosemont notes, however, not all IWW cartoonists were amateurs. Well-known leftist cartoonists like Art Young and Robert Minor at times drew for the Wobblies, and even a few professional illustrators working in the "capitalist press" donated their work under pen names. "And the First Great Step" is signed by "Van Dilman," presumably a rank-and-file Wobbly.[36]

Like Anderson's "Upward and Into the Light," Van Dilman's cartoon features an allegorical female figure and the directional metaphor of climbing. In both, education is a path toward freedom; however, this cartoon places Lady Liberty atop a pyramid away from a shirtless male figure who struggles to climb up to her, calling out, "Let's get *up* fellow workers." In this representation, education is just "the first great step" followed by organization and emancipation, echoing the union's motto. Why education is such a big step is evident from the other figures in the foreground. On the right, a female figure with bare midriff and feet taunts the rebel worker, saying, "Above lies illusion. Joys of the flesh are close to the ground." On the far left, a male figure with arms akimbo and hat pulled over his face asks, "Why don't the damn fool be satisfied with what he has? He knows the law won't let him climb!" In the middle foreground, a policeman with a billy club, a soldier with a rifle, and a hooded Klansman with a pistol advance on the would-be working-class intellectual.

Darker and less hopeful than most cartoons about education, "And the First Great Step" was accompanied by explanatory text that seemed at odds with its visual message. Identifying the many demons of working-class life, the caption nevertheless asserts that "the working class is still, on the whole, untainted and uncowed." Despite this, the cartoon presents a number of realistic barriers. Just as the "HUNGER" beast in Anderson's drawing suggests his personal experience as a child laborer, this IWW artist likely knew intimately what he was drawing. The first challenges facing self-taught working people would have been close at hand—neighbors, friends, and family who were doubtful that education would do any good—and the tempting "joys of the flesh" that were only a paycheck away. Notably absent from the image are those who might reach down to help the worker up, either real or allegorical. No one is leading the way. If anything, the drawing suggests that 1925 was a lonely year to be a Wobbly autodidact.

Artists associated with the Brotherhood of Sleeping Car Porters (BSCP), the nation's largest African American union, put their own spin on the iconography of ignorance and enlightenment. Drawing on the fashions and cultures of urban black communities, they depicted union members as well-dressed "New Negros" who rejected the paternalism of the Pullman Company; unorganized porters appeared as Uncle Toms and Sambos. The young cartoonist Ted Carroll, who grew up in Harlem and went on to a career as a boxing illustrator,

Living in the midst of the disgusting debaucheries of the capitalistic hogs who wallow in the products of modern industry, and continually menaced by the persecutions of their filthy gunmen, thugs, and murderers, the working class is still, on the whole, untainted and uncowed. It continually strives towards the three things the I. W. W. takes as its motto: Education, Organization, Emancipation. It not only tries in individual cases to mount this staircase towards the stars, but it is socially minded, and each member calls on his fellow to rise along with him.

A worker seeking emancipation must pass many challenges, but "the first great step is education" according to this IWW cartoon. Following the conventions of nineteenth-century radical imagery, the artist depicted emancipation as in female form, suggesting an association between freedom and heterosexual pairing. *Industrial Pioneer*, February 1926.

penned a series of remarkable images for the BSCP in the 1920s. In "The Modern Gulliver," Carroll drew on Jonathan Swift's story by depicting a porter as the giant Gulliver held down by the bonds of long hours and low wages. "Uncle Toms and Stool Pigeons" played the part of the Lilliputians, along with "Hungry Editors" in the black press who did management's bidding. Wielding the sword of unionism, A. Philip Randolph arrives to cut these bonds and allow the porter to stand tall on his own.[37] The nonunion workers appear as stooping caricatures in this and other cartoons by Carroll, confused by their own weakness and hungry for the crumbs offered by the boss. In one cartoon the wife of a porter tells her husband to join the union because, "you will have to organize eventually, why not now?" His son, pointing to a group of nonunion porters, asks, "Daddy, why do those men stand with their heads bowed?" The message was that unionism and the family wage would return to porters their rightful, manly place in the family.[38]

Like the contrast between Gulliver bound and the unionized porter standing in dignity, the distance between working-class aspirants and the knowledge they sought was a persistent theme of labor's iconography. Sometimes workers looked to the sun or a star, sometimes a union logo, and sometimes across great distances to symbols of political and intellectual power. Distance and attention signaled desire, or at least they advertised the things artists believed that their viewers ought to desire. For instance, the cover of the February 1916 *International Socialist Review* pictured a workman sitting down to his lunch amid factory buildings and power lines that open onto a view of a distant capitol building.[39] Recruiting posters for the Workers Summer Schools at Bryn Mawr and the University of Wisconsin played with similar imagery. In one, a woman looks up from her sewing machine and preoccupied workmates, gazing at a cathedral-like university building atop a hill. Another ("Job Doubtful? Try Study") reverses the view. A male figure dressed in a suit looks out upon an industrial landscape from beneath an archway that suggests a university building. In each, knowledge and power occupy high ground that allows for a clearer view in comparison to the cluttered and crowded working-class neighborhoods.

The temple on a hill, like the rising sun, is a symbol that artists and illustrators have deployed to represent everything from national power to religious conversion, from working-class revolution to superior consumer products. A pervasive symbol in labor and radical literature, the rising sun has symbolized both collective power and private escape. The title page of the 1935 ILGWU Education Department pamphlet "You and Your Union," for instance, shows two women and two men

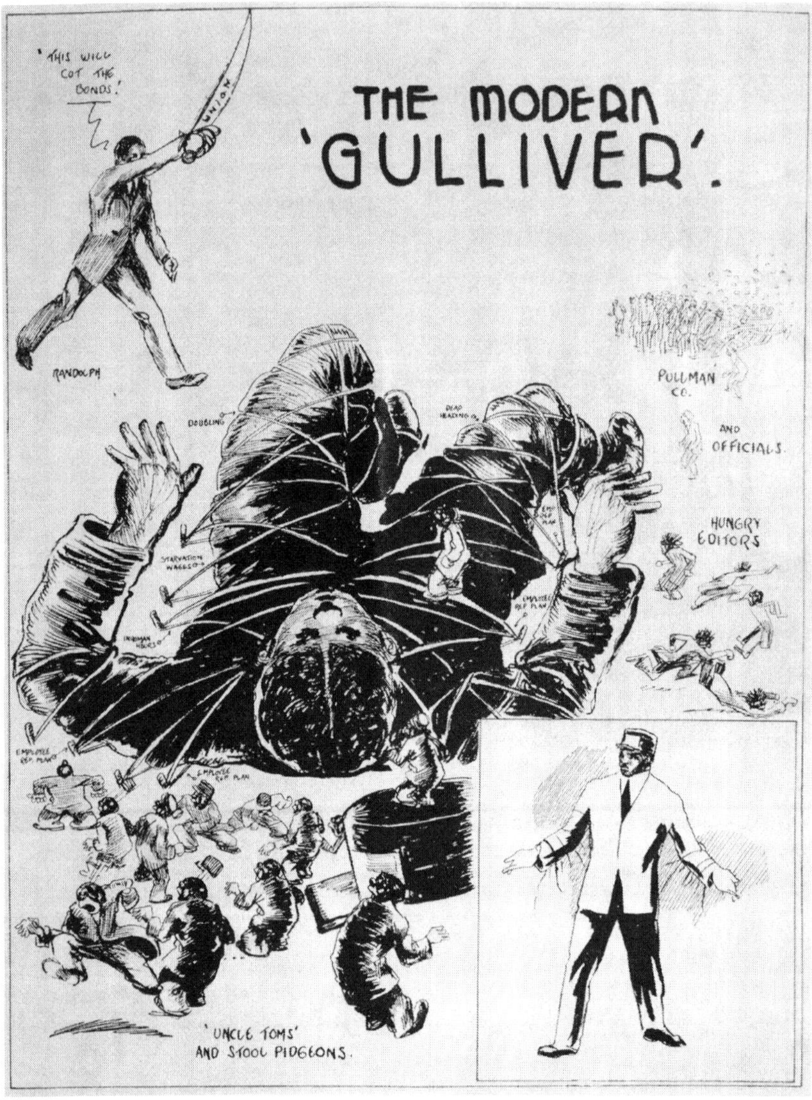

The Brotherhood of Sleeping Car Porters would cut the bindings of the black working class, depicted as a "Modern Gulliver." In other cartoons for A. Philip Randolph's *Messenger*, artist Ted Carroll depicted unionists as well-dressed, modern family men standing tall against weak-willed "Uncle Toms" who did the bidding of management. Ted Carroll, "The Modern Gulliver," *Messenger*, October 1926. Courtesy, Newberry Library, Chicago (Pullman Company Records, 06/01, box 17).

looking up from their sewing machines and irons toward a female figure. In one hand she holds aloft the logo of the union (radiating shafts of light), and points to the words "Knowledge Is Power" at the center of the image. Under her arm she holds a set of books. The distance between workers and their goal, and the relative clarity of the object they gaze at, reinforces the message that the union and workers' education are the path to liberation. On the pamphlet's cover, the "Knowledge Is Power" image sits atop a rising sun, out of which well-dressed workingwomen and -men stride forcefully toward the reader. A pile of books, some open to text and images, lies between the viewer (a rank-and-file union member) and the powerful ranks of labor. The composite illustration links the individual and the shop group to the overall collective force of the union, suggesting both that reading is a crucial instrument of collective power and that the purchasing power won by the union will make books, and the good life they represent, more accessible.[40]

Although the distance between workers and their own enlightenment was a staple of labor's iconography, many other images aimed to resolve this divide, imagining worker-intellectuals and powerful knowledge. Inviting actual readers to see themselves engaged in intellectual pursuits, images of readers and learners refracted the idea of intelligence into a gendered spectrum of individual and collective identities. The refinement of formal schooling had long been associated with women and feminized men—schoolteachers, eggheads, and intellectuals who had brains but did not know how to use them. Working-class masculinity, on the other hand, most often cohered to the informal knowledge of craft, or the rough knowledge of the street. Some artists depicted these two aspects of intelligence working together; others imagined one or the other leading the way. But an educated working class demanded reading men as well as women, and the iconography of workers' education had to find ways to portray education as manly.

The solution to this challenge was quite often an image of a solitary male reader heroically mastering the text as if in single combat. Each book in the Workers Education Bureau "Workers Bookshelf" series, for instance, featured the Lincolnesque image of a silhouetted male worker reading before the firelight of an open hearth. Likewise, radical magazines like the *Industrial Pioneer* featured the solo reader who read late into the night at a desk strewn with technical and social scientific books. The masthead for the book review section of *Industrial Pioneer* featured a detailed illustration of a male worker reading late into the night by lantern light. Drawn by "Dust" (thought to be a pseudonym for a commercial artist who donated his work to the IWW), the image carries the title "Ruler of Tomorrow."[41] A similar image with the same title (but created by a different illustrator) accompanies an article titled "The Diffusion of Knowledge,"[42] which evokes heroic thinkers of the past and

Forging Freedom's Weapons

Together, Man and Woman, forging the instrument by which to reach a free destiny. Side by side, helpful, sympathetic, determined; happy to labor together in a common cause. Today woman is in the industries; industrial freedom means her freedom as well as the freedom of man. United for this goal let them forge the weapon of organization, shape the sledge to beat down the walls of this economic prison.

Male and female workers forge "freedom's weapons" through complementary labor in an image that adorned the back cover of the IWW's monthly magazine, *Industrial Pioneer* (January 1925).

From A. Philip Randolph's *Messenger* (September 1926), a male figure labeled "the Brotherhood" (of Sleeping Car Porters) and a female figure labeled "Education" hammer the chains of low wages, prejudice, and the Pullman Company union. The hammers are labeled "Truth" and "Union." Courtesy, Newberry Library, Chicago (Pullman Company Records, 06/01, box 17).

points to the current need for applied rather than purely theoretical knowledge. These images reminded working-class autodidacts that they read with manly purpose, unlike their leisure-class opponents.[43]

A variant of the heroic individual reader was the companionate pairing of two workers, typically in didactic conversation about a book.[44] For instance, the cover art of an IWW pamphlet titled "An Economic Interpretation of the Job" depicts two workers sitting on a bench discussing something in confidence—one man appears to be talking and the other listening. Similarly, the logo of the University of Wisconsin School for Workers evoked a kind of division of labor between the worker who studies and his workmate who continues operating the machinery of industry. With his hands on levers controlling a machine, one worker reads over the shoulder of his workmate. In different ways these images insinuated reading, teaching, and learning into the daily lives of workers. They also reflect the organic social learning that educational activists hoped to build upon. Self-taught working men and women could easily recognize themselves in these images of late-night readers.

If workers staring into the distance signaled longing and desire, another mode of looking signaled connection. In picture after staged picture, in organizational logos and illustrations, working people performed the quintessential tasks of self-education: reading, listening to lecturers, and using libraries. To some extent the iconography of working class self-education took cues from Americanization and Canadianization programs, which circulated images of immigrants in classrooms as a sign of their mental transformation into national, rather than radical or ethnic, subjects.[45] A common image in union and radical

Reading late into the night was the "ruler of tomorrow," according to the IWW illustrator known as "Dust." The image ran above the book review section in the *Industrial Pioneer* during the early 1920s, portraying self-education as heroic, individual, and male.

publications was the group portrait in which members of reading clubs and union locals proudly displayed the publications and symbols of their organization. Trade unions with significant educational programs, like the IBEW and the ILGWU, also frequently portrayed their members in study groups or listening to lectures. These images were meant to promote union programs, but they also served to affirm members' status as individuals interested in living modern lives, including modern domestic life. For instance, one image from the ILGWU quietly celebrated leisure reading as a form of solidarity in the "corner of the reading room at local 62," a space that resembled a middle-class

"Knowledge Is Power," said the International Ladies Garment Workers Union, and they backed it up with an elaborate educational program. This union of immigrant working women and men favored images of groups of workers to represent the working class. This image appeared in many of the union's educational pamphlets during the mid-1930s. It features members of a shop group lifting their eyes to a female figure holding books and the logo of the union.

Members of ILGWU Local 62 read together in a setting that evokes the living room of a comfortable home. With night classes, music, theater, and sports, the ILGWU sought to bridge the differences among their multiethnic membership. From *Growing Up: 21 Years of Education with the I.L.G.W.U.* (1938).

living room with stuffed couches and easy chairs, bookshelves, and framed art on the walls.[46]

In contrast, the largely male and high-wage membership of the IBEW frequently viewed images that highlighted the relationship between book learning, craft knowledge, manly control, and aspiring middle-class status. In a cartoon titled "The Coping Stone," a lone worker clad in overalls and holding a whistle in his mouth directs the placement of carved stones that make up a new building. Among the stones already in place are "Organization," "Union Principles," "Codes," and a toolbox representing "Practical Ability." The final (coping) stone is in the form of a book titled "Theory of the Trade: Economic and Scientific." And whereas the ILGWU pictured its female members reading together in a cozy corner of their union hall, the IBEW imagined its members at home in their easy chairs reading the union journal, presumably while their wives cooked dinner. In either case, the unions signified the modernity of working-class subjects through the variegated social practice of reading.

Imagining Knowledge as Power

When Falkowski and his fellow Brookwooders performed Karel Čapek's robot play for a group of visiting educators in 1927, they were taking part in a global

A union of skilled tradesmen, the International Brotherhood of Electrical Workers often used images of powerful, individual men to symbolize their union and the working class. The drawing titled "The Coping Stone" suggested that book learning was a final element of skill, to be added only once a firm foundation of "practical ability" and "union principles" was in place. *Journal of Electrical Workers and Operators* (1926).

dialogue about the character of working-class politics. The play's robotic protagonists were assumed to be a metaphor for the world's proletarians. When their rebellion came, as it had in Russia, would the resulting society more closely resemble the regimentation of a factory or the liberty of Eden? In this way, robots were part of a field of imagery that interpreted widely held concerns about the effects of mass production on humankind. By 1940 robots were no longer part of this iconography of workers' critical consciousness. Instead they symbolized capital's power to enforce ignorance and destroy human potential. For instance, in 1948, when the University of Michigan shut down its Workers Educational Service in response to complaints by a General Motors executive, the autoworkers union portrayed the episode as a giant GM-produced robot crushing a town and tearing up the words of Abraham Lincoln.

Čapek's Robots had offered a different way to think through the modern dilemma. The Robots of *R.U.R.* were the proletarian masses with all their potential for development and destruction. Their consciousness, and their rebellion, derived from their structural position within the play's version of capitalism: cheap to produce and maintain, they solved the problem of the social reproduction of wage labor. Beyond the bounds of the play, robots changed from nearly human to mostly machine and lost a lot of their interpretive potential. Much as scientific managers divided workers' fluid movements into discrete actions, and then mandated the same motions over and over again in order to maximize productivity, the image of the robot became systematized. The image and idea of the machine robot fit more easily with the modern divisions between mind and body, thinker and worker, than had the organic robot worker. So the machine robot appeared in forms that were only loosely connected to the original concept. Robot Hamlets and robot Hoovers displaced robot revolutionaries as an all-purpose symbol of dissatisfaction with modern life and politics. By drawing a sharper distinction between workers and machines, activist artists asserted workers' humanity against the alienating power of industry. The earlier, murkier meaning of the robot as a hybrid between humanity and machinery, however, made workers more threatening and placed their claims to full humanity at the center of the cultural life of modernity.[47]

Social movement imagery was part of a broader strategy designed to generate identification between individual worker-readers and the collective. We can surmise that frequently repeated motifs, and popular characters such as the robot or Mr. Block, resonated with readers. Most of this iconography conformed to the conventions of heterosexual masculinity or femininity, as was commonplace in the interwar labor and radical movements. However, there were some obvious variations. Artists drawing for craft unions with an almost exclusively male membership sought to depict workingmen as readers and thinkers who retained their manly independence despite their visual association with the feminine realm of education and the collectivity of the union. Images of men reading at home

When the University of Michigan closed its popular Workers Education Service in 1948 following complaints from General Motors executives, the autoworkers' union published an image of the company as a giant robot trashing the community and America's cherished democratic traditions. Walter P. Reuther Library, Archives of Labor and Urban Affairs, Wayne State University.

in their easy chairs, or utilizing the knowledge they gained in study and training to orchestrate activity in the public sphere, aligned with craft union's male-breadwinner worldview. In contrast, the imagery of the ILGWU, with its largely female membership, more often suggested that reading was a collective activity, one that women did together in safe and comfortable environments. For both male and female audiences, enlightenment was frequently depicted as something distant but attainable. The eyes of worker-readers and students were drawn to images of the rising sun, labor colleges, and myriad union logos. These symbols of enlightenment signified workers' attention to the challenges of organizing their fellow workers, publishing union newspapers, and situating their own lives in a broader context. Images of ignorance also marked the distance traveled for the reader who imagined himself or herself enlightened. Just as trade unionists and radicals sometimes cheered the victory of the Robots in *R.U.R.*, the self-educated could see a little bit of their former selves in the travails of Mr. Block. The iconography of ignorance and enlightenment backed up the textual and oral culture of workers' education. If many could agree with John Brophy that "ideas *are* a power," labor's imagemakers made this connection visually immediate and memorable.

The gender of enlightenment on display in these didactic images most often followed traditional lines, embodying labor's mind within reproductive families, or linking the desire for knowledge with the desire for opposite-sex bodies. Desire for knowledge, however, transcended the physical world. It connected mind, body, and something like the soul. Workers who read on the job or late into the night were like the Robots whose love made them human. They stole time, space, and their own bodies from their industrial masters. They asserted the right to remake themselves on their own terms, one book at a time.

CONCLUSION

Self-Education in the Shadow of the Cold War

A week after Richard Nixon was sworn in as president of the United States in January 1969, CBS News aired an hour-long conversation between respected newsman Eric Sevareid and Eric Hoffer, a best-selling author known as the "longshoreman philosopher." Through a thick German accent and a cloud of cigarette smoke, Hoffer mixed the folksy wisdom of a plain workingman with references to the great works of Western philosophy. He assailed American intellectuals as power-hungry and antidemocratic. He condemned leaders of the Black Power movement as "phony." He predicted Nixon would make a "good President," but he praised Lyndon Johnson as "one of us" and "something very special."[1] Notably, this was the second hour-long interview to air on primetime national television with the man who had spent his working life as a laborer on the San Francisco docks. Hoffer's 1967 interview with Sevareid had earned him an invitation to the Johnson White House and an honorary post as a research scientist at the University of California's restive Berkeley campus. The working class, it seemed, had reached the heights of power and influence through this singular individual.

Hoffer's analysis of contemporary politics was a balm for political leaders who were eager to defuse the era's volatile social movements. For many radicals, Hoffer's performance was confirmation that prosperity had drained the unionized working class of its fighting spirit. The labor scholar Stan Weir, himself a former longshoreman, noted wryly that Hoffer's intellectual achievements rested on a material base secured by his union's contract. In addition to high wages, the ILWU's control of hiring had allowed Hoffer to take time off to write his books and to return to work with no loss of seniority.[2] These details were invisible to most who saw in Hoffer something they believed was truly unique: a self-educated workingman, a rank-and-file union member who could write and talk about ideas, and a thinker who rejected the label of "intellectual." Decades later the aura of Hoffer's uniqueness remains, especially among conservatives. His authorized biographer, the journalist Tom Bethell, asked in admiration of Hoffer's achievement, "Was there any precedent for this in the life of the nation?"[3]

If you have read this far, you know the correct answer is "yes." Hoffer's literary achievements were unusual for a man with no formal schooling, but as a worker with an extensive reading list and a love of ideas, he was one of many. Although most American workers in Hoffer's generation never finished high school, and fewer attended college, working-class Americans with a desire to learn could find their way to the world of ideas and have plenty of company along the way. Few working-class autodidacts published best sellers or appeared on national media, but Hoffer was not alone in penning books, pamphlets, songs, and articles that reached eager audiences. Given the uneven growth of formal education and the need for paying work that forced many to quit school, many among the reading public of the early and mid-twentieth century were themselves "unschooled." Their desire to understand the world or to enjoy the pleasure of reading and mental engagement generated a profitable market for low-cost newspapers, books, and magazines. The need to sell books and pamphlets, both as consumer products and as vehicles for ideas, placed many authors and advocates before their reading public on street corners, public parks, and in popular lecture series in most American cities. Hoffer was a product of this working-class public sphere rather than its antithesis.

Hoffer was also representative of the way many Americans imagined the relationship between "intellectuals and other people," to use the title of historian Merle Curti's 1954 address to the American Historical Association. "Americans have had faith in the rational," Curti told his highly educated colleagues, "but at the same time have tended to be suspicious of the life of reason."[4] The staging of Hoffer's television appearance reenacted a common depiction of American intellectual life as a feedback loop between plebian common sense and the erudite but cramped thinking of middle-class intellectuals. The image of Sevareid in suit and tie sitting opposite Hoffer is reminiscent of the face-off in Art Young's 1922 cartoon that featured a beefy "manual worker" pronouncing to a thin, bespectacled "brain worker," "You may have more brains than I've got, but you don't know how to use them." And Hoffer's gruff rebuttals to some of Sevareid's questions came close to the retort Ralph Ellison received from the opera-loving coal heavers he met in Harlem in the 1930s: "What the hell can we do for *you*?"

As no less an intellectual than Ralph Waldo Emerson noted, "Public opinion commends the practical man" while it regards fancy thinking as "subversive of social order and comfort." This assessment was as much playing to an audience as it was cultural analysis. Not only was Emerson making a living delivering lectures to ordinary Americans, as Curti noted, but those same "farmers and villagers were digging into their pockets to keep open the academies and colleges that enabled scholars to live and to train more of their kind."[5] Political parties that advocated wider access to the ballot also voted to fund new state universities, and in 1862 the Morrill Act provided a system of funding new universities by transferring federal lands to states to sell or use as campuses. When Southern states used the funding for their all-white universities, Congress required that they establish colleges for their African American residents. Cooperative agricultural extension programs, funded jointly by state and federal funds beginning in 1914, spread the reach of higher education to nearly every county in the United States. Celebrating the popular mind while fostering systems of formal education—systems that required large numbers of formally trained instructors—presented no contradiction for American politicians.

In a lightly bureaucratized society, the line between formal and informal education was less stark than it is today. Universities were one part of a more diffuse field of educational practices that included popular lectures and home study. It was only after World War II that modern universities sought to claim the field of higher education as their exclusive domain. Their success is measured in the degree to which contemporary society seems unable to fathom a different outcome. Labor unions went through a similar process after 1945. As institutionalized forms of collective bargaining became the norm, the possible scope of action for the labor movement narrowed. Before 1940 it was common to understand the "labor movement" as consisting of unions, working-class political parties and community-based organizations, and cooperatives. Higher education was also a more difuse and less bureaucratic social field before World War II. As we saw in the first chapters of this book, this broader social context helped support incipient educational institutions like the open forums and labor colleges, created points of access for many more working people, and fostered cross-class coalitions. We can think of "the university" and "the movement" not only as institutions but also as overlapping fields of social practice that brought together activists from very different parts of society. The relationships in these fields of practice were often contentious and messy, but they also created the potential for radically new ways of addressing persistent and emerging social problems. As unions became more institutionalized, the social movement organizations that did not engage in collective bargaining fell away from the public conception of the "labor movement," and unions themselves pushed many people out the door in a bid for political respectability. In the short term, narrowing the focus of unions delivered impressive benefits but also cut unions off from broader popular support. The shared field of social action between "the university" and "the movement," which was carefully tended by activists in both arenas, became much more difficult to maintain after 1945.

The world of working-class self-education had already receded from popular attention by the time Hoffer gained notoriety. The mobilization of millions of working-class people for the war effort absorbed much of the social energy that had gone into sustaining precarious venues of learning. After the war, substantial segments of the working class moved out of dense urban neighborhoods and into the suburbs, further eroding the audience for independent education. Those who found themselves leaders of new local unions were often consumed with the day-to-day functions of their organizations and were most interested in practical training they believed would make their unions successful. As many unions developed their own education departments, training for leaders and activists was less likely to bring members of different unions and different labor market sectors into personal contact. Finally, anticommunist sentiment and persecution shuttered some of the most creative independent workers' schools, and enforced moderation on those that survived. With a dwindling public presence, the movement for working-class self-education became increasingly unknown, allowing Hoffer's fame to burn brighter and seem all the more exceptional.

Universities also changed after the war. Responding to the demands of returning veterans, the federal government pumped billions of dollars into the expansion of university campuses and tuition support. Between 1940 and 1970 the proportion of American adults with some college experience doubled to 20 percent. In another thirty years it would top 50 percent. Perceptions of society's class structure changed as greater numbers of working-class youth attended college, an achievement that was supposed to mark their graduation to the middle class. On campus, however, students were becoming something of a class unto themselves, especially in public universities with their giant lecture halls and distant faculty. As Clark Kerr noted in *The Uses of the University*, "If the faculty looks upon itself as a guild, the undergraduate students are coming to look upon themselves more as a 'class,' some may even feel like a 'lumpen proletariat.'"[6] While a growing portion of this "student class" went back to working-class households after final exams, Kerr's ironic comment gestured to the cultural impossibility of inhabiting both categories. There would be no worker-students in mass higher education. Aspiring working-class youth would be students only, a temporary identity that would prepare them to rise above their parents' station.

The vastly expanded domains of collective bargaining and higher education created an ideal climate for scholars of industrial relations like Kerr. Some of the discipline's leaders soon become university administrators and applied their mediation skills to conflicts between radical students and conservative university governing boards. While the student movement struck a militant stance that was anathema to the mediating instincts of industrial relations professors, the two groups shared academic, social, and political commitments. Intellectually oriented toward political economy, industrial relations researchers and student organizers often had personal connections with working-class communities and shared a desire to modernize the management of public universities. Kerr tried to mollify the free speech movement in 1964, only to lose his position at the hands of conservative regents and a newly elected governor, Ronald Reagan. At the University of Michigan, Professor Robin Fleming was more successful. As a liberal critic of the war in Vietnam, he used public appearances to appeal to more moderate students. He also created new policies designed to arbitrate student grievances before they led to mass organizing, included students in some curricular decisions, and sought to diversify the university's student body and governing board.[7]

Beyond the walls of the university, social movements of the 1950s and 1960s continued to be sites of innovative popular education, sometimes with the support of labor unions. The autoworkers union built its own training campus in the woods of northern Michigan and offered funding programs for civil rights leaders at the Highlander Folk School in Tennessee. Drawing on the labor college experience of the 1930s, Highlander's Miles Horton helped to train a generation of organizers who went into the South to establish freedom schools.[8] As social movements spread far beyond the workplace and the control of union leaders, community-based popular education became a pervasive practice. African American activists established more than twenty community schools for children and adults in the late 1960s and 1970s, according to historian Russell Rickford, in "the attempt to build the prospective infrastructure for an independent black nation." Native American and Latino community activists followed suit with their own freedom schools, discussion groups, and publication programs. While these communities organized around issues of segregation, economic development, and cultural survival, women's and gay liberation groups deployed consciousness-raising methods to build tight communities of action as well.[9] Liberal observers decried what they considered to be the balkanization of the public sphere into identity-based interest groups. But the proliferation of communities of action looked something like the working-class public sphere of the early twentieth century, which amplified critical messages about the emerging capitalist order. Activist networks embedded in communities generated local knowledge and plans of action, engaged one another in contentious debate over the nature of the social order, and sometimes found intersecting interests and plans of action. The elaboration of new ways of seeing the world—new forms of social knowledge—was central to this development.

This creative wave of educational organizing rolled back over American universities as young people mounted a vigorous campaign of sit-ins and hunger strikes demanding the humanization of the modern university. The response of administrators echoed their predecessors' handling of workers education on campuses in the 1930s and 1940s. As a group, campus management and senior faculty wavered between outright hostility and cautious support, and they used their control over university structures to influence the outcome of the struggle. The existing industrial relations programs often played a mediating role in this process. When UCLA administrators acceded to student demands for a Center for Afro-American Studies, one of the first in the nation, they appointed as its director Robert Singleton, a Freedom Rider and local NAACP leader who had been a staff researcher at the Institute of Industrial Relations.[10] While Singleton left the position to finish his doctorate, the program received major funding from the Ford Foundation as part of its effort to foster the managed diversification of American institutions. Ford and other foundations aimed to promote civic dialogue as a way to soften the sharpening conflict between emerging social forces and the status quo, much as the Carnegie Endowment had done in the 1920s by underwriting the American Association of Adult Education.[11]

Within universities, however, ethnic studies departments and scholars often faced institutional pressures to throttle back their engagement with the communities that had demanded their creation in favor of scholarly publication. As a Ford Foundation report noted in 1978, Chicano scholars at UCLA had been rebuffed in their efforts to combine scholarship and community service. Even supportive faculty considered "direct community action as too political and inconsistent with the role of a university."[12] Resistance to community engagement grew in the Reagan years as university administrators and public commentary turned sharply against politically engaged scholarship. As unions began a steep decline, many industrial relations programs shifted resources away from labor education and toward professionalized management studies. With social movements and unions politically weakened and distracted by more immediate struggles, both labor education and ethnic studies programming became easy targets in budget battles.

Some people see in this history an inverse relationship between the politics of race and gender on the one hand and the politics of class on the other. To use historian Jefferson Cowie's evocative phrase, the 1970s were the "last days of the working class," after which the prospects for broad-based social democratic politics withered as narrow political agendas starved the public sphere. There is little doubt that deindustrialization and management antiunionism helped to break the fractious Democratic coalition in the 1970s. But this was hardly the end of the working class. Industries with large proportions of women and people of color became the new dynamic centers of the economy. The leadership of labor unions, however, remained in the hands of white men, many of whom resented the demands of their newly diverse membership for greater representation. Rank-and-file insurgencies had a mixed record of success in the steel and autoworkers' unions, while rebel teamsters were just starting a decades-long struggle for union democracy. Parallel to these efforts in traditionally unionized industries, young workers—often women, African Americans, and immigrants—launched innovative drives among clerical and service workers.[13]

As these insurgencies gained ground, their leaders often created strategic partnerships with university-based researchers. The Coalition of Labor Union Women, founded in 1974 to amplify the voices of women union members, partnered with university labor educators to revive the pre-1945 system of regional summer labor schools.[14] In Los Angeles progressive researchers and artists rallied to the new union insurgencies among janitors and hotel workers. UCLA's Institute of Industrial Relations launched an undergraduate program that placed students in internships with unions and community organizations, eventually creating a pipeline of new organizers. A few years later, the University of Massachusetts established a residential graduate program for labor union leaders. The 1990s also saw the revival of unionization efforts among university teaching and research assistants, a process that diverted talented organizers out of the academy and into the labor movement.[15] Despite these instances of deepening connections between university intellectuals and the labor movement, budget austerity in many states has left labor education programs in an ever more precarious position.[16]

A century after Ed Falkowski reluctantly left school to work in a Pennsylvania coal mine, Americans are still attracted to what he called the "high school of life."

We now expect all young people to earn a diploma from an actual high school, and want most to go to college, but the idea of "learning by doing" remains alluring.[17] This is partly true because formal schooling, systematically deprived of funding, often fails to inspire young minds and increasingly burdens them with student loan debt. The rapid advance of digital communication technologies seems to hold out the chance for a more engaged style of learning. As former secretary of education Arne Duncan noted in 2011, "Today's technology-enabled, information-rich, deeply interconnected world means learning not only can—but *should*—happen anywhere, anytime."[18] Likewise, the overhyped promise of MOOCs (Massive Open Online Courses) reflects the appeal of self-guided learning at the college level and the popular unease with the cost and value of higher education.[19] Libertarian venture capitalist Peter Thiel went so far as to establish a fellowship that paid young people *not to go to college*, based on the theory that formal education stifles innovation. Of course, the wealthy continue to send their children to private schools and colleges with ample and well-trained human instructors. But we can learn something from Thiel's gloomy assessment of the twentieth century and the chances for liberty in the twenty-first. The PayPal billionaire, early Facebook investor, and Donald Trump supporter thinks things have been all downhill since the 1920s, which he called "the last decade in American history during which one could be genuinely optimistic about politics." Ever since, he vented in an autobiographical article, "the vast increase in welfare beneficiaries and the extension of the franchise to women . . . have rendered the notion of 'capitalist democracy' into an oxymoron."[20] Thiel sees hope only where there are no living, breathing humans: the internet, under the oceans, and in outer space. These are solutions for a humanity greatly diminished in numbers and quality of life. Like these billionaire dream-futures, the logic of internet-based self-education abandons the goal of universal human development in favor of a fantasy of personal salvation. The assumption is that much of humanity is beyond saving.

In ways that most of today's self-styled education reformers are loath to admit, public education and the labor movement are modern phenomena that grew together and need each other. For more than a century, the American labor movement has been one of the most powerful advocates of greater funding for public schools and colleges. Like Mike Gold, who said he was haunted by education, and Rosella Burke, who felt "chilly inside" when she dropped out of school to go to work, Falkowski felt "cheated from the very start" because, as he observed, although he was better read than most college graduates, "it is credits and diplomas rather than the content of one's mind that goes farthest in the world of opportunity."[21] All three were happy to be partisans in the cause of working-class emancipation; however, whether haunted, chilly, or cheated, these and other working-class autodidacts were also right to feel society had robbed them of opportunity. This is why so many working people and unions championed public funding of high schools and colleges. They wanted their children to have the chance to develop their minds free from the compulsion to work. Of course, they also wanted their children to get good jobs, but our current obsession with making students "career ready" would have been unrecognizable for these education advocates of the past.

A new debate about learning, experience, and authenticity broke into the global public sphere after the financial crisis of 2008. But while movements of every political outlook featured what we can recognize as popular self-education, the right and the left have very different orientations toward formal education. The insurgent conservative movement associated with the so-called Tea Party championed a folksy, untutored conservatism in the personas of Sarah Palin and Joe the Plumber—a postmodern version of the "school of hard knocks." The presidential campaign of Donald Trump took this logic to a new extreme. The real estate tycoon and reality television star portrayed himself as the defender of forgotten industrial workers and as a man who said exactly what was on his mind, regardless of what the "media elites" thought was appropriate or true. Trump and his political allies are notably hostile to higher education and scholarly expertise in general.

On the other side of the political spectrum, the youth-led politics of occupying public spaces and confronting police violence also mobilize the power of experience through the strategic sharing of personal narratives and video on social media. Campus occupations in 2009 and the 2011 occupations of the Wisconsin capitol building and Zuccotti Park in New York (along with many of the local occupations that followed) each featured a free lending library and often a volunteer-run "People's University." The immigrant rights movement has found a resonant message in the defense of so-called Dreamers, mainly students in public schools and universities, while immigrant-worker centers use popular education to organize and defend undocumented wage earners. In the 2016 presidential campaign, many of the young insurgents coalesced around Bernie Sanders and his demand for free college and student loan forgiveness. A key demand of the Movement for Black Lives is "full and free access" to education at all levels. The vitality of the immigrant rights movement and the Movement for Black Lives, the surge of local organizing that followed the January 2017 Women's March, and the surprising renewal of interest in socialism among young organizers point to the emergence of a multicentered movement. The networks that link these organizations and tendencies look quite a bit like the pre–New Deal labor movement—a movement that had unions at its institutional core but that also included social justice organizations, immigrant community organizations, and heterodox political activists.[22]

The links between these movements and the academic knowledge machine that is the postmodern university are not always clear. But the history I have encountered in the archives of universities and labor colleges suggests that the separation between academics and everyone else has been a *project* that required careful tending. All the more reason to nurture and defend our spaces of collaboration and to pull our public universities back toward a more democratic future.

Notes

Introduction

1. Ralph Ellison, "The Little Man at Chehaw Station: The American Artist and His Audience," *American Scholar* 47(Winter 1977/1978): 45–46.

2. Ibid., 48.

3. Hutchins Hapgood, *The Spirit of Labor*, introduction and notes by James R. Barrett (1907; Urbana: University of Illinois Press, 2004), 16–17.

4. Ibid., 324.

5. Don D. Lescohier Papers, box 1, folder 1, State Historical Society of Wisconsin, emphasis in original; Don D. Lescohier, "With the I.W.W. in the Wheat Lands," *Harper's Monthly Magazine* 147 (July 1923): 374–75; and Frank Tobias Higbie, *Indispensable Outcasts: Hobo Workers and Community in the American Midwest, 1880–1930* (Urbana: University of Illinois Press, 2003), 205–206.

6. Oral history interview with Broadus Mitchell, August 14 and 15, 1977, interview B-0024, Southern Oral History Program Collection (#4007), Southern Historical Collection, Wilson Library, University of North Carolina at Chapel Hill, http://docsouth.unc.edu/sohp/B-0024/excerpts/excerpt_3992.html#fulltext; Broadus Mitchell, foreword to Rose Pesotta, *Bread Upon the Waters* (New York: Dodd, Mead, 1945), vii; and Elaine Leeder, *The Gentle General: Rose Pesotta, Anarchist and Labor Organizer* (Albany: SUNY Press, 1993).

7. Tom Snyder, ed., *120 Years of Education: A Statistical Portrait*, National Center for Educational Statistics, 1993, https://nces.ed.gov/naal/lit_history.asp#illiteracy; Claudia Goldin, "School Enrollment and Pupil-Teacher Ratios, by Grades K–8 and 9–12 and by Public-Private Control: 1869–1996," Table Bc7–18 in *Historical Statistics of the United States, Earliest Times to the Present: Millennial Edition*, ed. Susan B. Carter, Scott Sigmund Gartner, Michael R. Haines, Alan L. Olmstead, Richard Sutch, and Gavin Wright (New York: Cambridge University Press, 2006), http://dx.doi.org/10.1017/ISBN-9780511132971.Bc1-

50910.1017/ISBN-9780511132971.Bc1-509; U.S. Census Bureau, *Statistical Abstract of the United States* (Washington, DC: GPO, 2003), Table HS-22; U.S Census Bureau, "Educational Attainment of the Population 25 Years Old and Over, 1940," http://www.census.gov/hhes/socdemo/education/data/cps/1946/p10–8/tables.html; Harvey J. Graff, *The Legacies of Literacy: Continuities and Contradictions in Western Culture and Society* (Bloomington: Indiana University Press, 1987), 366–68; and Lawrence A. Cremin, *American Education: The Metropolitan Experience, 1876–1980* (New York: Harper and Row, 1988).

8. U.S. Census Bureau, *Statistical Abstract of the United States* (Washington, DC: GPO, 2003), Table HS-22; Snyder, ed., *120 Years of Education*; and U.S. Census Bureau, *CPS Historical Time Series Tables*, Tables A-1 and A-2, https://www.census.gov/data/tables/time-series/demo/educational-attainment/cps-historical-time-series.html.

9. Craig Phelan, *Grand Master Workman: Terence Powderly and the Knights of Labor* (Westport, CT: Greenwood Press, 2000), 11–12; and Samuel Gompers, *Seventy Years of Life and Labor: An Autobiography* (New York: E. P. Dutton, 1925), 6–8.

10. Lothrop Stoddard, *Revolt against Civilization: The Menace of the Underman* (New York: Scribner's, 1922), 143.

11. Ibid.; Henry Ford, *Today and Tomorrow* (1926), quoted in Stuart Chase, *Men and Machines* (New York: Macmillan, 1929); and Frederick W. Taylor, *Principles of Scientific Management* (New York: Harper and Brothers, 1911), 40.

12. Upton Sinclair, *The Flivver King: A Story of Ford-America* (1937; Chicago: Charles H. Kerr, 2006), 15.

13. Horace Kallen, *Education, the Machine, and the Worker: An Essay in the Psychology of Education in Industrial Society* (New York: New Republic, 1925), 89, 64.

14. Whiting Williams, *What's on the Worker's Mind, by One Who Put on Overalls to Find Out* (New York: C. Scribner's Sons, 1920); James E. Cronin and Carmen Sirianni, eds. *Work, Community, and Power: The Experience of Labor in Europe and America, 1900–1925* (Philadelphia: Temple University Press, 1983); Elspeth H. Brown, *The Corporate Eye: Photography and the Rationalization of American Commercial Culture, 1884–1929* (Baltimore: Johns Hopkins University Press, 2005); Steven Meyer, *Five Dollar Day: Labor Management and Social Control in the Ford Motor Company, 1908–1921* (Albany: SUNY Press, 1981); and Bohuslava R. Bradbrook, *Karel Čapek: In Pursuit of Truth, Tolerance, and Trust* (Brighton, Eng.: Sussex Academic Press, 1998).

15. Selig Perlman, *A Theory of the Labor Movement* (New York: Macmillan, 1928), 280–81.

16. William F. Dunne, *Worker Correspondents: What, Where, When, Why, How? The Little Red Library 4* (Chicago: Daily Worker Publishing, 1925); Antonio Gramsci, *Selections from the Prison Notebooks of Antonio Gramsci*, ed. and trans. Quintin Hoare and Geoffrey Nowell Smith (New York: International Publishers, 1971), 8–10; and Robert Michels, "Intellectuals," *Encyclopedia of the Social Sciences* (New York: Macmillan, 1930–1935), 118. On labor priests, see Heath W. Carter, *Union Made: Working People and the Rise of Social Christianity in Chicago* (New York: Oxford University Press, 2015); and Erik S. Gellman

and Jarod Roll, *The Gospel of the Working Class: Labor's Southern Prophets in New Deal America* (Urbana: University of Illinois Press, 2011).

17. See Jonathan Rose, *The Intellectual Life of the British Working Classes* (New Haven, CT: Yale University Press, 2001); and Joseph F. Kett, *The Pursuit of Knowledge under Difficulties: From Self-Improvement to Adult Education in America, 1750–1990* (Stanford, CA: Stanford University Press, 1994).

18. Carter, *Union Made*; Gellman and Roll, *Gospel of the Working Class*; Tony Michels, *Fire in Their Hearts: Yiddish Socialists in New York* (Cambridge, MA: Harvard University Press, 2005); Paul Lubienecki, "Catholic Labor Education and the Association of Catholic Trade Unionists: Instructing Workers to Christianize the Workplace," *Journal of Catholic Education* 18 (March 2015); and Elizabeth Fones-Wolf and Ken Fones-Wolf, *Struggle for the Soul of the Postwar South: White Evangelical Protestants and Operation Dixie* (Urbana: University of Illinois Press, 2016).

19. Charles Taylor, *Modern Social Imaginaries* (Durham, NC: Duke University Press, 2004).

20. On the debate over experience in history, see, among others, Joan Scott, "The Evidence of Experience," *Critical Inquiry* 17, no. 4 (1991): 773–97; William H. Sewell Jr., "Refiguring the 'Social' in Social Science: An Interpretivist Manifesto," in Sewell, *Logics of History: Social Theory and Social Transformation* (Chicago: University of Chicago Press, 2005); Frederick Cooper, "Identity," in *Colonialism in Question: Theory, Knowledge, History* (Berkeley: University of California Press, 2005); and James C. Scott, *Seeing Like a State: How Certain Schemes to Improve the Human Condition Have Failed* (New Haven, CT: Yale University Press, 1998).

21. Philip Bump, "There Are Fewer Coal Miners Than You Might Realize," *Washington Post*, March 20, 2017, https://www.washingtonpost.com/news/politics/wp/2017/03/20/there-are-fewer-coal-miners-than-you-might-realize; "National Occupational Employment and Wage Estimates" (May 2016), U.S. Bureau of Labor Statistics, https://www.bls.gov/oes/current/oes_nat.htm.

Part I. Reading the Marks of Capital

1. J. H. Larsh, "Experience versus Thinking," *Industrial Pioneer*, April 1924, 29.

2. On Commons and Foster, see James R. Barrett, *William Z. Foster and the Tragedy of American Radicalism* (Urbana: University of Illinois Press, 1999), 115; Tim Lacy, *The Dream of a Democratic Culture: Mortimer J. Adler and the Great Books Idea* (New York: Palgrave Macmillan, 2013), 23–24; and Alex Beam, *A Great Idea at the Time : The Rise, Fall, and Curious Afterlife of the Great Books* (New York: Public Affairs, 2008), 21–22.

Chapter 1. "A little avenue to self-mastery": The Social World of Working-Class Readers

1. Edward Falkowski, "Personal Record and Self-Analysis," folder 1–2; and Edward Falkowski, "Diary of Edward Fulsky," entry for October 2, 1916, folder 1–5, both in Edward

J. Falkowski Papers, Walter P. Reuther Archives of Labor and Urban Affairs, Wayne State University (hereafter EJFP).

2. Edward Falkowski, "Radicalism" and "In the Mines," undated writings, EJFP; and Edward Falkowski, "Transit, Book 1," Edward Falkowski Papers, Tamiment Library, New York University.

3. Ed Falkowski, "New Plans for Self Improvement," (undated) box 4, folder 9, EJFP.

4. James Maurer, "How I Became a Rebel. Part 2," *Labor Herald*, July 1922, 24.

5. Jack Conroy reading "The Disinherited" and interview, American Audio Prose Library, October 1980, Jack Conroy Papers, Newberry Library, Chicago; and Douglas C. Wixson, *Worker-Writer in America: Jack Conroy and the Tradition of Midwestern Literary Radicalism, 1898–1990* (Urbana: University of Illinois Press, 1994).

6. David Montgomery, *Fall of the House of Labor: The Workplace, the State, and American Labor Activism, 1865–1925* (Cambridge, UK: Cambridge University Press, 1987), 2; and Thomas A. Guglielmo, "Encountering the Color Line in the Everyday: Italians in Interwar Chicago," *Journal of American Ethnic History* 23, no. 4 (2004): 45–77. On learning in contemporary workplaces, see Mike Rose, *The Mind at Work: Valuing the Intelligence of the American Worker* (New York: Penguin Books, 2005); and Steven P. Vallas and John P. Beck, "The Transformation of Work Revisited: The Limits of Flexibility in American Manufacturing," *Social Problems* 43 (August 1996): 345–46.

7. Ben Reisman, "Why I Came to America," in *My Future Is in America: Autobiographies of Eastern European Jewish Immigrants*, ed. and trans. Jocelyn Cohen and Daniel Soyer (New York: New York University Press, 2006), 77.

8. Stanley Mathewson, *Restriction of Output among Unorganized Workers* (New York: Viking Press, 1931), 68–69.

9. "Harmony?" in ibid., 127.

10. Frank Tobias Higbie, *Indispensable Outcasts: Hobo Workers and Community in the American Midwest, 1880–1930* (Urbana: University of Illinois Press, 2003), 119; "The Symbolic Jacket," Andria T. Hourwich and Gladys L. Palmer, *I Am a Woman Worker: A Scrapbook of Autobiographies* (New York: Affiliated Schools for Workers, 1936), 22–23.

11. Steve Nelson, James R. Barrett, and Rob Ruck, *Steve Nelson: American Radical* (Pittsburgh: University of Pittsburgh Press, 1981), 5; Robert Saunders, "The Road," Western Historical Manuscripts, University of Missouri, St. Louis; and Kristine Stilwell, "'If You Don't Slip': The Hobo Life, 1911–1916" (PhD diss., University of Missouri, 2004).

12. Floyd Dell, *Moon-Calf* (New York: Alfred A. Knopf, 1920), 198.

13. Rosella Burke, "Autobiography," Brookwood Labor College Collection, Walter P. Reuther Archive, Wayne State University.

14. "E. Calloway Dies, Labor Activists," *St. Louis Post-Dispatch* (MO), January 4, 1990, A1, A9.

15. The examples in this paragraph are drawn from Solon De Leon, ed., *The American Labor Who's Who* (New York: Hanford Press, 1925). Of over thirteen hundred labor, radical, and civil liberties leaders, only about fifty directly identified themselves as "self-

educated." A larger number indicated they entered the workforce by age fifteen, suggesting limited schooling.

16. Hutchins Hapgood, *The Spirit of Labor. Introduction and Notes by James R. Barrett* (1907; Urbana: University of Illinois Press, 2004); Annelise Orleck, *Common Sense and a Little Fire: Women and Working-Class Politics in the United States, 1900–1965* (Chapel Hill: University of North Carolina Press, 1995); and John P. Frey, *An American Molder* (Cincinnati: S. Rosenthal, 1910).

17. Douglas Waples and Ralph Tyler, *What People Want to Read About: A Study of Group Interests and a Survey of Problems in Adult Reading* (Chicago: University of Chicago Press, 1931), 86–92. See also William S. Gray and Ruth Munroe, *The Reading Interests and Habits of Adults: A Preliminary Report* (New York: Macmillan, 1929); and Rhey Boyd Parsons, "A Study of Adult Reading" (MA thesis, University of Chicago, 1923), 68–71.

18. William Frank Rasche, "The Reading Interests of Young Workers" (PhD diss., University of Chicago, 1936), 44–52; and William F. Rasche, *The Reading Interests of Young Workers* (Milwaukee: Milwaukee Vocational School, 1925).

19. Rasche, *Reading Interests of Young Workers*, 20–42, 67–70; Erin A. Smith, *Hard-Boiled: Working-Class Readers and Pulp Magazines* (Philadelphia: Temple University Press, 2000), 23–32; and Ann Fabian, "Making a Commodity of Truth: Speculations on the Career of Bernarr Macfadden," *American Literary History* 5, no. 1 (1993): 51–76. On nineteenth-century working-class reading, see Michael Denning, *Mechanic Accents: Dime Novels and Working-Class Culture in America* (London: Verso, 1987), especially chapter 3; and Jennifer Scanlon, *Inarticulate Longings: The Ladies' Home Journal, Gender, and the Promises of Consumer Culture* (New York: Routledge, 1995).

20. Letter from Louise Dieffenbacher to Dr. Eliza Edwards, April 13, 1926, box 1, General Correspondence, Students, University of Wisconsin School for Workers Records, Archives Department, University of Wisconsin–Madison Libraries; see also Mary Frederickson, "Citizens for Democracy: The Industrial Programs of the YWCA," in *Sisterhood and Solidarity: Workers' Education for Women, 1914–1984*, ed. Joyce Kornbluh and Mary Frederickson (Philadelphia: Temple University Press, 1984); Rose, *Intellectual Life*, 4–6; Abraham Bisno, *Abraham Bisno, Union Pioneer* (Madison: University of Wisconsin Press, 1967), 49; Richard Wright, *Black Boy (American Hunger): A Record of Childhood and Youth* (1944; New York: Harper Perennial, 2006), 151.

21. Floyd Dell, "Books and Writers," *Progressive Woman* (September 1912): 11.

22. U.S. Census of Manufactures, 1914, vol. 2, 653, as cited in Robert Park, *The Immigrant Press and Its Control* (New York: Harper, 1922), 17.

23. Rasche, "Reading Interests of Young Workers," 84.

24. Park, *Immigrant Press*, 7; and Jon Bekken, "The Chicago Newspaper Scene: An Ecological Perspective," *Journalism and Mass Communication Quarterly* 74, no. 3 (1997): 492. The Chicago Foreign Language Press Survey, a New Deal–era translation project, reviewed the pages of more than one hundred ethnic newspapers publishing in Chicago from the 1860s to the 1930s. See Chicago Public Library Omnibus Project, *The Chicago*

Foreign Language Press Survey: A General Description of Its Contents (Chicago: Work Projects Administration, 1942), 7–12, and the online version created by the Newberry Library at http://flps.newberry.org. Varpu Lindstrom-Best, "'Fist Press': A Study of Finnish Canadian Handwritten Newspapers," in *Essays on the Scandinavian–North American Radical Press, 1880s–1930s*, ed. Dirk Hoerder, 100–11 (Bremen: Labor Newspaper Preservation Project, 1984); and Dirk Hoerder and Christiane Harzig, *The Immigrant Labor Press in North America, 1840s–1970s: An Annotated Bibliography* (New York: Greenwood Press, 1987).

25. Solon De Leon, ed., *The American Labor Press Directory* (New York: Rand School of Social Science, 1925).

26. Mary Anderson, *Woman at Work: The Autobiography of Mary Anderson as told to Mary N. Winslow* (Minneapolis: University of Minnesota Press 1951), 14; and Park, *Immigrant Press*, 7–9.

27. Jon Bekken, "Negotiating Class and Ethnicity: The Polish-Language Press in Chicago," *Polish American Studies* 57, no. 2 (2000): 5–29; and Frederick J. Augustyn Jr., "Together and Apart: Lithuanian and Polish Immigrant Adult Literacy Programs in Chicago, 1890–1930," *Polish American Studies* 57, no. 2 (2000): 31–44.

28. Park, *Immigrant Press*, 49–67; Benedict Anderson, *Imagined Communities: Reflections on the Origin and Spread of Nationalism* (London: Verso, 1991); James R. Barrett, "Americanization from the Bottom Up," *Journal of American History* 79, no. 3 (1992): 996–1020; Werner Sollors, *Ethnic Modernism* (Cambridge, MA: Harvard University Press, 2008), 13–14; and Werner Sollors, ed., *The Invention of Ethnicity* (New York: Oxford University Press, 1989), x-xii.

29. Tony Michels, *A Fire in Their Hearts: Yiddish Socialists in New York* (Cambridge, MA: Harvard University Press, 2005), 3, 104–105; and Mordecai Soltes, *The Yiddish Press: An Americanizing Agency* (New York: Teachers College of Columbia University, 1924), 24. On the role of urban public libraries in serving foreign-language readers, see Esther Johnston, "Readers of a Foreign Neighborhood," *The Survey* (April 2, 1921): 7–8.

30. Michels, *Fire in Their Hearts*, 112–13; and Orleck, *Common Sense*, 40–41.

31. Michels, *Fire in Their Hearts*, 181–89.

32. Frederick Douglass, *Narrative of the Life of Frederick Douglass, an American Slave* (London: G. Kershaw and Sons, 1852), 33.

33. Elizabeth McHenry, *Forgotten Readers: Recovering the Lost History of African American Literary Societies* (Durham, NC: Duke University Press, 2002); Steven Hahn, *A Nation under Our Feet: Black Political Struggles in the Rural South from Slavery to the Great Migration* (Cambridge, MA: Harvard University Press, 2003), 461–62; Heather A. Williams, *Self-Taught: African American Education in Slavery and Freedom* (Chapel Hill: University of North Carolina Press, 2005); Kimberley L. Phillips, *Alabama North: African-American Migrants, Community, and Working-Class Activism in Cleveland, 1915–45* (Urbana: University of Illinois Press, 1999), 183–88; Jeffrey B. Perry, *Hubert Harrison: The Voice of Harlem Radicalism, 1883–1918* (New York: Columbia University Press, 2009), chapter 9; Erik S.

McDuffie, *Sojourning for Freedom : Black Women, American Communism, and the Making of Black Left Feminism* (Durham, NC: Duke University Press, 2011); and Keisha N. Blain, *Set the World on Fire: Black Nationalist Women and the Global Struggle for Freedom* (Philadelphia: University of Pennsylvania Press, 2018).

34. James R. Grossman, *Land of Hope: Chicago, Black Southerners, and the Great Migration* (Chicago: University of Chicago Press, 1989); and James N. Gregory, *The Southern Diaspora: How the Great Migrations of Black and White Southerners Transformed America* (Chapel Hill: University of North Carolina Press, 2005).

35. Horace Cayton and George S. Mitchell, *Black Workers and the New Unions* (Chapel Hill: University of North Carolina Press, 1939), 352–53.

36. Higbie, *Indispensable Outcasts*, chapters 1 and 4; and Nigel Sellars, *Oil, Wheat, and Wobblies: The Industrial Workers of the World in Oklahoma, 1905–1930* (Norman: University of Oklahoma Press, 1998). The classic general history of the IWW is Melvyn Dubofsky and Joseph McCartin, *We Shall Be All: A History of the Industrial Workers of the World* (Urbana: University of Illinois Press, 2000). On the cultural world of the IWW, see Salvatore Salerno, *Red November, Black November: Culture and Community in the Industrial Workers of the World* (Albany: SUNY Press, 1989). On the global history of the IWW, see Peter Cole, David Struthers, and Kenyon Zimmer, eds., *Wobblies of the World: A Global History of the IWW* (London: Pluto Press, 2017).

37. Michael Denning, *The Cultural Front: The Laboring of American Culture in the Twentieth Century* (New York: Verso, 1997), 5. On the relationships between the communist and non-communist left across the early twentieth century, see Shelton Stromquist, *Reinventing "The People": The Progressive Movement, the Class Problem, and the Origins of Modern Liberalism* (Urbana: University of Illinois Press, 2006); Nick Salvatore, *Eugene V. Debs: Citizen and Socialist* (Urbana: University of Illinois Press, 1982); James R. Barrett, *William Z. Foster and the Tragedy of American Radicalism* (Urbana: University of Illinois Press, 1999); and Andrew Hemingway, *Artists on the Left: American Artists and the Communist Movement, 1926–1956* (New Haven, CT: Yale University Press, 2002).

38. Agnes Nestor, *Woman's Labor Leader: An Autobiography of Agnes Nestor* (Rockford, IL: Bellevue Books Publishing, 1954), 43–44.

39. Rose Schneiderman, *All for One* (New York: Paul S. Erikson, 1967), 39–50; and Orleck, *Common Sense*, 35–41.

40. Gary R. Mormino, "The Reader and the Worker: 'Los Lectores' and the Culture of Cigarmaking in Cuba and Florida," *International Labor and Working Class History* 54 (1998): 1–18; and Patricia A. Cooper, *Once a Cigarmaker: Men, Women, and Work Culture in American Cigar Factories, 1900–1919* (Urbana: University of Illinois Press, 1987), 66.

41. Josiah Flynt, *Notes of an Itinerant Policeman* (Boston: L. C. Page, 1900), 216–17; and Daniel Horsley, "What the Hobo Reads," Nels Anderson Field Notes, Document 150, Ernest W. Burgess Papers, Special Collections, University of Chicago Library.

42. James R. Green, "The 'Salesmen-Soldiers' of the 'Appeal' Army: A Profile of Rank-and-File Socialist Agitators," in *Socialism in the Cities*, ed. Bruce M. Stave (Port Washington,

NY: Kennikat Press, 1975), 14; and Tim Davenport, "*The Appeal to Reason*: Forerunner of Haldeman-Julius Publications," *Big Blue Newsletter* 3 (2004), http://www.haldeman-julius.org/historical-notes/the-appeal-to-reason.html.

43. Allen Ruff, *"We Called Each Other Comrade": Charles H. Kerr and Company, Radical Publishers* (Urbana: University of Illinois Press, 1997), 160–99. In 1927 Kerr transferred ownership of the company to the Proletarian Party, a communist group whose leader, John Keracher, was an autodidact.

44. "World's Famous Books," *Labor Herald* (March 1922); Albert Mordell, comp. *The World of Haldeman-Julius* (New York: Twayne Publishers, 1960); Stuart McConnell, "E. Haldeman-Julius and the Little Blue Bookworms: The Bridging of Cultural Styles, 1919–1951," *Prospects: An Annual of American Cultural Studies* 11 (1987): 59–79; and Dale Marvin Herder, "Education for the Masses: The Haldeman-Julius Little Blue Books as Popular Culture during the Nineteen-Twenties" (PhD diss., Michigan State University, 1975). On Durant, see Joan Shelley Rubin, *The Making of Middlebrow Culture* (Chapel Hill: University of North Carolina Press, 1992), 231–34. On the *Appeal to Reason*, see John Graham, *"Yours for the Revolution": The* Appeal to Reason, *1895–1922* (Lincoln: University of Nebraska Press, 1990).

45. "The Modern Library," *International Socialist Review* 18 (November–December 1917); and Gordon B. Neavill, "The Modern Library Series and American Cultural Life," *Journal of Library History* 16 (Spring 1981): 241–52.

46. Advertisement for "The Trial and Death of Socrates," inside back cover of *De Maupassant's Stories*, People's Pocket Series No. 6 (Girard, KS: Appeal to Reason, n.d.).

47. Ed Falkowski to Jack Conroy, November 25, 1977, box 8, folder 458, Jack Conroy Papers, Newberry Library, Chicago.

48. Jesse L. Ralph to Dale Herder, quoted in Herder, "Education for the Masses," 260; Carl Sullivan to Dale Herder, quoted in Herder, "Education for the Masses," 263; and Tad Tekla to Dale Herder, quoted in Herder, "Education for the Masses," 258.

49. Stewart H. Holbrook, "What the Loggers Read," *The Bookman* 65 (July 1927): 528–31.

50. Larry Peterson, "The Intellectual World of the IWW: An American Worker's Library in the First Half of the 20th Century," *History Workshop Journal* 22 (1986): 153–72.

51. Rasche, *Reading Interests of Young Workers*, 143–44.

52. Guide to the Gordon and Anna Watkins Papers, Online Archive of California, California Digital Library, http://www.oac.cdlib.org/findaid/ark:/13030/kt3p3037b7/entire_text.

53. Charles A. Hale, "Frank Tannenbaum and the Mexican Revolution," *Hispanic American Historical Review* 75, no. 2 (1995): 215–46.

54. Maurice Neufeld, ed., "Portrait of the Labor Historian as a Boy and Young Man. Excerpts from the Interviews of Philip Taft by Margot Honig," *Labor History* 19 (Winter 1978): 39–63, 67–70; and University of Wisconsin Admission Record for Philip Taft, September 20, 1928, Archives Department, University of Wisconsin–Madison Libraries.

55. Rose Pesotta, *Days of Our Lives* (Boston: Excelsior, 1958), 178.

56. Ibid., 130–32, 178–201.

57. Ibid., 247.

58. Ibid., 254.

59. Rose Pesotta, *Bread Upon the Waters* (New York: Dodd-Mead, 1945), 16, 91.

60. Harry Haywood, *Black Bolshevik: Autobiography of an Afro-American Communist* (Chicago: Liberator Press, 1978), 96–97.

61. Ibid., 98–101, 128–29, 148–75. For Richard Wright's experiences in the Communist Party, see *Black Boy (American Hunger)*, 315–28.

62. Tillie Olsen, *Silences* (New York: Delacorte Press/Seymour Lawrence, 1978), 13.

63. Michel Folsom, "The Education of Michael Gold," in *Proletarian Writers of the Thirties*, ed. David Madden (Carbondale: Southern Illinois University Press, 1968), 224.

64. Ed Falkowski, "Transit, Book 1," March 16, 1928, box 1, folder 1, Edward Falkowski Papers, Tamiment Library, New York University.

65. Richard Sennett and Jonathan Cobb, *The Hidden Injuries of Class* (New York: Knopf, 1972).

66. Stromquist, *Re-inventing the People*, 3.

Chapter 2. "All sorts of wild, impassioned talk": Open Forums and the Working-Class Public Sphere

1. Kenneth Rexroth, *Autobiographical Novel* (Garden City, NY: Doubleday, 1966), 105–106; and interview with Slim Brundage, College of Complexes "janitor" on the *Studs Terkel Radio Program*, WFMT-FM, Chicago, 1967 (audio recording), Chicago Historical Society, Archives and Manuscripts Collections.

2. Nancy Franser, "Rethinking the Public Sphere," chapter 5 in *Habermas and the Public Sphere*, ed. Craig Calhoun (Cambridge: MIT Press, 1992); Stanley Aronowitz, "Unions as Counter-Public Spheres," in *Masses, Classes, and the Public Sphere*, ed. Mike Hill and Warren Montag (London: Verso, 2000), 83–101; and Charles Taylor, *Modern Social Imaginaries* (Durham, NC: Duke University Press, 2004), 83–107.

3. Robin D. G. Kelley, "'We Are Not What We Seem': Rethinking Black Working-Class Opposition in the Jim Crow South," *Journal of American History* 80 (June 1993): 75–112.

4. Gordon Parks, *A Choice of Weapons* (1965; St. Paul: Minnesota Historical Society Press, 1986), see 110–14 for the entire passage. See Werner Sollors, *Ethnic Modernism* (Cambridge, MA: Harvard University Press, 2008), chapter 13.

5. Ernestine Rose, "Serving New York's Black City," *Legacy: A Journal of American Women Writers* 31 (2014): 107–12 (originally published in *Library Journal*, March 15, 1921).

6. Barbara Ransby, *Ella Baker and the Black Freedom Movement: A Radical Democratic Vision* (Chapel Hill: University of North Carolina Press, 2003), 69. On adult programming at the Harlem public library in the 1930s, see Ernestine Rose, "Racial Development and Cooperation: A Record of Two Experiments," *Journal of Adult Education* (January 1933): 53–55; and Celeste Tibbets, *Ernestine Rose and the Origins of the Schomburg Center*

(New York: Schomburg Center for Research in Black Culture, New York Public Library, 1989).

7. Liesl Olson, *Chicago Renaissance: Literature and Art in the Midwest Metropolis* (New Haven, CT: Yale University Press, 2017), 251–53.

8. Rose Pesotta, *Bread Upon the Waters* (New York: Dodd, Mead, 1945), 24–27; Rose Pesotta, "The City of Angels,'" *Labor Age*, October 1931, 23–24; Pesotta to A. J. Muste, April 7, 1932; and Pesotta to A. J. Muste, June 2, 1932, Brookwood Labor College Collection, Walter P. Reuther Library, Archives of Labor and Urban Affairs, Wayne State University, Detroit. On street life in Los Angeles, see Mark Wild, *Street Meeting: Multiethnic Neighborhoods in Early Twentieth-Century Los Angeles* (Berkeley: University of California Press, 2005).

9. Keene Wallis, "A Harvest Stiff Comes Back to Town," *Workers Monthly* (November 1924): 17–18.

10. Solon De Leon and Nathan Fine, eds., *American Labor Press Directory* (New York: Rand School of Social Science, 1925).

11. Nels Anderson, "Document 60: Notes on an Afternoon's Series of Talks," box 127, folder 1, Ernest W. Burgess Papers—Other's Work, Individual Students and Collaborators, Nels Anderson, Special Collections, University of Chicago Library.

12. "The Safety of Free Speech," *Chicago Commons* (November 1896), 8–9; and Graham Taylor, *Pioneering on Social Frontiers* (Chicago: University of Chicago Press, 1930), 312–30.

13. "Men's Work: Annual Report, 1921–22," box 12, folder 1, Chicago Commons Papers, Chicago History Museum.

14. See "Annual Report of the Adult Education Department, 1933–34," box 12, and undated scripts, box 16, Chicago Commons Papers, Chicago History Museum.

15. Auditor's Report, May 20, 1926, lists the Midwest Council for Social Discussion as the major donor, while a later history identified B'nai B'rth as the first donor; see also "Some Adult Education Council Accomplishments [c. 1964]," box 3, folder 26, and Chicago Forum Council charter, August 1929, box 1, folder 12, both in Adult Education Council of Greater Chicago, University of Illinois at Chicago (hereafter AECGC).

16. Franklin Rosemont, ed., *From Bughouse Square to the Beat Generation: Selected Ravings of Slim Brundage* (Chicago: Charles H. Kerr Publishers, 1997), 93; Sophia Fagin, *Public Forums in Chicago* (Chicago: Work Projects Administration, 1940).

17. "Du Bois Shatters Stoddard's Cultural Theories in Debate. Thousands Jam Hall to Hear Du Bois Debate," *Chicago Defender*, March 23, 1929; and Chicago Forum Attendance Report, 1929–1930, box 3, folder 26, AECGC.

18. John Studebaker, *Choosing Our Way: The Story of a Forum Program Sponsored by the Office of Education and the Results of a Survey of 431 Forums under Various Sponsorships* (Washington, DC: United States Department of the Interior, Office of Education, 1938).

19. Chicago Foreign Language Press Survey, http://flps.newberry.org.

20. "What Is Most Important for Danish-Americans?," *Revyen*, March 27, 1909, box 9, Chicago Foreign Language Press Survey, University of Chicago Library, Special Collections (hereafter CFLPS). See also Fred M. Schied, *Learning in Social Context: Workers*

and Adult Education in Nineteenth-Century Chicago (DeKalb: LEPS Press, Northern Illinois University, 1995).

21. Roger Waldinger, *The Cross-Border Connection: Immigrants, Emigrants, and Their Homelands* (Cambridge, MA: Harvard University Press, 2015), chapter 8.

22. "Plan to Establish Lithuanian Lecture Forum in Chicago," *Lietuva*, August 3, 1917; "Women's Progressive Association Sponsors Lecture," *Naujienos*, April 5, 1916, box 29, CFLPS; "The Ingersollova Racionalisticka Spolecnost Founded," *Denni Hlasatel*, April 9, 1922; and "Thought Is the Thing," *Vek Rozumn*, October 21, 1937, box 3, CFLPS.

23. Samuel Putnam, "Red Days in Chicago," *American Mercury* 30 (September 1933): 65; Elizabeth Gurly Flynn, *The Rebel Girl: An Autobiography. My First Life (1906–1926)* (New York: International Publishers, 1955), 86–88; James R. Barrett, *William Z. Foster and the Tragedy of American Radicalism* (Urbana: University of Illinois Press, 1999), 73; Ben Reitman, "Highlights of Dill Pickle History," supplement 2, folder 87, Ben Reitman Papers, Special Collections, University of Illinois at Chicago Library; and Roger Bruns, *The Damndest Radical: The Life and World of Ben Reitman, Chicago's Celebrated Social Reformer, Hobo King, and Whorehouse Physician* (Urbana: University of Illinois Press, 1987). See also Christine Stansell, *American Moderns: Bohemian New York and the Creation of a New Century* (New York: Henry Holt, 2000); and James R. Barrett, introduction to Hutchins Hapgood, *The Spirit of Labor* (1907; Urbana: University of Illinois Press, 2004).

24. John Drury, *Chicago in Seven Days* (New York: Robert M. McBride, 1928), 12, 199–201.

25. Dick Arman, "The Bug Club, *Chicago Tribune*, July 9, 1921, 6; and "Park Board File Answer in Suit of the 'Bug Club,'" *Chicago Tribune*, September 15, 1921, 12.

26. Roger Didier, "What Do These Radicals Think about Us Fish?," *Chicago Defender*, April 14, 1923, 5. Other *Defender* writers criticized Reitman for expressing negative views on African Americans. See "Ben Reitman Flays Race on Culture: Inferior to Whites Is His Idea," *Chicago Defender*, July 5, 1924, 4.

27. "Near North Side. Bug Park, etc.," box 214, folder 9, Ernest W. Burgess Papers, Addendum, Special Collections, University of Chicago Library.

28. Illinois Writers' Program, *Public Forums in Chicago*, (Chicago, 1940), 38–46; Chad Heap, *Slumming: Sexual and Racial Encounters in American Nightlife, 1885–1940* (Chicago: University of Chicago Press, 2009); and Kevin Mumford, *Interzones: Black/White Sex Districts in Chicago and New York in the Early Twentieth Century* (New York: Columbia University Press, 1997). On bohemia clubs in Los Angeles, see Daniel Hurewitz, *Bohemian Los Angeles and the Making of Modern Politics* (Berkeley: University of California Press, 2007).

29. Joanne J. Meyerowitz, *Women Adrift: Independent Wage Earners in Chicago, 1880–1930* (Chicago: University of Chicago Press, 1988); and Frank Tobias Higbie, *Indispensable Outcasts: Hobo Workers and Community in the American Midwest, 1880–1930* (Urbana: University of Illinois Press, 2003).

30. Fagin, *Public Forums in Chicago.*

31. Carolyn Toll, "Ghosts Fill the Air as Bughouse Square of Old Dies," *Chicago Tribune*, June 24, 1971, S1.

32. Interview with Slim Brundage on the "Studs Terkel Radio Program," Chicago Historical Society.

33. Theda Skocpol, *Diminished Democracy: From Membership to Management in American Civic Life* (Norman: University of Oklahoma Press, 2003), 46–56; Robyn Muncy, *Creating a Female Dominion in American Reform, 1890–1935* (New York: Oxford University Press, 1991); Elizabeth McHenry, *Forgotten Readers: Recovering the Lost History of African American Literary Societies* (Durham, NC: Duke University Press, 2002); and Hahn, *Nation under Our Feet*, 461–63.

34. Solon De Leon, *The American Labor Who's Who* (New York: Hanford Press, 1925). The Odd Fellows and the Knights of Pythias were among the top ten, the Moose were number 17, the Eagles and Knights of Columbus were numbers 20 and 21.

35. Geoffrey R. Stone, *Perilous Times: Free Speech in Wartime* (New York: W. W. Norton, 2004), 158.

36. On free speech fights, see Higbie, *Indispensable Outcasts*, 139, 144–51; on San Diego, see Bruns, *Damndest Radical*, 118–32.

37. Kenyon Zimmer, *Immigrants against the State: Yiddish and Italian Anarchism in America* (Urbana: University of Illinois Press, 2015), 147–56; and Katherine Benton-Cohen, *Borderline Americans: Racial Division and Labor War in the Arizona Borderlands* (Cambridge, MA: Harvard University Press, 2009).

38. Robert C. Cottrell, *Roger Nash Baldwin and the American Civil Liberties Union* (New York: Columbia University Press, 2000), 72–74.

39. Risa Lauren Goluboff, *Vagrant Nation: Police Power, Constitutional Change, and the Making of the 1960s* (New York: Oxford University Press, 2016).

40. Oliver Wendell Holmes, dissent, *Abrams v. United States*, 250 U.S. 616 (1919).

41. David M. Rabban, *Free Speech in Its Forgotten Years* (Cambridge, UK: Cambridge University Press, 1997), 347–55; and Holmes, dissent, *Abrams v. United States*.

42. Holmes, dissent, *Abrams v. United States*; and Oliver Wendell Holmes, majority, *Debs v. United States*, 249 U.S. 211.

43. Don Mitchell, "The Liberalization of Free Speech; or, How Protest in Public Space Is Silenced," *Stanford Agora* (vol. 4), http://agora.stanford.edu/agora/volume4/mitchell.shtml; and Don Mitchell, *The Right to the City: Social Justice and the Fight for Public Space* (New York: Guilford Press, 2003).

44. Doug McAdam, Sidney Tarrow, and Charles Tilly, *Dynamics of Contention* (New York: Cambridge University Press, 2001), 4–9; and Florence Passy and Gian-Andrea Monsch, "Do Social Networks Really Matter in Contentious Politics?," *Social Movement Studies* 13, no. 1 (2014): 22–47.

45. Julie Greene, *Pure and Simple Politics: The American Federation of Labor and Political Activism, 1881–1917* (New York: Cambridge University Press, 1998); Jennifer Luff, *Commonsense Anticommunism: Labor and Civil Liberties between the World Wars* (Chapel Hill:

University of North Carolina Press, 2012); and Craig Phelan, *William Green: Biography of a Labor Leader* (Albany: SUNY Press, 1989).

46. See, for instance, Harvey Warren Zorbaugh, *The Gold Coast and the Slum: A Sociological Study of Chicago's Near North Side* (1929; Chicago: University of Chicago Press, 1983); Nels Anderson, *The Hobo: The Sociology of the Homeless Man (1923; Chicago: University of Chicago Press, 1961)*; and Fagin, *Public Forums in Chicago*. The open forums appear in Richard Wright's *American Hunger*, Jack Conroy's *The Disinherited* (1933; Cambridge, MA: R. Bentley, 1979); James T. Farrell's *The Young Manhood of Studs Lonigan* (New York: Vanguard Press, [c. 1934]); and the poetry Frank Marshall Davis, among others.

47. Carolyn Toll, "Ghosts Fill the Air as Bughouse Square of Old Dies," *Chicago Tribune*, June 24, 1971, S1.

48. See advertisements for Reconciliation Tours, 1928–1934; "Exploring Chicago with a Sociologist," Ben Reitman Papers, supplement 2, folder 93, University of Illinois at Chicago Library, Special Collections (hereafter BRP); Drury, *Chicago in Seven Days*, 178–202; and "Free Chicago Tours for Chicagoans: Dill Pickle Club, August 8, 1936," box 30, folder 373, BRP; see also "Educational tours—itineraries: May 1928–March 1940," supplement 2, folder 93, BRP.

49. "The Curriculum: Official Neurosis of the College of Complexes," June [1963], Slim Brundage Papers, Newberry Library.

50. Gordon Poole, personal correspondence with the author, March 27, 2015.

51. Ruff, "*We Called Each Other Comrade*"; Franklin Rosemont, *The Rise and Fall of the Dill Pickle: Jazz-Age Chicago's Wildest and Most Outrageously Creative Hobohemian Nightspot* (Chicago: Charles H. Kerr Publishers, 2004); Frank Orman Beck, *Hobohemia: Emma Goldman, Lucy Parsons, Ben Reitman, and Other Agitators and Outsiders in 1920s/30s Chicago* (Chicago: Charles H. Kerr, 2000); and Slim Brundage and Franklin Rosemont, *From Bughouse Square to the Beat Generation: Selected Ravings* (Chicago: Charles H. Kerr, 1997).

52. Interview with Slim Brundage, College of Complexes "janitor," on the "Studs Terkel Radio Program," WFMT-FM, Chicago, 1967, Chicago Historical Society.

53. Denise DeClue, "The Siege of Sandburg Village," *Chicago Reader*, January 20, 1978, http://www.chicagoreader.com/chicago/the-siege-of-sandburg-village/Content?oid=3295234.

54. Jack Lait and Lee Mortimer, *Chicago: Confidential!* (New York: Crown Publishers, 1950), 64–65, 289.

55. Jean Latz Griffin, "Bughouse Square Clean-up Driving out 'Undesirables,'" *Chicago Tribune*, July 8, 1982, N1.

56. "Come to the Reopening of Washington Square Park," July 4, 1976, box 6, folder 242, Events, Newberry Library Archives.

57. "Rocking the Boat Raw: Bughouse Square #2," *Media Burn Archive*, 1998, http://mediaburn.org/video/rocking-the-boat-raw-bughouse-square-2.

58. See, for instance, Aimee Levitt, "The Migration of the Hipster. A Chicago History: 1898–present," *Chicago Reader*, October 3, 2013, 17–23.

59. Stephen Kinzer, "In Chicago, an Ambiguous Memorial to the Haymarket Attack," *New York Times*, September 15, 2004, http://www.nytimes.com/2004/09/15/us/in-chicago-an-ambiguous-memorial-to-the-haymarket-attack.html; Karen Ann Cullotta, "Passion of Haymarket Affair Resonates 125 Years Later," *New York Times*, April 21, 2011, sec. U.S., http://www.nytimes.com/2011/04/22/us/22cnchaymarket.html?_r=2; and James R. Green, *Taking History to Heart: The Power of the Past in Building Social Movements* (Amherst: University of Massachusetts Press, 2000).

Chapter 3. "To see and hear things that have always been there": Labor's Pedagogy of the Organized

1. John Brophy, "Miners' Problems and Workers' Education," Report of *Proceedings of First National Conference on Workers' Education in the United States*, 65–67, https://archive.org/stream/workerseducatiooooamergoog/workerseducatiooooamergoog_djvu.txt.

2. Ibid. See also, John Brophy, *How to Run Coal: Suggestions for a Plan of Public Ownership, Public Control, and Democratic Management in the Coal Industry* (Altoona, PA: Nationalization Research Committee, United Mine Workers of America, 1922), 8; and Alan Singer, "John Brophy's 'Miners' Program': Workers' Education in UMWA District 2 during the 1920s," *Labor Studies Journal* 13 (Winter 1988): 50.

3. John Brophy, *A Miner's Life* (Madison: University of Wisconsin Press, 1964), 155–56, 204–206; and Singer, "John Brophy's 'Miners' Program,'" 50–64.

4. Goodman, "Students Who Work."

5. See, for instance, Daniel Katz, *All Together Different: Yiddish Socialists, Garment Workers, and the Labor Roots of Multiculturalism* (New York: New York University Press, 2011); Tony Michels, *A Fire in Their Hearts: Yiddish Socialists in New York* (Cambridge, MA: Harvard University Press, 2005); Erik Gellman and Jarod Roll, *The Gospel of the Working Class: Labor's Southern Prophets in New Deal America* (Urbana: University of Illinois Press, 2011); Jane F. McAlevey, *No Shortcuts: Organizing for Power in the New Gilded Age* (New York: Oxford University Press, 2016); Charles Payne, *I've Got the Light of Freedom: The Organizing Tradition of the Mississippi Freedom Struggle* (Berkeley: University of California Press, 2007); and Barbara Ransby, *Ella Baker and the Black Freedom Movement: A Radical Democratic Vision* (Chapel Hill: University of North Carolina Press, 2003).

6. Tim Davenport, "The Formation of the Proletarian Party of America, 1913–1923. Part 1: John Keracher's Proletarian University and the Establishment of the Communist Party of America" (Corvallis, OR: 1000 Flowers Publishing, 2011), https://www.marxists.org/history/usa/parties/ppa/1933/0000-davenport-formationofppa.pdf, 4–5; and *Historical Catechism of American Unionism* (Chicago: Educational Bureau, IWW, 1923), https://www.marxists.org/history/usa/unions/iww/1923/catechism.htm.

7. Paolo Freire, *Pedagogy of the Oppressed*, trans. Myra Bergman Ramos (New York: Herder and Herder, 1970); and Myles Horton and Paolo Freire, *We Make the Road by Walking: Conversations on Education and Social Change*, ed. Brenda Bell, John Gaventa, and John Peters (Philadelphia: Temple University Press, 1990).

8. Among the many studies of popular education in the period are Marius Hansome, *World Workers' Educational Movements: Their Social Significance* (New York: Columbia University Press, 1931); Mary K. Vaughan, *Cultural Politics in Revolution: Teachers, Peasants, and Schools in Mexico, 1930–1940* (Tucson: University of Arizona Press, 1997); Alfred Fitzpatrick, *The University in Overalls: A Plea for Part-time Study* (Toronto: Frontier College Press, 1920); Alan L. Jones, "Gaining Self-Consciousness while Losing the Movement: The American Association for Adult Education, 1926–1941" (PhD diss., University of Wisconsin–Madison, 1991); Joyce L. Kornbluh and Mary Frederickson, eds., *Sisterhood and Solidarity: Workers' Education for Women, 1914–1984* (Philadelphia: Temple University Press, 1984); Joyce L. Kornbluh, *A New Deal for Workers' Education: The Workers' Service Program, 1933–1942* (Urbana: University of Illinois Press, 1987); Tom Woodin, "Working-Class Education and Social Change in Nineteenth- and Twentieth-Century Britain," *History of Education* 36, nos. 4–5 (2007): 483–96; and Marvin Gettleman, "'No Varsity Teams': New York's Jefferson School of Social Science, 1943–1956," *Science and Society* 66 (Fall 2002): 336–59.

9. See, for instance, Robert Park, *The Immigrant Press and Its Control* (New York: Harper and Brothers, 1922); and Michels, *Fire in Their Hearts*. There are more than two thousand articles in the Chicago Foreign Language Press Survey (flps.newberry.org) that touch on the subjects of adult education, literary societies and classes, and public lectures.

10. Katz, *All Together Different*, 64–65; Douglas J. Ollila Jr., "The Work People's College: Immigrant Education for Adjustment and Solidarity," in *For the Common Good: Finish Immigrants and the Radical Response to Industrial America*, ed. Michael G. Karni and Douglas J. Ollila Jr., 87–118 (Superior, WI: Tyomies Society, 1977); and Samuel H. Holland, "The Workers Institute (1915–1920): An Experiment in Workers Education," Labor Education Division of Roosevelt University, Chicago Historical Museum Collection.

11. "More Mind," *National Women's Trade Union League of America* [1923?], 2, WTUL Papers, Harvard University Library; Margaret T. Hodgen, *Workers' Education in England and the United States* (New York: E. P. Dutton, 1925), 225–26; and Elizabeth Anne Payne, *Reform, Labor, and Feminism: Margaret Dreier Robins and the Women's Trade Union League* (Urbana: University of Illinois Press, 1988).

12. In 1918 there were about eight hundred industrial clubs nationally, with a combined membership of thirty thousand. See Mary Frederickson, "Citizens for Democracy: The Industrial Programs of the YWCA," in Kornbluh and Frederickson, *Sisterhood and Solidarity*, 77; and Industrial Department, National Board of the YWCA, *The Young Women's Christian Association and Industry* (New York, 1928), 29.

13. Annelise Orleck, *Common Sense and a Little Fire: Women and Working-Class Politics in the United States, 1900–1965* (Chapel Hill: University of North Carolina Press, 1995); Jennifer Guglielmo, *Living the Revolution: Italian Women's Resistance and Radicalism in New York City, 1880–1945* (Chapel Hill: University of North Carolina Press, 2010); and Katz, *All Together Different*, 67–68.

14. Janice Fine, *Worker Centers: Organizing Communities at the Edge of the Dream,* (Ithaca, NY: Cornell University Press, 2006); and Janice Fine, "Worker Centers," Economic Policy Institute Briefing Paper 159, December 2005, http://www.epi.org/publication/bp159. See also Kent Wong and Victor Narro, "Educating Immigrant Workers for Action," *Labor Studies Journal* 32, no. 1 (2007): 113–18; and Jane McAlevey, "The High-Touch Model: Make the Road New York's Participatory Approach to Immigrant Organizing," in *New Labor in New York: Precarious Workers and the Future of the Labor Movement,* ed. Ruth Milkman and Ed Ott (Ithaca, NY: Cornell University Press, 2014).

15. Abraham Epstein, "The Replies to the Questionnaire on Workers Education in the United States," *Workers' Education in the United States: Proceedings of the National Convention* (New York: Workers' Education Bureau of America, 1921), 133–34.

16. Leilah Danielson, *American Gandhi: A. J. Muste and the History of Radicalism in the Twentieth Century* (Philadelphia: University of Pennsylvania Press, 2014), 84–86; Richard J. Altenbaugh, *Education for Struggle: The American Labor Colleges of the 1920s and 1930s* (Philadelphia: Temple University Press, 1990); "Plans for Workers' College," *New York Times,* April 1, 1921, 23; "Aims of Workers' College," *New York Times,* June 16, 1921, 8; "Labor College Grafted on Tree of Knowledge," *Chicago Daily Tribune,* April 2, 1921, 3; and Walton H. Hamilton, "The Educational Policy of 'A Labor College,'" *Journal of Social Forces* 2 (January 1924): 204–208.

17. Karyn L. Hollis, *Liberating Voices: Writing at the Bryn Mawr Summer School for Women Workers* (Carbondale: Southern Illinois University Press, 2004), 15–19; and Ernest E. Schwarztrauber, *The University of Wisconsin School for Workers: Its First Twenty-Five Years* (Madison: University of Wisconsin School for Workers, 1950), 12. The Boston Trade Union College drew on university faculty but located classes in the central labor union hall and rested control with the union; see Hodgen, *Workers' Education,* 218–19.

18. William Cobb, *Radical Education in the Rural South: Commonwealth College, 1922–1940* (Detroit: Wayne State University Press, 2000); John M. Glen, *Highlander: No Ordinary School, 1932–1962* (Lexington: University Press of Kentucky, 1988); and Gellman and Roll, *Gospel of the Working Class.*

19. Jess Rigelhaupt, "'Education for Action': The California Labor School, Radical Unionism, Civil Rights, and Progressive Coalition Building in the San Francisco Bay Area, 1934–1970" (PhDdiss., University of Michigan, 2005); "Time Table of Critical Events in the Life of the California Labor School," [1957], 20th Century Organization Files, Southern California Library; Randi Storch, *Red Chicago: American Communism at Its Grassroots, 1928–1935* (Urbana: University of Illinois Press, 2007); and Gettleman, "'No Varsity Teams,'" 336–59.

20. Charles F. Howlett, *Brookwood Labor College and the Struggle for Peace and Social Justice in America* (Lewiston, NY: Edwin Mellen Press, 1993), 217.

21. Benjamin Stolberg, *Tailor's Progress: The Story of a Famous Union and the Men Who Made It* (Garden City, NY: Doubleday, Doran, 1944), 289–91; and Horace M. Kallen,

Education, the Machine, and the Worker: An Essay in the Psychology of Education in Industrial Society (New York: New Republic, 1925), 69.

22. "The Communist Protest" (open letter from communist students of the Western School for Workers, 1935, CU-5, series 2, 1935, folder 308, Office of the President Records, University of California.

23. Arthur Gleason, *Workers' Education* (New York: Bureau of Industrial Education, 1921), 5–6.

24. Ibid., 5, 10.

25. Alfred Dwight Sheffield, *Joining in Public Discussions: A Study of Effective Speechmaking for Members of Labor Unions, Conferences, Forums, and Other Discussion Groups* (New York: George H. Doran, [c.1922]), v-xv.

26. Ibid., 156–57.

27. Edward Falkowski, "In Transit, March 20," Edward Falkowski Papers, box 1, folder 2, Tamiment Library, New York University; and John Troxell, "Wisconsin's Summer School for Working Women," *American Federationist*, October 1925, 944.

28. Workers Education Bureau of America, *Workers Education in the United States, Report of Proceedings, First National Conference on Workers Education in the United States Held at the New School for Social Research, New York City, April 2–3, 1921* (New York: Workers Education Bureau of America, 1921), 84–85.

29. Chris Sproger, "The Value of Workers Education," and Mary Goff, "The Newcomer," in ibid., 85, 94; and Richard Wright, *Black Boy (American Hunger): A Record of Childhood and Youth* (New York: Harper Perennial, 1944), 169.

30. Sarah Shapiro, "What I Learned in Class," in Workers Education Bureau of America, *Workers Education*, 87; and Jennie Matyos, "The Working Girl and Labor Education," in Workers Education Bureau of America, *Workers Education*, 95–96. Despite the alternate spelling, this is most likely Jennie Matyas, who became an ILGWU organizer in San Francisco in the 1930s. Bertolt Brecht, "Questions from a Worker Who Reads" (1935), https://www.marxists.org/subject/art/literature/brecht.

31. Box 10, folder 12, Brookwood Labor College Records, Walter Reuther Library, Archives of Labor and Urban Affairs, Wayne State University, Detroit (hereafter BLCR).

32. Kallen, *Education, the Machine, and the Worker*, 187–88.

33. Schwartztrauber, *University of Wisconsin School for Workers*, 24–25.

34. Hollis, *Liberating Voices*, 61–66.

35. Ibid.

36. Amy Hewes, "How to Build on the Workers' Experience," in *The Promotion and Maintenance of Workers' Education. Third Annual Conference of Teachers in Workers' Education at Brookwood, February 19–22, 1926* (Katonah, NY: Brookwood Labor College, 1926), 61; and Amy Hewes, "The First Job," *Vocational Education Magazine*, December 1922, 305–309, http://hdl.handle.net/2027/mdp.39015079968668?urlappend=%3Bseq=63.

37. Hewes, "How to Build on Workers' Experience," 62.

38. William Mann Fincke, introduction to *I Am a Woman Worker: A Scrapbook of Autobiographies*, ed. Andria Taylor Hourwich and Gladys L. Palmer (New York: Affiliated Schools for Workers, 1936), 1.

39. "This Winter Live and Learn at Work People's College," Work People's College brochure, box 11, School for Workers Records, Archives Department, University of Wisconsin–Madison Libraries (hereafter SWR).

40. Harold J. Newton interview (1982), tape 1, side 2 Wisconsin Labor Oral History Project, State Historical Society of Wisconsin.

41. "Summer School for Women Workers, University of Wisconsin, 1927," box 4, folder 6, General Correspondence, Students, SWR; Hollis, *Liberating Voices*; and Schwarztrauber, *University of Wisconsin School for Workers*.

42. Letter to Zona Gale, June 24, 1927, box 1, folder 9, General Correspondence, Cities; handwritten report by Alice Shoemaker, July 3, 1929, box 16; Faculty Reports and Minutes for 1933, box 14; Letters from Members of the 1933 Summer School for Workers in Industry, University of Wisconsin; "Field Trips, 1934–35," box 1, 18/5/37-12, all in SWR; and "Benefit Plans for Scholarship Are Carried Out," *Chicago Defender*, April 21, 1934, 7.

43. Pauli Murray, *Pauli Murray : The Autobiography of a Black Activist, Feminist, Lawyer, Priest, and Poet* (Knoxville: University of Tennessee Press, 1989), 106–108.

44. Anna M. Pyott (YWCA) to Don Lescohier, July 24, 1924, box 1, 18/5/37-2, SWR. See also Industrial Department, YWCA, *The Young Women's Christian Association and Industry*, 24–25; and Ernest E. Schwarztrauber, *Workers' Education: A Wisconsin Experiment* (Madison: University of Wisconsin Press, 1942), 60.

45. Schwartztrauber, *University of Wisconsin School for Workers*, 7–14; Edwin E. Witte, "The University and Labor Education," *Industrial and Labor Relations Review* 1 (October 1947): 3–17; Solon De Leon, *The American Labor Who's Who* (New York: Hanford Press, 1925), 178; Wisconsin Historical Society, *Dictionary of Wisconsin History*, https://www.wisconsinhistory.org/Records/Article/CS11326; and Robert Bussel, *Fighting for Total Person Unionism: Harold Gibbons, Ernest Calloway, and Working-Class Citizenship* (Urbana: University of Illinois Press, 2015), 17.

46. Irving M. Ives, "The New York State School of Industrial and Labor Relations—A New Venture in Education," *Journal of Educational Sociology* 19 (September 1945): 40–42; and Mark Starr and Edmund Ezra Day, "Re: 'Education in Industrial and Labor Relations,'" *Industrial and Labor Relations Review* 3 (July 1, 1950): 575–80.

47. Memorandum on Institute of Labor Relations, January 11, 1946, series 2/9/1, box 103, Arthur C. Willard Papers, University of Illinois Archives (hereafter ACWP); Horace Gray to A. J. Harno, January 12, 1943, series 9/5/22, box 1, Horace M. Gray Papers, University of Illinois Archives (hereafter HMGP); Report of the Committee on Future Programs in the Social Sciences [August 1944], series 7/1/2, box 2, University of Illinois Archives, Graduate College Dean's Office; Institute of Labor Relations at the University of Illinois, Statement of Policy and Program, February 11, 1946; and Chicago Bridge and Iron Co. to President Willard, April 5, 1946, series 2/9/1, box 103, ACWP.

48. Sadie Goodman Questionnaire for Prospective Brookwood Students (1923), box 66, folder 25; Rose Schneiderman to A. J. Muste, April 25, 1923, box 66, folder 26, BLCR; Recruiting Committee to Miss Zona Gale, June 24, 1927, 18/5/37, box 1; Application of Sadie Goodman, May 19, 1927, 18/5/37, box 4, SWR; and Sadie Goodman to A. J. Muste, July 15, 1927, box 84, folder 24, BLCR.

49. Don D. Lescohier to Clara Kaiser, December 15, 1927, 18/5/37, box 1, SWR.

50. Sadie Goodman, "The Birth of the Western Summer School for Workers," *The Crusader* (1935), [no pagination]. Mimeographed magazine produced by students in the Western School for Workers, CU-5, series 2, 1935, folder 308; John L. Kerchen, "Historically Speaking," *Solidarity* (student publication of the Western Summer School for Workers (1937); and "Class Record: Summer School for Industrial Workers, Occidental College, August 1933," Pacific Coast Labor School Collection, Mary Norton Clapp Library, Occidental College. On Pesotta's connection, see "Questionnaires for Short History of Brookwood's contribution to the labor movement," box 14, folder 11, BLCR.

51. Rose Pesotta to *Labor Age* (October 1931), 23–24; Rose Pesotta to A. J. Muste, April 7, 1932; Pesotta to Muste, June 2, 1932, BLCR; Rose Pesotta, *Bread Upon the Waters*, 24–27; Pesotta to A. J. Muste, April 7, 1932; Pesotta to A. J. Muste, June 2, 1932, BLCR; and Goodman, "Students Who Work."

52. "History," *Class Record, Summer School for Industrial Workers, Occidental College, August 1933*, 1–3, Presidential Papers of Remsen Bird, Special Collections Department, Occidental College Library.

53. Robert Sproul to Carl McDowell, September 12, 1935, UC Office of the President Records, Bancroft Library.

54. Leon Richardson to Monroe Deutsch, July 28, 1937, CU-5, series 2, 1937.

55. John L. Kerchen to Robert Sproul, October 3, 1935.

56. George Hedley to Ernest Schwarztrauber, May 2, 1938, 18/5/37-3, box 9, School for Workers Records, University of Wisconsin Archives.

57. Assembly Bill 878, introduced by Messrs. Dills, Tenney, King, Reaves, Doyle, Bennett, Hawkins, Atkinson, Pelletier, Massion, and Richie, January 18, 1939; news clipping, January 18, 1939, CU-18, box 55, Labor Extension Bill, Records of the University Extension, Bancroft Library, University of California, Berkeley (hereafter RUE); and Preliminary Report of the Committee on Labor Education, AFT College Section, Los Angeles, Eric Beecroft, chairman, March 25, 1938 (cover letter and pp. 4, 5), CU-18, box 55, RUE.

58. Boyd Rakestraw (Assistant Director [Extension]) to Professor F. L. Paxson (University Extension Advisory Board Chair), February 8, 1939.

59. Rakestraw to Heineman, April 16, 1942, box 5, Pacific Coast Labor School Collection, Special Collections, Occidental College Library.

60. [Haynes Foundation] to Irene Heineman, April 24, 1942, box 5, Pacific Coast Labor School Collection, Occidental College; "Paul A. Dodd: Looking from Los Angeles at President Sproul, An Interview Conducted by Suzanne Riess," 1984; and "A Ten-Year Report of the Institute of Industrial Relations on the Los Angeles Campus, 1946–1956,"

UCLA Institute for Research on Labor and Employment (hereafter IRLE) Records. Also during the war, the director of the UC Extension joined the advisory board of the California Labor School, suggesting the general acceptance of progressive politics at the time.

61. P.A.D. [Paul A. Dodd]"Memorandum to Provost Dykstra Re: Institute of Industrial Relations," July 3, 1945, and text of Chapter 1416 Statutes of California, 1945; "Tentative Proposals for the Establishment of an Institute of Industrial Relations on the Berkeley and Los Angeles Campuses of the University of California (Pursuant to the obligation placed upon the University in the enactment of Assembly Bill No. 391 as amended)" [July 4, 1945]; and "Institute of Industrial Relations at UCLA Announces New Additions to Staff," press release, September 23, 1946, all in IRLE Records.

62. Abbott Kaplan, "Summary of Extension Services," box 54, folder 30, Institute of Industrial Relations Records, UCLA, August 1947, CU-18; "Ten-Year Report," 59–60, IRLE Records; and P.A.D. [Paul A. Dodd], "To Members of the Departments of Economics and Business Administration," September 24, 1945, IRLE Records.

63. Report of the Coordinating Committee on the Institute of Industrial Relations [1946], IRLE Records.

64. Leon Fink, "'Intellectuals' versus 'Workers': Academic Requirements and the Creation of Labor History," *American Historical Review* 96, no. 2 (1991): 395–421; and Dorothy Ross, *The Origins of American Social Science* (New York: Cambridge University Press, 1991).

65. Box 12, folders 1–5, Charles Stuart Kennedy Papers, Bentley Historical Library, University of Michigan. See also *UAW-CIO Ammunition* (November 1948).

66. "To CIO Affiliates in Southern California," August 12, 1948, box 1, folder 14, California CIO Council Union Research and Information Services, Southern California Library; "Once They Did It to Speakeasies, Now They Do It to Schools!," 20th Century Organization Files, California Labor School, Southern California Library; David Jenkins, "David Jenkins: The Union Movement, the California Labor School, and San Francisco Politics, 1926–1988," Regional Oral History Office, Bancroft Library, University of California, Berkeley; and Rigelhaupt, "'Education for Action.'"

67. "Ten-Year Report," 59–64, 104–107; First Annual Report, Institute of Industrial Relations—Southern Division, July 1946–June 1947, IRLE Records; and Abbott Kaplan, "Summary of Extension Services, Institute of Industrial Relations, University of California, Los Angeles, August 1947," CU-18, box 54, folder 34, RUE.

68. "Ten-Year Report," 59–64.

69. Rose Pesotta (comment), "The Promotion and Maintenance of Workers' Education," Third Annual Conference of Teachers in Workers' Education at Brookwood, February 19–22, 1926 (Katonah, NY: Brookwood Labor College, 1926), 15.

70. "Jennie Matyas and the ILGWU," interview by University of California Oral History Project; and *Yearbook of the Eighth Annual Summer Session, Pacific Coast School for Workers* (Berkeley: Pacific Coast School for Workers, 1940), 40, 54.

71. Sarah Rozner, "YIVO Questionnaire for Union Members (1955)," box 1, folder 1, Sarah Rozner Collection, Southern California Library; interview with Sarah Rozner by Sherna Gluck, March 27, 1973, California State University Virtual Oral/Aural History Archive; and Sherna Gluck, ed., "What Is It We Want, Brother Levin? Reminiscences of a Nonconforming Shop Girl, 1892–1980," 39–51, mss 024, box 1, folder 2, Sarah Rozner Collection, Southern California Library.

Part II. Imagining Critical Consciousness

1. Tillie Lerner, "Thousand-Dollar Vagrant," *New Republic*, August 29, 1934, 67–69; and Constance Coiner, *Better Red: The Writing and Resistance of Tillie Olsen and Meridel Le Sueur* (New York: Oxford University Press, 1995), 166–67.

2. Tillie Lerner, "The Strike," *Partisan Review* (September–October 1934), 3–9; Coiner, *Better Red*, 167–70.

3. Tillie Olsen, *Silences* (New York: Delacourt Press/Seymour Lawrence, 1978), 10; and Coiner, *Better Red*, 145–73. Olsen completed and published her long-abandoned novel in 1974; see Tillie Olsen, *Yonnondio: From the Thirties* (New York: Delacourt Press, 1974).

4. Raymond Williams, *Problems in Materialism and Culture: Selected Essays* (London: Verso, 1980), 31–49; Nicholas Mirzoeff, *The Right to Look: A Counterhistory of Visuality* (Durham, NC: Duke University Press, 2011), 27–29; Lawrence W. Levine, "The Folklore of Industrial Society: Popular Culture and Its Audiences," *American Historical Review* 97 (1992): 1369–99; Charles Taylor, *Modern Social Imaginaries* (Durham, NC: Duke University Press, 2004); William H. Sewell Jr., *Logics of History: Social Theory and Social Transformation* (Chicago: University of Chicago Press, 2005); and James C. Scott, *Seeing Like a State: How Certain Schemes to Improve the Human Condition Have Failed* (New Haven, CT: Yale University Press, 1998).

5. Roland Marchand, *Creating the Corporate Soul: The Rise of Public Relations and Corporate Imagery in American Big Business* (Berkeley: University of California Press, 1998); Roland Marchand, *Advertising the American Dream: Making Way for Modernity, 1920–1940* (Berkeley: University of California Press, 1985); Steven J. Ross, *Working-Class Hollywood: Silent Film and the Shaping of Class in America* (Princeton, NJ: Princeton University Press, 1998); Elizabeth Faue, *Community of Suffering and Struggle: Women, Men, and the Labor Movement in Minneapolis, 1915–1945* (Chapel Hill: University of North Carolina Press, 1991), chapter 3; Michael Cohen, "'Cartooning Capitalism': Radical Cartooning and the Making of American Popular Radicalism in the Early Twentieth Century," *International Review of Social History* 52 (2007): 35–58; Paul Buhle, "The Iconographics of American Labor," in *From the Knights of Labor to the New World Order: Essays on Labor and Culture* (New York: Garland Publishing, 1997), 161–200; and Lincoln Cushing and Timothy W. Drescher, *Agitate! Educate! Organize! American Labor Posters* (New York: Cornell University Press, 2009). On photography, see Carol Quirke, *Eyes on Labor: News Photography and America's Working Class* (New York: Oxford University Press, 2012); Elizabeth Abel, "Cultural Memory and the Conditions of Visibility: The Circulation of Jim Crow

Photographs," *Signs of the Times: The Visual Politics of Jim Crow* (Berkeley: University of California Press, 2010), chapter 3; Linda Gordon, "Dorothea Lange: The Photographer as Agricultural Sociologist," *Journal of American History* 93 (December 2006), 698–727; and Levine, "Folklore of Industrial Society."

6. J. C. Scott, *Seeing Like a State*; C. Taylor, *Modern Social Imaginaries*.

Chapter 4. Brain Workers in the House of Labor: Life Stories and the Politics of Experience

1. "How I Became a Rebel. A Symposium. Part 1," *Labor Herald*, June 1922, 23–25, and "How I Became a Rebel. A Symposium. Part 2," *Labor Herald*, July 1922, 23–26.

2. "How I Became a Rebel, Part 1," 23–24; "How I Became a Rebel, Part 2," 24.

3. Mary Jo Maynes, *Taking the Hard Road: Life Course in French and German Workers' Autobiographies in the Era of Industrialization* (Chapel Hill: University of North Carolina Press, 1995), 3; Virginia Yans-McLaughlin, "Metaphors of Self in History: Subjectivity, Oral Narrative, and Immigration Studies," *Immigration Reconsidered: History, Sociology, and Politics*, ed. Virginia Yans-McLaughlin (New York: Oxford University Press, 1990), 254–90; and Diane P. Koenker, "Scripting the Revolutionary Worker Autobiography: Archetypes, Models, Inventions, and Markets," *International Review of Social History* 49 (2004): 371–400. See also George Steinmetz, "Reflections on the Role of Social Narrative in Working-Class Formation: Narrative Theory in the Social Sciences," *Social Science History* 16, no. 3 (1992): 489–516. See also Elizabeth Faue, *Writing the Wrongs: Eva Valesh and the Rise of Labor Journalism* (Ithaca, NY: Cornell University Press, 2002); Elliott J. Gorn, *Mother Jones: The Most Dangerous Woman in America* (New York: Hill and Wang, 2002). See also Adelheid Popp, *The Autobiography of a Working Woman* (Chicago: F. G. Browne, 1913); and Ingrun Lafleur, "Adelheid Popp and Working-Class Feminism in Austria," *Frontiers* (Autumn 1975): 86–105.

4. William Z. Foster, *From Bryan to Stalin* (New York: International Publishers, 1937), 13.

5. James Clifford, *The Predicament of Culture: Twentieth-Century Ethnography, Literature, and Art* (Cambridge, MA: Harvard University Press, 1988); Daniel Bender, *American Abyss: Savagery and Civilization in the Age of Industry* (Ithaca, NY: Cornell University Press, 2009); Dorothy Ross, *The Origins of American Social Science* (New York: Cambridge University Press, 1991); Ann Fabian, *The Unvarnished Truth: Personal Narratives in Nineteenth-Century America* (Berkeley: University of California Press, 2000); Jacqueline Anne Hatton, "'True Stories: Working-Class Mythology, American Confessional Culture, and 'True Story Magazine,' 1919–1929'" (PhD diss., Cornell University, 1997); and Martin Jay, *Songs of Experience: Modern American and European Variations on a Universal Theme* (Berkeley: University of California Press, 2005).

6. "How I Became a Rebel, Part 1," 23.

7. Nick Salvatore, *Eugene V. Debs: Citizen and Socialist* (Urbana: University of Illinois Press, 1982), 149–50.

8. Eugene Debs, "How I Became a Socialist," *New York Comrade*, 1902, in *Debs: His Life, Writings, and Speeches*, ed. Bruce Rogers (Girard, KS: Appeal to Reason, 1908), 79–84; and Dave Burns, "The Soul of Socialism: Christianity, Civilization, and Citizenship in the Thought o Eugene Debs," *Labor* 5 (Summer 2008): 83–116.

9. Elizabeth Gurley Flynn, "How I Became a Rebel. A Symposium. Part 2," *Labor Herald*, July 1922, 23–24. On Irish nationalism in labor politics, see James R. Barrett, *The Irish Way: Becoming American in the Multiethnic City* (New York: Penguin Press, 2012), chapter 6.

10. Elizabeth Gurley Flynn, *The Rebel Girl: An Autobiography. My First Life (1906–1926)* (New York: International Publishers, 1955), 42–48; and Helen C. Camp, *Iron in Her Soul: Elizabeth Gurley Flynn and the American Left* (Pullman: Washington State University Press, 1995).

11. Flynn, *Rebel Girl*, 79.

12. Ibid., 112–14.

13. Foster, *From Bryan to Stalin*, 14–15.

14. Ibid., 20–21.

15. William Z. Foster, *Pages from a Worker's Life* (New York: International Publishers, 1939), foreword.

16. Ibid., 42–43; Earl C. Ford and William Z. Foster, *Syndicalism* (1912; Chicago: Charles H. Kerr, 1990); and Foster, *Pages from a Worker's Life*, 280.

17. William Ross Knudsen, Application for U.S. Passport, July 18, 1922 (accessed on ancestry.com, March 28, 2012); Thirteenth Census of the U.S., 1910 (accessed on ancestry.com, March 28, 2012); Fourteenth Census of the U.S., 1920, Cleveland Ward 24 (accessed on ancestry.com, February 2017); Philip S. Foner, *History of the Labor Movement in the United States*, vol. 10: *The TUEL to the End of the Gompers Era* (New York: International Publishers, 1991), 173; and *Statement of Candidates to be Voted for at General Municipal Elections, November 6, 1923* (San Francisco: Board of Election Commissioners, [1923]), 6–7. See also Solon De Leon, *The American Labor Who's Who* (New York, 1925), 127.

18. James Maurer, "How I Became a Rebel," *Labor Herald*, July 1922, 24.

19. James Hudson Maurer, *It Can Be Done. The Autobiography of James Hudson Maurer* (New York: Rand School Press, 1938), 36.

20. Ibid., 63–64, 83–84.

21. Ibid., 86.

22. Ibid., 85–87.

23. Ibid., 118.

24. Ibid., 87.

25. Lincoln Steffens, "How I Became a Rebel," *Labor Herald*, June 1922, 24–25; Upton Sinclair, "How I Became a Rebel," *Labor Herald*, June 1922, 24.

26. Robert Minor, "How I Became a Rebel," *Labor Herald*, July 1922, 25–26. See also De Leon, *American Labor Who's Who*, 162; and Robert Minor obituary in the *New York Times*, November 28, 1952, 25.

27. Minor, "How I Became a Rebel," 25–26.

28. Robert Minor, "I Change My Mind a Little," *Liberator* (October 1920), 6. See also Robert Minor, "Answer to My Critics," *Liberator* (November 1920), 10–11.

29. Joseph North, *Robert Minor, Artist and Crusader: An Informal Biography* (New York: International Publishers, 1956), 122–23.

30. William J. Maxwell, *New Negro, Old Left: African American Writing and Communism between the Wars* (New York: Columbia University Press, 1999), 99–104; and Daniel Aaron, *Writers on the Left* (New York: Avon Books, 1965).

31. Alan M. Wald, *Exiles from a Future Time: The Forging of the Mid-Twentieth Century Literary Left* (Chapel Hill: University of North Carolina Press, 2002), 39–70; Maxwell, *New Negro, Old Left*, 104–112; and Michael Folsom, "The Education of Michael Gold," in *Proletarian Writers of the Thirties*, ed. David Madden (Carbondale: Southern Illinois University Press, 1968), 222–51.

32. Claude McKay, *A Long Way from Home* (New York: Lee Furman, 1937), 3–4; 31–32. For Max Eastman's early assessment, see Claude McKay, *Harlem Shadows* (New York: Harcourt Brace, 1922), ix-xxi.

33. Mike Gold, "Drunk with Sunlight," *New Masses* (July 1929), 17; Claude McKay, *Long Way from Home*, 138–41; and Claude McKay, "Birthright," *Liberator* (August 1922), 15–16.

34. James R. Barrett, *William Z. Foster and the Tragedy of American Radicalism* (Urbana: University of Illinois Press, 1999), 111–17; and Bryan D. Palmer, *James P. Cannon and the Origins of the American Revolutionary Left, 1890–1928* (Urbana: University of Illinois Press, 2007), 42–51.

35. Mike Gold, *Jews without Money* (New York: Liveright, 1930), 304.

36. Folsom, "Education of Michael Gold," 224–26.

37. Michael Denning, *The Cultural Front: The Laboring of American Culture in the Twentieth Century* (New York: Verso, 1997), 200–229.

38. Dale Kramer, *Chicago Renaissance: The Literary Life in the Midwest, 1900–1930* (New York: Appleton, 1966); Max Eastman, "Floyd Dell's Double Life," in *Art and the Life of Action, with Other Essays* (New York: A. A. Knopf, 1934), 134–60; De Leon, *American Labor Who's Who*, 58; Floyd Dell, *Moon-Calf, a Novel* (New York: A. A. Knopf, 1920); Floyd Dell, *The Briary-Bush, a Novel* (New York: A. A. Knopf, 1921); and Floyd Dell, *Homecoming: An Autobiography* (New York: Farrar and Rinehart, 1933).

39. Floyd Dell, "A Psycho-Analytic Confession," *Liberator* (April 1920), 15–19.

40. Michael Gold, "Thoughts of a Great Thinker," *Liberator* (March 1922), 23–25.

41. Michael Gold, "Palm Sunday in the Coal Fields," *Liberator* (May 1922), 5–9.

42. Michael Gold, "The Jesus-Thinkers," *Liberator* (September 1922), 11–12; and Upton Sinclair, "The 'Jesus-Thinkers,'" *Liberator* (October 1922), 15.

43. Floyd Dell, "Apologies and Explanations," *Liberator* (June 1922), 25–26.

44. William Mann Fincke, introduction to *I Am a Woman Worker: A Scrapbook of Autobiographies*, ed. Andria Taylor Hourwich and Gladys L. Palmer (New York: Affili-

ated Schools for Workers, 1936), 1; Karyn L. Hollis, *Liberating Voices: Writing at the Bryn Mawr Summer School for Women Workers* (Carbondale: Southern Illinois University Press, 2004); and Frank Tobias Higbie, *Indispensable Outcasts: Hobo Workers and Community in the American Midwest, 1880–1930* (Urbana: University of Illinois Press, 2003), 89–92.

45. Application of George McCray, School for Workers Papers, Archives Department, University of Wisconsin, Madison.

46. Application of John Alspaugh, School for Workers Papers, Archives Department, University of Wisconsin, Madison. See also Application of George McCray, ibid.

47. Elsie Faxon, "Employment History of E. Faxon. (Eliminating dates and names of employers)," Accepted Applications, School for Workers Papers, Archives Department, University of Wisconsin, Madison.

48. Elsie Faxon, "Application for Scholarship, 1932," in ibid.

49. H. H. Giles, "Reports on Students, 1932," General Correspondence, Faculty Reports; Faxon, "Application for Scholarship, 1932." Le Galliene's intimate relationships with other women were widely known, although she did not identify as a lesbian, according to her biographer. See Helen Sheehy, *Eva Le Galliene: A Biography* (New York: Alfred A. Knopf, 1996).

50. Werner Sollors, *Ethnic Modernism* (Cambridge, MA: Harvard University Press, 2008).

51. Application of Rosella Burke, Brookwood Labor College Records, Archives of Labor and Union Affairs, Walter P. Reuther Library, Wayne State University, Detroit (hereafter BLCR).

52. Rosella Burke, "Autobiography," BLCR.

53. Ibid. On communist anti-eviction and youth organizing in Chicago, see Randi Storch, *Red Chicago: American Communism at Its Grassroots, 1928–1935* (Urbana: University of Illinois Press, 2007), 99–101, 189–95.

54. Abe "Ben" Calderon, "Concerning 'Ben,'" BLCR.

55. Ibid.

56. Edward Falkowski, "The Age of How-We-Got-There," March 4, 1937; and Rose to Ed, September 29, 1945, box 1, folder 1, Edward Falkowski Papers, Tamiment Library.

57. Falkowski, "The Age of How-We-Got-There."

58. Edward Falkowski, "Our Fathers and We (Three Generations)," in *Polish Authors of Today and Yesterday: Bartkiewicz, Falkowski, Gojawiczynska, Morska, Muszal, Olechowski, Orzeszko, Prus, Rey, Reymont, Sienkiewicz, Szymanski [and] Zeromski*, ed. Irena Morska (New York: S. F. Vanni, 1947), 11–27. On the difficulty of publishing radical stories in the late 1940s, see Alexander Saxton, "Introduction," *The Great Midland* (Urbana: University of Illinois Press, 1997), xx–xxiv.

59. Marshall Ganz, "What Is Public Narrative?" Kennedy School, 2007; and Ganz, "Public Narrative, Collective Action, and Power," chapter 18 in *Accountability through Public Opinion: From Inertia to Public Action*, ed. Sina Odugbemi and Taeku Less (Washington, DC: World Bank), 273–89. The website "We Are the 99%" captures this process. Thou-

sands of individuals contributed personal stories in a simple format: brief, handwritten narratives captured along with the author's face by a computer camera. The cumulative effect was to personalize the fallout of the 2008 global financial crisis that had been relatively absent from mainstream media. See posts for the month of September 2011 on the "We Are the 99%" Tumbler site: http://wearethe99percent.tumblr.com/archive/2011/9.

60. Liesl Olson, *Modernism and the Ordinary* (New York: Oxford University Press, 2009).

61. Carlos Bulosan, "My Education," *Amerasia* 6, no. 1 (1979): 113–19.

62. Richard Wright, *Black Boy (American Hunger)): A Record of Childhood and Youth* (1944; New York: Harper Perennial, 2006), 39.

63. Ralph Chaplin, *Wobbly: The Rough-and-Tumble Story of an American Radical* (Chicago: University of Chicago Press, 1948), 3.

64. "Jennie Matyas and the I.L.G.W.U.," 2, Regional Oral History Office, Bancroft Library, University of California, Berkeley, 1955.

65. As the compilers of the *American Labor Who's Who* noted, "Many stalwart workers who would face any hardship or danger for the movement have shrunk from setting forth in print their eventful careers. Some organizations have an established policy against personal publicity. Other individuals, who recognized the value of the publication, were held back by fear of being victimized if they attracted attention." De Leon, *American Labor Who's Who*, iii.

Chapter 5. Icons of Ignorance and Enlightenment: The Visual Culture of Critical Consciousness

1. Karel Čapek, *R.U.R. (Rossum's Universal Robots). A Fantastic Melodrama*, trans. Paul Selver (New York: Doubleday, Page, 1923), 46, 91; and American Federation of Teachers, *Adult Education vs. Workers' Education: Fourth Annual Conference of Teachers in Workers' Education at Brookwood, February 18–20, 1927* (Katonah, NY: Brookwood Labor College, 1927), 55. I preserve Čapek's capitalization of the term "Robot" when referring specifically to the play, and use lowercase for the more general term.

2. A. J. Muste, "Education and the Unorganized," *Labor Age* 17 (April 1928): 9.

3. Joshua Brown, *Beyond the Lines: Pictorial Reporting, Everyday Life, and the Crisis of Gilded-Age America* (Berkeley: University of California Press, 2002), 68–70; and Elizabeth Faue, *Community of Suffering and Struggle: Women, Men, and the Labor Movement in Minneapolis, 1915–1945* (Chapel Hill: University of North Carolina Press, 1991), chapter 3. See also Michael Cohen, "'Cartooning Capitalism': Radical Cartooning and the Making of American Popular Radicalism in the Early Twentieth Century," *International Review of Social History* 52, no. 15 (2007): 35–58; Barbara Melosh, *Engendering Culture: Manhood and Womanhood in New Deal Public Art and Theater* (Washington, DC: Smithsonian Institution Press, 1991), 1–10; John Ott, "Graphic Consciousness: The Visual Cultures of Integrated Industrial Unions at Midcentury," *American Quarterly* 66 (December 2014): 883–917; and Eric Hobsbawm, "Man and Woman in Socialist Iconography," *History Workshop Journal* 6(September 1978): 121–38.

4. See, for instance, "Mr. Block: He Fails to Interest Mrs. Block in Democracy" and "Mr. Block: He Has Some Uplifting Done," in Ernest Riebe, *Mr. Block: Twenty-Four IWW Cartoons* (Chicago: Charles H. Kerr Publishing, 1984).

5. Ernest Riebe, *Mr. Block and the Profiteers* (Chicago: All-American Publishing, 1919), 45.

6. Ibid., 83.

7. Edward Frank, "Čapek's R.U.R.: America Turns to Czechoslovak Drama," *Czechoslovak Review* 6 (November 1922): 297.

8. William J. Perlman, "To the Dramatic Editor," *New York Times*, February 25, 1923, X2. Responding specifically to John Corbin, "The Critic and His Orient," *New York Times*, December 24, 1922, 75, Perlman wrote: "The proletarian swept into power on the crest of the revolutionary wave has rid himself of the intellectual aristocracy and now finds himself starving because he has not enough intelligence to reproduce the tools and implements by which he must live."

9. Roland Holt, "Plays Tough and Tender," *The Forum* (December 1922): 974.

10. Robert Allerton Parker, "Drama: Satire from Czecho-Slovakia," *The Independent* November 25, 1922, 320.

11. Ibid.

12. John Corbin, "The Revolt against Civilization," *New York Times*, October 15, 1922, 99.

13. Horace M. Kallen, *Education, the Machine, and the Worker* (New York: New Republic, 1925), 89. For an example of workers' "spells," see "The Effects of Employment on One's Health, in Hourwich and Palmer, *I Am a Woman Worker*, 54–55.

14. Hyacinthe Dubreuil, *Robots or Men? A French Workman's Experience in American Industry* (New York: Harper and Brothers, 1930), 182–84.

15. Kallen, *Education*, 64. See also Anson Rabinbach, *The Human Motor: Energy, Fatigue, and the Origins of Modernity* (Berkeley: University of California Press, 1992); and David Hounshell, *From the American System to Mass Production, 1800–1932 : The Development of Manufacturing Technology in the United States* (Baltimore: Johns Hopkins University Press, 1984).

16. Kallen, *Education*, 89.

17. Ibid., 67.

18. Ibid., 63.

19. "R.U.R.: Story of the Play," in Karel Čapek, *R.U.R. (Rossum's Universal Robots): A Fantastic Melodrama in Three Acts and an Epilogue* (English version by Paul Selver and Nigel Playfair) (New York: Doubleday, Page, 1923). Translating the meaning of "robot" was a common element of reviews, suggesting various emphases: worker, drudge, labor, slave, and so on.

20. Playbill for "R.U.R. (Rossum's Universal Robots)," Lee Simonson Papers, State Historical Society of Wisconsin.

21. Amy Sue Bix, *Inventing Ourselves Out of Jobs? America's Debate over Technological Unemployment, 1929–1981* (Baltimore: Johns Hopkins University Press, 2001), 9.

22. "A Typical Meeting of the Shop Committee, *Labor Age*, October 1926, 17; and "An Industry Epoch," *Labor Age*, February 1927, 1. A 1936 article about steel industry company unions becoming more active was titled "Steel Robots That Came Alive"; see *Nation*, February 5, 1936, 160–61.

23. *Labor Age*, November 1927, 11.

24. "We Interview Mr. Televox, Mechanical Man," *Journal of Electrical Workers and Operators* 28 (January 1929), 6. See also Waldemar Kaempffert, "Science Produces the 'Electrical Man,'" *New York Times*, October 23, 1927, 21.

25. Stephen P. Rice, *Minding the Machine: Languages of Class in Early Industrial America* (Berkeley: University of California Press, 2004), 29–30; and David Roediger, *Wages of Whiteness: Race and the Making of the American Working Class* (New York: Verso, 1991), 44–47.

26. "Slaves" (General Electric advertisement), *Journal of Electrical Workers and Operators* 25 (December 1926), 635. William F. Ogburn, *You and Machines* (Chicago: University of Chicago Press, 1934), also compared slaves, robots, and machinery.

27. "Topics of the Times: Not Čapek's Robot," *New York Times*, July 18, 1933, 16.

28. Carroll W. Pursell, *The Machine in America: A Social History of Technology* (1995; Baltimore: Johns Hopkins University Press, 2007), 231. See also the Westinghouse promotional film *The Middleton Family at the New York World's Fair*, (1939), *Internet Archive*, http://www.archive.org/details/middleton_family_worlds_fair_1939.

29. "'Fiddling' While Rome Burns" (advertisement), *Literary Digest* 108 (January 24, 1931), 37; and "The Pied Piper Today" (advertisement), *Literary Digest* 108 (February 21, 1931), 41.

30. The idea that modernity was disrupting normal sexual reproduction was commonplace in European and North American culture during the early twentieth century, and Čapek's biographers suggest the theme was related to his own sexual frustrations. Bohuslava R. Bradbrook, *Karel Čapek: In Pursuit of Truth, Tolerance, and Trust* (Brighton, Eng.: Sussex Academic Press, 1998), 45; and William E. Harkins, *Karel Čapek* (New York: Columbia University Press, 1962), 90–92.

31. Victor Olander, "Know Thyself," *American Flint* (September 1927): 7–12; and Victor Olander, "The Machine Problem," *Cigar Maker's Official Journal* 21, no. 9 (1927): 24–31. Olander was the secretary-treasurer of the International Seamen's Union and the Illinois Federation of Labor.

32. Olander, "Machine Problem," 29.

33. For similar interpretations, see Leo Hartmann, "Review of R.U.R.," *American Labor Monthly* 1(January 1923), 88; and Stuart Chase, *Men and Machines* (New York: Macmillan, 1929), 167–68.

34. Daniel Bender, *American Abyss: Savagery and Civilization in the Age of Industry* (Ithaca, NY: Cornell University Press, 2009); and Mark Pittenger, *American Socialists and Evolutionary Thought, 1870–1920* (Madison: University of Wisconsin Press, 1993).

35. "Announcement," *Industrial Pioneer* (February 1921), 2.

36. Franklin Rosemont, "A Short Treatise on Wobbly Cartoons," in Joyce L. Kornbluh, ed., *Rebel Voices: An IWW Anthology* (Chicago: Charles H. Kerr Publishing, 1988).

37. Ted Carroll, "The Modern Gulliver," *Messenger*, October 1926, 294.

38. *Messenger*, January 1926, 11, 14.

39. The image was drawn by Leeland Stanford Chumley, the son of a civil engineer, who claimed to have started working at age nine and then worked as "migratory hotel worker" during his twenties. Like Ralph Chaplin, Chumley attended the Art Institute of Chicago and became an IWW artist and editor. DeLeon, *American Labor Who's Who*, 41–42.

40. "You and Your Union," ILGWU 1935; and Nan Enstad, *Ladies of Labor, Girls of Adventure: Working Women, Popular Culture, and Labor Politics at the Turn of the Twentieth Century* (New York: Columbia University Press, 1999).

41. *Industrial Pioneer*, April 1926.

42. *Industrial Pioneer*, March 1926.

43. *Industrial Pioneer*, August 1926.

44. Logo of the University of Wisconsin School for Workers; IWW pamphlet.

45. Merton E. Hill, *The Development of an Americanization Program* (Ontario, CA: Board of Trustees of the Chaffey Union High School and the Chaffey Junior College, 1928), 11; and Alfred Fitzpatrick, *Handbook for New Canadians* (Toronto: Ryerson Press, 1919), 56.

46. "Corner of the Reading Room, Local 62," *Growing Up: 21 Years of Education with the ILGWU* (New York: ILGWU Educational Department, 1938).

47. See, for instance, Donna Haraway, "A Cyborg Manifesto: Science, Technology, and Socialist-Feminism in the Late Twentieth Century," in *Simians, Cyborgs, and Women: The Reinvention of Nature* (New York: Routledge, 1991), 149–81.

Conclusion: Self-Education in the Shadow of the Cold War

1. Transcript, CBS News Special, "The Savage Heart—A Conversation with Eric Hoffer," January 28, 1969, mss 830, box 7, folder 26, Wolff Perry Papers, Wisconsin Historical Society.

2. Stan Weir, "Eric Hoffer: Far Right True Believer," in *Singlejack Solidarity*, (Minneapolis: University of Minnesota Press, 2004), 179. Although Hoffer was an ardent anticommunist, he spoke admiringly of the ILWU and its longtime leader Harry Bridges. See Tom Bethell, *Eric Hoffer: The Longshoreman Philosopher* (Stanford, CA: Hoover Institution Press, 2012), 10.

3. Bethell, *Eric Hoffer*, 10. See also Edmund Fuller, "Eric Hoffer's Essays Provoke and Stimulate," *New York Times*, February 17, 1967, 16. Hoffer claimed to have minimal formal schooling, but Bethell concludes that Hoffer fabricated the story of his early life.

4. Merle Curti, "Intellectuals and Other People," *American Historical Review* 60, no. 2 (1955): 260.

5. Ibid., 259–60.

6. Clark Kerr, *The Uses of the University* (Cambridge, MA: Harvard University Press, 2001), 78; and Mary Soo and Cathryn Carson, "Managing the Research University: Clark Kerr and the University of California," *Minerva: A Review of Science, Learning, and Policy* 42 (July 2004): 215–36.

7. Ronald Schatz, "A Portrait of the Founders of the Industrial Relations Research Association," *Labor Law Journal* 49 (September 1998).

8. Myles Horton and Paulo Freire, *We Make the Road by Walking: Conversations on Education and Social Change*, ed. Brenda Bell, John Gaventa, and John Peters (Philadelphia: Temple University Press, 1990); and Charles M. Payne, *I've Got the Light of Freedom: The Organizing Tradition and the Mississippi Freedom Struggle* (Berkeley: University of California Press, 2007).

9. Russell Rickford, *We Are an African People: Independent Black Education, Black Power, and the Radical Imagination* (New York: Oxford University Press, 2016), 3; Julie L. Davis, *Survival Schools: The American Indian Movement and Community Education in the Twin Cities* (Minneapolis: University of Minnesota Press, 2013); Mario T. Garcia, *Memories of Chicano History: The Life and Narrative of Bert Corona* (Berkeley: University of California Press, 1994); and Emily K. Hobson, *Lavender and Red: Liberation and Solidarity in the Gay and Lesbian Left* (Oakland: University of California Press, 2016).

10. Interview of Robert Singleton by Elston Carr, UCLA Oral History Program, 1999; and Martha Biondi, *The Black Revolution on Campus* (Berkeley: University of California Press, 2012), 190.

11. Jack Bass, *Widening the Mainstream of American Culture: A Ford Foundation Report on Ethnic Studies* (New York: Ford Foundation, 1978), 11–13, 34; and Noliwe M. Rooks, *White Money/Black Power: The Surprising History of African American Studies and the Crisis of Race in Higher Education* (Boston: Beacon Press, 2006).

12. Bass, *Widening the Mainstream*, 22.

13. Lane Windham, *Knocking on Labor's Door: Union Organizing in the 1970s and the Roots of a New Economic Divide* (Chapel Hill: University of North Carolina Press, 2017), see especially chapter 7.

14. Emily E. LB. Twarog, Jennifer Sherer, Brigid O'Farrell, and Cheryl Coney, "Labor Education and Leadership Development for Union Women: Assessing the Past, Building the Future," *Labor Studies Journal* 41 (2016): 14–15.

15. Karen Brodkin, *Making Democracy Matter: Identity and Activism in Los Angeles* (New Brunswick, NJ: Rutgers University Press, 2007); Ruth Milkman, *L.A. Story: Immigrant Workers and the Future of the Labor Movement* (New York: Russell Sage Foundation, 2006); and Susan Breitzer, "The Difference a Union Makes: Graduate Employee Activists' Engaged Scholarship and Their Working Lives," in *Civic Labors: Scholar Activism and Working-Class Studies*, ed. Dennis Deslipipe, Eric Fure-Slocum, and John W. McKerley (Urbana: University of Illinois Press, 2016).

16. Helena Worthen, "The Status of Labor Education in Higher Education in the US," report commissioned by the executive board of the United Association for Labor

Education, Fall 2015, http://uale.org/resources-list/publications/350-the-status-of-labor-education-in-higher-education-in-the-us.

17. Matthew Crawford, *Shop Class as Soulcraft : An Inquiry into the Value of Work* (New York: Penguin Press, 2009).

18. Arne Duncan, "Digital Badges for Learning," remarks by Secretary Duncan at 4th Annual Launch of the MacArthur Foundation Digital Media and Lifelong Learning Competition September 15, 2011, U.S. Department of Education, http://www.ed.gov/news/speeches/digital-badges-learning.

19. See, among others, Christopher Newfield, *The Great Mistake: How We Wrecked Public Universities and How We Can Fix Them* (Baltimore: Johns Hopkins University Press, 2016).

20. Vivek Wadhwa, "Billionaire's Failed Education Experiment Proves There's No Shortcut to Success," *Forbes* (September 11, 2013), http://www.forbes.com/sites/singularity/2013/09/11/peter-thiel-promised-flying-cars-instead-we-got-caffeine-spray; and Peter Thiel, "The Education of a Libertarian," *Cato Unbound*, April 13, 2009, https://www.cato-unbound.org/2009/04/13/peter-thiel/education-libertarian.

21. Michael Folsom, "The Education of Michael Gold," in *Proletarian Writers of the Thirties*, ed. David Madden (Carbondale: Southern Illinois University Press, 1968), 224; Burke, "Autobiography," Brookwood Labor College Papers, Walter P. Reuther Library, Archives of Labor and Urban Affairs, Wayne State University, Detroit; and Ed Falkowski, "Transit, Book 1," March 16, 1928, box 1, folder 1, Edward Falkowski Papers, Tamiment Library, New York University.

22. Milkman, *L.A. Story*, 4–5; Janice Fine, *Worker Centers: Organizing Communities at the Edge of the Dream* (Ithaca, NY: Cornell University Press, 2006); Jane McAlevey, *No Shortcuts: Organizing for Power in the New Gilded Age* (New York: Oxford University Press, 2016); "The Movement for Black Lives," https://policy.m4bl.org; and Ruth Milkman, "Millennial Movements: Occupy Wall Street and the Dreamers," *Dissent* 61 (Summer 2014): 55–59.

Bibliography

Archival Sources

CALIFORNIA

Bancroft Library, University of California, Berkeley
- Office of the President Records, CU-5, Series 2
- Records of the University Extension, CU-18
- Regional Oral History Office

Labor Archives and Research Center, San Francisco State University
- California Labor School Collection

Occidental College, Special Collections Department, Occidental College Library, Los Angeles
- Pacific Coast Labor School Collection
- Remsen Bird Papers

Southern California Library, Los Angeles
- 20th Century Organization Files
- Sarah Rozner Collection

UCLA Library Special Collections, Charles E. Young Research Library, Los Angeles
- Collection of Socialist and Labor Movement Pamphlets and Books, 1886–1962
- Institute of Industrial Relations Records
- John Randolph Haynes Papers
- University Extension. Course files (University Archives Record Series 56) and Administrative files (University Archives Record Series 284)

ILLINOIS

Newberry Library, Chicago
- Charles H. Kerr Company Records
- Dill Pickle Club Records

Floyd Dell Papers
Franklin and Penelope Rosemont Collection of IWW Publications and Ephemera
Graham Taylor Papers
Jack Conroy Papers
Newberry Library Archives
Pullman Company Records
Slim Brundage Papers
Theodore Kornweibel Research Papers
University of Chicago Library, Special Collections
Chicago Foreign Language Press Survey
Ernest W. Burgess Papers
Kermit Eby Papers
Chicago History Museum
Chicago Commons Papers
University of Illinois at Chicago Library, Special Collections
Adult Education Council of Greater Chicago
Ben Reitman Papers
Victor Olander Papers
University of Illinois, Urbana–Champaign Library, Special Collections
Arthur C. Willard Papers
Horace M. Gray Papers

MICHIGAN

Walter P. Reuther Library, Archives of Labor and Urban Affairs, Wayne State University, Detroit
Albert K. Williams Papers
Brookwood Labor College Records
Edward Falkowski Papers
Industrial Workers of the World Records
Katherine Pollak Ellickson Papers
United Automobile Workers, Education Department Records
University of Michigan Library (Special Collections Research Center), Ann Arbor
California Labor School Records
University of Michigan, Bentley Historical Library, Ann Arbor
Charles Stuart Kennedy Papers
University of Michigan Workers Education Service Records

NEW YORK

Tamiment Library/Robert F. Wagner Labor Archives, New York University
Edward Falkowski Papers, TAM 120

WASHINGTON, DC

American Catholic History Research Center, Catholic University of America
John Brophy Papers

WISCONSIN

State Historical Society of Wisconsin, Madison
American Labor Education Service Records
David J. Saposs Papers
Don D. Lescohier Papers
Lee Simonson Papers
Svend Godredsen Papers
Walter Uphoff Papers
Wisconsin Labor Oral History Project
University of Wisconsin–Madison Libraries, Archives Department
School for Workers Records, 1924–1969
Admission Records

Newspapers and Magazines

American Federationist
Chicago Defender
Chicago Reader
Chicago Tribune
Industrial Pioneer
International Socialist Review
Labor Age
Labor Herald
Liberator
Los Angeles Times
Marxian Labor College Bulletin
Masses, The
New Masses
New York Times
One Big Union Monthly
Progressive Woman

Articles, Books, and Dissertations

Aaron, Daniel. *Writers on the Left*. New York: Avon Books, 1965.
Abel, Elizabeth. *Signs of the Times: The Visual Politics of Jim Crow*. Berkeley: University of California Press, 2010.

Altenbaugh, Richard J. *Education for Class Struggle: The American Labor Colleges of the 1920s and 1930s*. Philadelphia: Temple University Press, 1990.

Anderson, Benedict. *Imagined Communities: Reflections on the Origin and Spread of Nationalism*. London: Verso, 1991.

Anderson, Mary. *Woman at Work: The Autobiography of Mary Anderson as told to Mary N. Winslow*. Minneapolis: University of Minnesota Press 1951.

Anderson, Nels. *The Hobo: The Sociology of the Homeless Man*. Chicago: University of Chicago Press, 1961. First published in 1923.

Aronowitz, Stanley. "Unions as Counter-Public Spheres." In *Masses, Classes, and the Public Sphere*, edited by Mike Hill and Warren Montag. London: Verso, 2000.

Augustyn, Frederick J. "Together and Apart: Lithuanian and Polish Immigrant Adult Literacy Programs in Chicago, 1890–1930." *Polish American Studies* 57, no. 2 (2000): 31–44.

Barrett, James R. "Americanization from the Bottom Up: Immigration and the Remaking of the Working Class in the United States, 1880–1930." *Journal of American History* 79, no. 3 (1992): 996–1020.

———. *The Irish Way: Becoming American in the Multiethnic City*. New York: Penguin Press, 2012.

———. *William Z. Foster and the Tragedy of American Radicalism*. Urbana: University of Illinois Press, 1999.

Bass, Jack. *Widening the Mainstream of American Culture: A Ford Foundation Report on Ethnic Studies*. New York: Ford Foundation, 1978.

Beam, Alex. *A Great Idea at the Time: The Rise, Fall, and Curious Afterlife of the Great Books*. New York: Public Affairs, 2008.

Beck, Frank Orman. *Hobohemia: Emma Goldman, Lucy Parsons, Ben Reitman, and Other Agitators and Outsiders in 1920s/30s Chicago*. Chicago: Charles H. Kerr, 2000.

Bekken, Jon. "The Chicago Newspaper Scene: An Ecological Perspective." *Journalism and Mass Communication Quarterly* 74, no. 3 (1997): 490–500.

———. "Negotiating Class and Ethnicity: The Polish-Language Press in Chicago." *Polish American Studies* 57, no. 2 (2000): 5–29.

Bender, Daniel. *American Abyss: Savagery and Civilization in the Age of Industry*. Ithaca, NY: Cornell University Press, 2009.

Benton-Cohen, Katherine. *Borderline Americans: Racial Division and Labor War in the Arizona Borderlands*. Cambridge, MA: Harvard University Press, 2009.

Bethell, Tom. *Eric Hoffer: The Longshoreman Philosopher*. Stanford, CA: Hoover Institution Press, 2012.

Biondi, Martha. *The Black Revolution on Campus*. Berkeley: University of California Press, 2012.

Bisno, Abraham. *Abraham Bisno, Union Pioneer*. Madison: University of Wisconsin Press, 1967.

Bix, Amy Sue. *Inventing Ourselves Out of Jobs? America's Debate over Technological Unemployment, 1929–1981*. Baltimore: Johns Hopkins University Press, 2001.

Blain, Keisha N. *Set the World on Fire: Black Nationalist Women and the Global Struggle for Freedom*. Philadelphia: University of Pennsylvania Press, 2018.

Bradbrook, Bohuslava R. *Karel Čapek: In Pursuit of Truth, Tolerance, and Trust*. Brighton, Eng.: Sussex Academic Press, 1998.

Breitzer, Susan. "The Difference a Union Makes: Graduate Employee Activists' Engaged Scholarship and Their Working Lives." In *Civic Labors: Scholar Activism and Working-Class Studies*, edited by Dennis Deslipipe, Eric Fure-Slocum, and John W. McKerley. Urbana: University of Illinois Press, 2016.

Brodkin, Karen. *Making Democracy Matter: Identity and Activism in Los Angeles*. New Brunswick, NJ: Rutgers University Press, 2007.

Brophy, John. *How to Run Coal: Suggestions for a Plan of Public Ownership, Public Control, and Democratic Management in the Coal Industry*. Altoona, PA: Nationalization Research Committee, United Mine Workers of America, 1922.

———. *A Miner's Life*. Madison: University of Wisconsin Press, 1964.

Brown, Elspeth H. *The Corporate Eye: Photography and the Rationalization of American Commercial Culture, 1884–1929*. Baltimore: Johns Hopkins University Press, 2005.

Brown, Joshua. *Beyond the Lines: Pictorial Reporting, Everyday Life, and the Crisis of Gilded-Age America*. Berkeley: University of California Press, 2002.

Brundage, Slim, and Franklin Rosemont. *From Bughouse Square to the Beat Generation: Selected Ravings*. Chicago: Charles H. Kerr, 1997.

Bruns, Roger. *The Damndest Radical: The Life and World of Ben Reitman, Chicago's Celebrated Social Reformer, Hobo Kind, and Whorehouse Physician*. Urbana: University of Illinois Press, 1987.

Buhle, Paul. "The Iconographics of American Labor." In *From the Knights of Labor to the New World Order: Essays on Labor and Culture*. New York: Garland Publishing, 1997.

Bulosan, Carlos. "My Education." *Amerasia* 6, no. 1 (1979): 113–19.

Burns, Dave. "The Soul of Socialism: Christianity, Civilization, and Citizenship in the Thought of Eugene Debs." *Labor* 5 (Summer 2008): 83–116.

Bussel, Robert. *Fighting for Total Person Unionism: Harold Gibbons, Ernest Calloway, and Working-Class Citizenship*. Urbana: University of Illinois Press, 2015.

Camp, Helen C. *Iron in Her Soul: Elizabeth Gurley Flynn and the American Left*. Pullman: Washington State University Press, 1995.

Čapek, Karel. *R.U.R. (Rossum's Universal Robots): A Fantastic Melodrama in Three Acts and an Epilogue*. English version by Paul Selver and Nigel Playfair. New York: Doubleday, Page, 1923.

Carter, Heath W. *Union Made: Working People and the Rise of Social Christianity in Chicago*. New York: Oxford University Press, 2015.

Cayton, Horace, and George S. Mitchell. *Black Workers and the New Unions*. Chapel Hill: University of North Carolina Press, 1939.

Chaplin, Ralph. *Wobbly: The Rough-and-Tumble Story of an American Radical*. Chicago: University of Chicago Press, 1948.

Chase, Stuart. *Men and Machines*. New York: Macmillan, 1929.

Chicago Public Library Omnibus Project. *The Chicago Foreign Language Press Survey: A General Description of Its Contents*. Chicago: Work Projects Administration, 1942.

Clifford, James. *The Predicament of Culture: Twentieth-Century Ethnography, Literature, and Art*. Cambridge, MA: Harvard University Press, 1988.

Cobb, William. *Radical Education in the Rural South: Commonwealth College, 1922–1940*. Detroit: Wayne State University Press, 2000.

Cohen, Michael. "'Cartooning Capitalism': Radical Cartooning and the Making of American Popular Radicalism in the Early Twentieth Century." *International Review of Social History* 52, no. 15 (2007): 35–58.

Coiner, Constance. *Better Red: The Writing and Resistance of Tillie Olsen and Meridel Le Sueur*. New York: Oxford University Press, 1995.

Cole, Peter, David Struthers, and Kenyon Zimmer, eds., *Wobblies of the World: A Global History of the IWW*. London: Pluto Press, 2017.

Conroy, Jack. *The Disinherited*. Cambridge, MA: R. Bentley, 1979. First published in 1933.

Cooper, Frederick. *Colonialism in Question: Theory, Knowledge, History*. Berkeley: University of California Press, 2005.

Cooper, Patricia A. *Once a Cigarmaker: Men, Women, and Work Culture in American Cigar Factories, 1900–1919*. Urbana: University of Illinois Press, 1987.

"Corner of the Reading Room, Local 62." *Growing Up: 21 Years of Education with the ILGWU*. New York: ILGWU Educational Department, 1938.

Cottrell, Robert C. *Roger Nash Baldwin and the American Civil Liberties Union*. New York: Columbia University Press, 2000.

Crawford, Matthew. *Shop Class as Soulcraft : An Inquiry into the Value of Work*. New York: Penguin Press, 2009.

Cremin, Lawrence A. *American Education: The Metropolitan Experience, 1876–1980*. New York: Harper and Row, 1988.

Cronin, James E., and Carmen Sirianni, eds. *Work, Community, and Power: The Experience of Labor in Europe and America, 1900–1925*. Philadelphia: Temple University Press, 1983.

Curti, Merle. "Intellectuals and Other People." *American Historical Review* 60, no. 2 (1955): 259–82.

Cushing, Lincoln, and Timothy W. Drescher. *Agitate! Educate! Organize! American Labor Posters*. New York: Cornell University Press, 2009.

Danielson, Leilah. *American Gandhi: A. J. Muste and the History of Radicalism in the Twentieth Century*. Philadelphia: University of Pennsylvania Press, 2014.

Davenport, Tim. "The Formation of the Proletarian Party of America, 1913–1923. Part 1: John Keracher's Proletarian University and the Establishment of the Communist Party of America." Corvallis, OR: 1000 Flowers Publishing, 2011.

Davis, Julie L. *Survival Schools: The American Indian Movement and Community Education in the Twin Cities*. Minneapolis: University of Minnesota Press, 2013.

De Leon, Solon, ed. *The American Labor Press Directory*. New York: Rand School of Social Science, 1925.

———. *The American Labor Who's Who*. New York: Hanford Press, 1925.

De Leon, Solon, and Nathan Fine, eds., *American Labor Press Directory* (New York: Rand School of Social Science, 1925.

Debs, Eugene V. "How I Became a Socialist," *New York Comrade*, 1902. In *Debs: His Life, Writings, and Speeches*, ed. Bruce Rogers, 79–84. Girard, KS: Appeal to Reason, 1908.

Dell, Floyd. *The Briary-Bush, a Novel*. New York: A. A. Knopf, 1921.

———. *Homecoming; an Autobiography*. New York: Farrar and Rinehart, 1933.

———. *Moon-Calf*. New York: Alfred A. Knopf, 1920.

Denning, Michael. *The Cultural Front: The Laboring of American Culture in the Twentieth Century*. New York: Verso, 1997.

———. *Mechanic Accents: Dime Novels and Working-Class Culture in America*. London: Verso, 1987.

Douglass, Frederick. *Narrative of the Life of Frederick Douglass, an American Slave*. London: G. Kershaw and Sons, 1852.

Drury, John. *Chicago in Seven Days*. New York: Robert M. McBride, 1928.

Dubofsky, Melvyn, and Joseph McCartin. *We Shall Be All: A History of the Industrial Workers of the World*. Urbana: University of Illinois Press, 2000.

Dubreuil, Hyacinthe. *Robots or Men? A French Workman's Experience in American Industry*. New York: Harper and Brothers, 1930.

Dunne, William F. *Worker Correspondents: What, Where, When, Why, How? The Little Red Library* 4 Chicago: Daily Worker Publishing, 1925.

Eastman, Max. *Art and the Life of Action, with Other Essays*. Freeport, NY: Books for Libraries Press, 1970. First published New York: A. A. Knopf, 1934.

Ellison, Ralph. "The Little Man at Chehaw Station: The American Artist and His Audience." *American Scholar* 47, no. 1 (1977/1978): 25–48.

Enstad, Nan. *Ladies of Labor, Girls of Adventure: Working Women, Popular Culture, and Labor Politics at the Turn of the Twentieth Century*. New York: Columbia University Press, 1999.

Epstein, Abraham. "The Replies to the Questionnaire on Workers Education in the United States." In *Workers Education in the United States: Proceedings of the National Convention*. New York: Workers' Education Bureau of America, 1921.

Fabian, Ann. "Making a Commodity of Truth: Speculations on the Career of Bernarr Macfadden." *American Literary History* 5, no. 1 (1993): 51–76.

———. *The Unvarnished Truth: Personal Narratives in Nineteenth-Century America*. Berkeley: University of California Press, 2000.

Falkowski, Edward. "Our Fathers and We (Three Generations)." In *Polish Authors of Today and Yesterday: Bartkiewicz, Falkowski, Gojawiczynska, Morska, Muszal, Olechowski, Orzeszko, Prus, Rey, Reymont, Sienkiewicz, Szymanski [and] Zeromski*, edited by Irena Morska, 11–27. New York: S. F. Vanni, 1947.

Farrell, James T. *The Young Manhood of Studs Lonigan*. New York: Vanguard Press, [c. 1934].

Faue, Elizabeth. *Community of Suffering and Struggle: Women, Men, and the Labor Movement in Minneapolis, 1915–1945*. Chapel Hill: University of North Carolina Press, 1991.

———. *Writing the Wrongs: Eva Valesh and the Rise of Labor Journalism*. Ithaca, NY: Cornell University Press, 2002.

Fincke, William Mann. Introduction to *I Am a Woman Worker: A Scrapbook of Autobiographies*. Edited by Andria Taylor Hourwich and Gladys L. Palmer. New York: Affiliated Schools for Workers, 1936.

Fine, Janice. *Worker Centers: Organizing Communities at the Edge of the Dream*. Ithaca, NY: Cornell University Press, 2006.

Fink, Leon. "'Intellectuals' versus 'Workers': Academic Requirements and the Creation of Labor History." *American Historical Review* 96, no. 2 (1991): 395–421.

Fitzpatrick, Alfred. *Handbook for New Canadians*. Toronto: Ryerson Press, 1919.

———. *The University in Overalls: A Plea for Part-time Study*. Toronto: Frontier College Press, 1920.

Flynn, Elizabeth Gurley. *The Rebel Girl: An Autobiography. My First Life (1906–1926)*. New York: International Publishers, 1955.

Flynt, Josiah. *Notes of an Itinerant Policeman*. Boston: L. C. Page, 1900.

Folsom, Michael. "The Education of Michael Gold." In *Proletarian Writers of the Thirties*, edited by David Madden. Carbondale: Southern Illinois University Press, 1968.

Foner, Philip S. *History of the Labor Movement in the United States*. Vol. 10, *The TUEL to the End of the Gompers Era*. New York: International Publishers, 1991.

Fones-Wolf, Elizabeth, and Ken Fones-Wolf. *Struggle for the Soul of the Postwar South: White Evangelical Protestants and Operation Dixie*. Urbana: University of Illinois Press, 2016.

Ford, Earl C., and William Z. Foster. *Syndicalism*. Chicago: Charles H. Kerr Publishing, 1990. First published in 1912.

Foster, William Z. *From Bryan to Stalin*. New York: International Publishers, 1937.

———. *Pages from a Worker's Life*. New York: International Publishers, 1939.

Frank, Edward. "Čapek's R.U.R.: America Turns to Czechoslovak Drama." *Czechoslovak Review* 6 (November 1922): 297.

Franser, Nancy. "Rethinking the Public Sphere." In *Habermas and the Public Sphere*, edited by Craig Calhoun. Cambridge: MIT Press, 1992.

Frederickson, Mary. "Citizens for Democracy: The Industrial Programs of the YWCA." In *Sisterhood and Solidarity: Workers' Education for Women, 1914–1984*, edited by Joyce L. Kornbluh and Mary Frederickson. Philadelphia: Temple University Press, 1984.

Freire, Paolo. *Pedagogy of the Oppressed*. Translated by Myra Bergman Ramos. New York: Herder and Herder, 1970.

Frey, John P. *An American Molder*. Cincinnati: S. Rosenthal, 1910.

Ganz, Marshall. "Public Narrative, Collective Action, and Power." In *Accountability through Public Opinion: From Inertia to Public Action*, ed. Sina Odugbemi and Taeku Less, 273–89. Washington, DC: World Bank.

Garcia, Mario T. *Memories of Chicano History: The Life and Narrative of Bert Corona*. Berkeley: University of California Press, 1994.

Gellman, Erik, and Jarod Roll. *The Gospel of the Working Class: Labor's Southern Prophets in New Deal America*. Urbana: University of Illinois Press, 2011.

Gettleman, Marvin. "'No Varsity Teams': New York's Jefferson School of Social Science, 1943–1956." *Science and Society* 66 (Fall 2002): 336–59.

Gleason, Arthur. *Workers' Education*. New York: Bureau of Industrial Education, 1921.

Glen, John M. *Highlander: No Ordinary School, 1932–1962*. Lexington: University Press of Kentucky, 1988.

Gold, Mike. *Jews without Money*. New York: Liveright, 1930.

Goluboff, Risa Lauren. *Vagrant Nation: Police Power, Constitutional Change, and the Making of the 1960s*. New York: Oxford University Press, 2016.

Gompers, Samuel. *Seventy Years of Life and Labor: An Autobiography*. New York: E. P. Dutton, 1925.

Gordon, Linda. "Dorothea Lange: The Photographer as Agricultural Sociologist." *Journal of American History* 93 (December 2006): 698–727.

Gorn, Elliott J. *Mother Jones: The Most Dangerous Woman in America*. New York: Hill and Wang, 2002.

Graff, Harvey J. *The Legacies of Literacy: Continuities and Contradictions in Western Culture and Society*. Bloomington: Indiana University Press, 1987.

Graham, John. *"Yours for the Revolution": The* Appeal to Reason, *1895–1922*. Lincoln: University of Nebraska Press, 1990.

Gramsci, Antonio. *Selections from the Prison Notebooks of Antonio Gramsci*. Edited and translated by Quintin Hoare and Geoffrey Nowell Smith. New York: International Publishers, 1971.

Gray, William S., and Ruth Munroe. *The Reading Interests and Habits of Adults: A Preliminary Report*. New York: Macmillan, 1929.

Green, James R. "The 'Salesmen-Soldiers' of the 'Appeal' Army: A Profile of Rank-and-File Socialist Agitators." In *Socialism in the Cities*, edited by Bruce M. Stave. Port Washington, NY: Kennikat Press, 1975.

Green, James R. *Taking History to Heart: The Power of the Past in Building Social Movements*. Amherst: University of Massachusetts Press, 2000.

Greene, Julie. *Pure and Simple Politics: The American Federation of Labor and Political Activism, 1881–1917*. New York: Cambridge University Press, 1998.

Gregory, James N. . The *Southern Diaspora: How the Great Migrations of Black and White Southerners Transformed America*. Chapel Hill: University of North Carolina Press, 2005.

Grossman, James R. *Land of Hope: Chicago, Black Southerners, and the Great Migration*. Chicago: University of Chicago Press, 1989.

Guglielmo, Jennifer. *Living the Revolution: Italian Women's Resistance and Radicalism in New York City, 1880–1945*. Chapel Hill: University of North Carolina Press, 2010.

Guglielmo, Thomas A. "Encountering the Color Line in the Everyday: Italians in Interwar Chicago." *Journal of American Ethnic History* 23, no. 4 (2004): 45–77.

Hahn, Steven. *A Nation under Our Feet: Black Political Struggles in the Rural South from Slavery to the Great Migration*. Cambridge, MA: Harvard University Press, 2003.

Hale, Charles A. "Frank Tannenbaum and the Mexican Revolution." *Hispanic American Historical Review* 75, no. 2 (1995): 215–46.

Hamilton, Walton H. "The Educational Policy of 'A Labor College.'" *Journal of Social Forces* 2 (January 1924): 204–208.

Hansome, Marius. *World Workers' Educational Movements: Their Social Significance*. New York: Columbia University Press, 1931.

Hapgood, Hutchins. *The Spirit of Labor*. Introduction and notes by James R. Barrett. Urbana: University of Illinois Press, 2004. First published in 1907.

Haraway, Donna. "A Cyborg Manifesto: Science, Technology, and Socialist-Feminism in the Late Twentieth Century." In *Simians, Cyborgs, and Women: The Reinvention of Nature*. New York: Routledge, 1991.

Harkins, William E. *Karel Čapek*. New York: Columbia University Press, 1962.

Hartmann, Leo. "Review of R.U.R." *American Labor Monthly* 1 (January 1923): 88.

Hatton, Jacqueline Anne. "'True Stories: Working-Class Mythology, American Confessional Culture, and 'True Story Magazine,' 1919–1929.'" PhD diss., Cornell University, 1997.

Haywood, Harry. *Black Bolshevik: Autobiography of an Afro-American Communist*. Chicago: Liberator Press, 1978.

Heap, Chad. *Slumming: Sexual and Racial Encounters in American Nightlife, 1885–1940*. Chicago: University of Chicago Press, 2009.

Hemingway, Andrew. *Artists on the Left: American Artists and the Communist Movement, 1926–1956*. New Haven, CT: Yale University Press, 2002.

Herder, Dale Marvin. "Education for the Masses: The Haldeman-Julius Little Blue Books as Popular Culture during the Nineteen-Twenties." PhD diss., Michigan State University, 1975.

Hewes, Amy. "How to Build on the Workers' Experience." In *The Promotion and Maintenance of Workers' Education. Third Annual Conference of Teachers in Workers' Education at Brookwood, February 19–22, 1926* (Katonah, NY: Brookwood Labor College, 1926).

Higbie, Frank Tobias. *Indispensable Outcasts: Hobo Workers and Community in the American Midwest, 1880–1930*. Urbana: University of Illinois Press, 2003.

———. "Unschooled but Not Uneducated: Print, Public Speaking, and the Networks of Informal Working-Class Education, 1900–1940." In *Education and the Culture of Print in Modern America*, ed. Adam R. Nelson and John L. Rudolph, 103–125. Madison: University of Wisconsin Press, 2010.

———. "Why Do Robots Rebel? The Labor History of a Cultural Icon." *Labor: Studies in Working Class History of the Americas* 10 (Spring 2013): 99–121.

Hill, Merton E. *The Development of an Americanization Program*. Ontario, CA: Board of Trustees of the Chaffey Union High School and the Chaffey Junior College, 1928.

Historical Statistics of the United States, Earliest Times to the Present: Millennial Edition. Edited by Susan B. Carter, Scott Sigmund Gartner, Michael R. Haines, Alan L. Olmstead, Richard Sutch, and Gavin Wright. New York: Cambridge University Press, 2006.

Hobsbawm, Eric. "Man and Woman in Socialist Iconography." *History Workshop Journal* 6 (September 1978): 121–38.

Hobson, Emily K. *Lavender and Red: Liberation and Solidarity in the Gay and Lesbian Left*. Oakland: University of California Press, 2016.

Hodgen, Margaret T. *Workers' Education in England and the United States*. New York: E. P. Dutton, 1925.

Hoerder, Dirk, and Christiane Harzig. *The Immigrant Labor Press in North America, 1840s–1970s: An Annotated Bibliography*. New York: Greenwood Press, 1987.

Holbrook, Stewart H. "What the Loggers Read." *The Bookman* 65 (July 1927): 528–31.

Hollis, Karyn L. *Liberating Voices: Writing at the Bryn Mawr Summer School for Women Workers*. Carbondale: Southern Illinois University Press, 2004.

Horton, Myles, and Paolo Freire. *We Make the Road by Walking: Conversations on Education and Social Change*. Edited by Brenda Bell, John Gaventa, and John Peters. Philadelphia: Temple University Press, 1990.

Hounshell, David. *From the American System to Mass Production, 1800–1932 : The Development of Manufacturing Technology in the United States*. Baltimore: Johns Hopkins University Press, 1984.

Hourwich, Andria T., and Gladys L. Palmer. *I Am a Woman Worker: A Scrapbook of Autobiographies*. New York: Affiliated Schools for Workers, 1936.

Howlett, Charles F. *Brookwood Labor College and the Struggle for Peace and Social Justice in America*. Lewiston, NY: Edwin Mellen Press, 1993.

Hurewitz, Daniel. *Bohemian Los Angeles and the Making of Modern Politics*. Berkeley: University of California Press, 2007.

Illinois Writers' Program. *Public Forums in Chicago*. Chicago: Work Projects Administration, 1940.

Industrial Department, National Board of the YWCA. *The Young Women's Christian Association and Industry*. New York, 1928.

Ives, Irving M. "The New York State School of Industrial and Labor Relations—A New Venture in Education." *Journal of Educational Sociology* 19 (September 1945): 40–42.

Jay, Martin. *Songs of Experience: Modern American and European Variations on a Universal Theme*. Berkeley: University of California Press, 2005.

Johnston, Esther. "Readers of a Foreign Neighborhood." *The Survey* (April 2, 1921), 7–8.

Jones, Alan L. "Gaining Self-Consciousness while Losing the Movement: The American Association for Adult Education, 1926–1941." PhD diss., University of Wisconsin–Madison, 1991.

Kallen, Horace M. *Education, the Machine, and the Worker: An Essay in the Psychology of Education in Industrial Society*. New York: New Republic, 1925.

Katz, Daniel. *All Together Different: Yiddish Socialists, Garment Workers, and the Labor Roots of Multiculturalism*. New York: New York University Press, 2011.

Kelley, Robin D. G. "We Are Not What We Seem: Rethinking Black Working-Class Opposition in the Jim Crow South." *Journal of American History* 80 (June 1993): 75–112.

Kerr, Clark. *The Uses of the University*. Cambridge, MA: Harvard University Press, 2001.

Kett, Joseph F. *The Pursuit of Knowledge under Difficulties: From Self-Improvement to Adult Education in America, 1750–1990*. Stanford, CA: Stanford University Press, 1994.

Koenker, Diane P. "Scripting the Revolutionary Worker Autobiography: Archetypes, Models, Inventions, and Markets." *International Review of Social History* 49 (2004): 371–400.

Kornbluh, Joyce L. *A New Deal for Workers' Education: The Workers' Service Program, 1933–1942*. Urbana: University of Illinois Press, 1987.

Kornbluh, Joyce L., and Mary Frederickson, eds., *Sisterhood and Solidarity: Workers' Education for Women, 1914–1984*. Philadelphia: Temple University Press, 1984.

Kramer, Dale. *Chicago Renaissance: The Literary Life in the Midwest, 1900–1930*. New York: Appleton, 1966.

Lacy, Tim. *The Dream of a Democratic Culture: Mortimer J. Adler and the Great Books Idea*. New York : Palgrave Macmillan, 2013.

Lafleur, Ingrun. "Adelheid Popp and Working-Class Feminism in Austria." *Frontiers* (Autumn 1975): 86–105.

Lait, Jack, and Lee Mortimer. *Chicago: Confidential!* New York: Crown Publishers, 1950.

Leeder, Elaine. *The Gentle General: Rose Pesotta, Anarchist and Labor Organizer*. Albany: SUNY Press, 1993.

Lerner, Tillie. "The Strike." *Partisan Review* (September–October 1934): 3–9.

———. "Thousand-Dollar Vagrant." *New Republic*, August 29, 1934, 67–69.

Lescohier, Don D. "With the I.W.W. in the Wheat Lands." *Harper's Monthly Magazine* 147 (July 1923): 374–75.

Levine, Lawrence W. "The Folklore of Industrial Society: Popular Culture and Its Audiences." *American Historical Review* 97 (1992): 1369–99.

Lindstrom-Best, Varpu. "'Fist Press': A Study of Finnish Canadian Handwritten Newspapers." In *Essays on the Scandinavian–North American Radical Press, 1880s–1930s*, edited by Dirk Hoerder. Bremen: Labor Newspaper Preservation Project, 1984.

Lubienecki, Paul. "Catholic Labor Education and the Association of Catholic Trade Unionists. Instructing Workers to Christianize the Workplace." *Journal of Catholic Education* 18 (March 2015): 99–124.

Luff, Jennifer. *Commonsense Anticommunism: Labor and Civil Liberties between the World Wars*. Chapel Hill: University of North Carolina Press, 2012.

Marchand, Roland. *Advertising the American Dream: Making Way for Modernity, 1920–1940*. Berkeley: University of California Press, 1985.

———. *Creating the Corporate Soul: the Rise of Public Relations and Corporate Imagery in American Big Business*. Berkeley: University of California Press, 1998.

Mathewson, Stanley Bernard. *Restriction of Output among Unorganized Workers*. Carbondale: Southern Illinois University Press, 1969. First published New York: Viking Press, 1931.

Maurer, James Hudson. *It Can Be Done. The Autobiography of James Hudson Maurer*. New York: Rand School Press, 1938.

Maxwell, William J. *New Negro, Old Left: African American Writing and Communism between the Wars*. New York: Columbia University Press, 1999.

Maynes, Mary Jo. *Taking the Hard Road: Life Course in French and German Workers' Autobiographies in the Era of Industrialization*. Chapel Hill: University of North Carolina Press, 1995.

McAdam, Doug, Sidney Tarrow, and Charles Tilly. *Dynamics of Contention*. New York: Cambridge University Press, 2001.

McAlevey, Jane. "The High-Touch Model: Make the Road New York's Participatory Approach to Immigrant Organizing." In *New Labor in New York: Precarious Workers and the Future of the Labor Movement*, edited by Ruth Milkman and Ed Ott, 173–86. Ithaca, NY: Cornell University Press, 2014.

McAlevey, Jane F. *No Shortcuts: Organizing for Power in the New Gilded Age*. New York: Oxford University Press, 2016.

McConnell, Stuart. "E. Haldeman-Julius and the Little Blue Bookworms: The Bridging of Cultural Styles, 1919–1951." *Prospects: An Annual of American Cultural Studies* 11 (1987): 59–79.

McDuffie, Erik S. *Sojourning for Freedom: Black Women, American Communism, and the Making of Black Left Feminism*. Durham, NC: Duke University Press, 2011.

McHenry, Elizabeth. *Forgotten Readers: Recovering the Lost History of African American Literary Societies*. Durham, NC: Duke University Press, 2002.

McKay, Claude. *Harlem Shadows*. New York: Harcourt Brace, 1922.

———. *A Long Way from Home*. New York: Lee Furman, 1937.

Melosh, Barbara. *Engendering Culture: Manhood and Womanhood in New Deal Public Art and Theater*. Washington, DC: Smithsonian Institution Press, 1991.

Meyer, Steven. *Five Dollar Day: Labor Management and Social Control in the Ford Motor Company, 1908–1921*. Albany: SUNY Press, 1981.

Meyerowitz, Joanne J. *Women Adrift: Independent Wage Earners in Chicago, 1880–1930*. Chicago: University of Chicago Press, 1988.

Michels, Tony. *A Fire in Their Hearts: Yiddish Socialists in New York*. Cambridge, MA: Harvard University Press, 2005.

Milkman, Ruth. *L.A. Story: Immigrant Workers and the Future of the Labor Movement*. New York: Russell Sage Foundation, 2006.

———. "Millennial Movements: Occupy Wall Street and the Dreamers." *Dissent* 61(Summer 2014): 55–59.

Mirzoeff, Nicholas. *The Right to Look: A Counterhistory of Visuality*. Durham, NC: Duke University Press, 2011.

Mitchell, Don. *The Right to the City: Social Justice and the Fight for Public Space*. New York: Guilford Press, 2003.

Montgomery, David. *Fall of the House of Labor: The Workplace, the State, and American Labor Activism, 1865–1925*. Cambridge, UK: Cambridge University Press, 1987.

Mordell, Albert, comp. *The World of Haldeman-Julius*. New York: Twayne Publishers, 1960.

Mormino, Gary R. "The Reader and the Worker: 'Los Lectores' and the Culture of Cigarmaking in Cuba and Florida." *International Labor and Working Class History* 54 (1998): 1–18.

Mumford, Kevin. *Interzones: Black/White Sex Districts in Chicago and New York in the Early Twentieth Century*. New York: Columbia University Press, 1997.

Muncy, Robyn. *Creating a Female Dominion in American Reform, 1890–1935*. New York: Oxford University Press, 1991.

Murray, Pauli. *Pauli Murray: The Autobiography of a Black Activist, Feminist, Lawyer, Priest, and Poet*. Knoxville: University of Tennessee Press, 1989.

Neavill, Gordon B. "The Modern Library Series and American Cultural Life." *Journal of Library History* 16 (Spring 1981): 241–52.

Nelson, Steve, James R. Barrett, and Rob Ruck. *Steve Nelson: American Radical*. Pittsburgh: University of Pittsburgh Press, 1981.

Nestor, Agnes. *Woman's Labor Leader. An Autobiography of Agnes Nestor*. Rockford, IL: Bellevue Books Publishing, 1954.

Neufeld, Maurice, ed. "Portrait of the Labor Historian as a Boy and Young Man. Excerpts from the Interviews of Philip Taft by Margot Honig." *Labor History* 19 (Winter 1978): 39–63, 67–70.

Newfield, Christopher. *The Great Mistake: How We Wrecked Public Universities and How We Can Fix Them*. Baltimore: Johns Hopkins University Press, 2016.

North, Joseph. *Robert Minor, Artist and Crusader: An Informal Biography*. New York: International Publishers, 1956.

Ogburn, William F. *You and Machines*. Chicago: University of Chicago Press, 1934.

Olander, Victor. "Know Thyself," *American Flint* (September 1927): 7–12.

———. "The Machine Problem." *Cigar Maker's Official Journal* 21, no. 9 (1927): 24–31.

Ollila, Douglas J. "The Work People's College: Immigrant Education for Adjustment and Solidarity." In *For the Common Good: Finish Immigrants and the Radical Response to Industrial America*, edited by Michael G. Karni and Douglas J. Ollila Jr., 99–122. Superior, WI: Tyomies Society, 1977.

Olsen, Tillie. *Silences*. New York: Delacorte Press/Seymour Lawrence, 1978.

———. *Yonnondio: From the Thirties*. New York: Delacorte Press, 1974.

Olson, Liesl. *Chicago Renaissance: Literature and Art in the Midwest Metropolis*. New Haven, CT: Yale University Press, 2017.

———. *Modernism and the Ordinary*. New York: Oxford University Press, 2009.

Orleck, Annelise. *Common Sense and a Little Fire: Women and Working-Class Politics in the United States, 1900–1965*. Chapel Hill: University of North Carolina Press, 1995.

Ott, John. "Graphic Consciousness: The Visual Cultures of Integrated Industrial Unions at Midcentury." *American Quarterly* 66 (December 2014): 883–917.

Palmer, Bryan D. *James P. Cannon and the Origins of the American Revolutionary Left, 1890–1928*. Urbana: University of Illinois Press, 2007.

Park, Robert. *The Immigrant Press and Its Control*. New York: Harper and Brotl ers, 1922.

Parks, Gordon. *A Choice of Weapons*. St. Paul: Minnesota Historical Society Press, 1986. First published in 1965.

Parsons, Rhey Boyd. "A Study of Adult Reading." MA thesis, University of Chicago, 1923.

Passy, Florence, and Gian-Andrea Monsch. "Do Social Networks Really Matter in Contentious Politics?" *Social Movement Studies* 13, no. 1 (2014): 22–47.

Payne, Charles. *I've Got the Light of Freedom: The Organizing Tradition of the Mississippi Freedom Struggle*. Berkeley: University of California Press, 2007.

Payne, Elizabeth Anne. *Reform, Labor, and Feminism: Margaret Dreier Robins and the Women's Trade Union League*. Urbana: University of Illinois Press, 1988.

Perlman, Selig. *A Theory of the Labor Movement*. New York: Macmillan, 1928.

Perry, Jeffrey B. *Hubert Harrison: The Voice of Harlem Radicalism, 1883–1918*. New York: Columbia University Press, 2009.

Pesotta, Rose. *Bread Upon the Waters*. New York: Dodd, Mead, 1945.

———. *Days of Our Lives*. Boston: Excelsior, 1958.

Peterson, Larry. "The Intellectual World of the IWW: An American Worker's Library in the First Half of the 20th Century." *History Workshop Journal* 22 (1986): 153–72.

Phelan, Craig. *Grand Master Workman: Terence Powderly and the Knights of Labor*. Westport, CT: Greenwood Press, 2000.

———. *William Green: Biography of a Labor Leader*. Albany: SUNY Press, 1989.

Phillips, Kimberley L. *Alabama North: African-American Migrants, Community, and Working-Class Activism in Cleveland, 1915–45*. Urbana: University of Illinois Press, 1999.

Pittenger, Mark. *American Socialists and Evolutionary Thought, 1870–1920*. Madison: University of Wisconsin Press, 1993.

Popp, Adelheid. *The Autobiography of a Working Woman*. Chicago: F. G. Browne, 1913.

Pursell, Carroll W. The *Machine in America: A Social History of Technology*. Baltimore: Johns Hopkins University Press, 2007. First published in 1995.

Putnam, Samuel. "Red Days in Chicago." *American Mercury* 30 (September 1933): 64–71.

Quirke, Carol. *Eyes on Labor: News Photography and America's Working Class*. New York: Oxford University Press, 2012.

Rabban, David M. *Free Speech in Its Forgotten Years*. Cambridge, UK: Cambridge University Press, 1997.

Rabinbach, Anson. *The Human Motor: Energy, Fatigue, and the Origins of Modernity*. Berkeley: University of California Press, 1992.

Ransby, Barbara. *Ella Baker and the Black Freedom Movement: A Radical Democratic Vision*. Chapel Hill: University of North Carolina Press, 2003.

Rasche, William F. *The Reading Interests of Young Workers*. Milwaukee: Milwaukee Vocational School, 1925.

Rasche, William Frank. "The Reading Interests of Young Workers." PhD diss., University of Chicago, 1936.

Reisman, Ben. "Why I Came to America." In *My Future Is in America: Autobiographies of Eastern European Jewish Immigrants*, edited and translated by Jocelyn Cohen and Daniel Soyer. New York: New York University Press, 2006.

Rexroth, Kenneth. *Autobiographical Novel*. Garden City, NY: Doubleday, 1966.

Rice, Stephen P. *Minding the Machine: Languages of Class in Early Industrial America*. Berkeley: University of California Press, 2004.

Rickford, Russell. *We Are an African People: Independent Black Education, Black Power, and the Radical Imagination*. New York: Oxford University Press, 2016.

Riebe, Ernest. *Mr. Block and the Profiteers*. Chicago: All-American Publishing, 1919.

Rigelhaupt, Jess. "'Education for Action': The California Labor School, Radical Unionism, Civil Rights, and Progressive Coalition Building in the San Francisco Bay Area, 1934–1970." PhD diss., University of Michigan, 2005.

Roediger, David. *Wages of Whiteness: Race and the Making of the American Working Class*. New York: Verso, 1991.

Rooks, Noliwe M. *White Money/Black Power: The Surprising History of African American Studies and the Crisis of Race in Higher Education*. Boston: Beacon Press, 2006.

Rose, Ernestine. "Racial Development and Cooperation: A Record of Two Experiments." *Journal of Adult Education* (January 1933): 53–55.

———. "Serving New York's Black City." *Legacy: A Journal of American Women Writers* 31 (2014): 107–12. First published in *Library Journal*, March 15, 1921.

Rose, Jonathan. *The Intellectual Life of the British Working Classes*. New Haven, CT: Yale University Press, 2001.

Rose, Mike. *The Mind at Work: Valuing the Intelligence of the American Worker*. New York: Penguin Books, 2005.

Rosemont, Franklin, ed., *From Bughouse Square to the Beat Generation: Selected Ravings of Slim Brundage*. Chicago: Charles H. Kerr Publishers, 1997.

———. *The Rise and Fall of the Dill Pickle: Jazz-Age Chicago's Wildest and Most Outrageously Creative Hobohemian Nightspot*. Chicago: Charles H. Kerr Publishers, 2004.

———. "A Short Treatise on Wobbly Cartoons." In *Rebel Voices: An IWW Anthology*, edited by Joyce L. Kornbluh. Chicago: Charles H. Kerr Publishing, 1988.

Ross, Dorothy. *The Origins of American Social Science*. New York: Cambridge University Press, 1991.

Ross, Steven J. *Working-Class Hollywood: Silent Film and the Shaping of Class in America*. Princeton, NJ: Princeton University Press, 1998.

Rubin, Joan Shelley. *The Making of Middlebrow Culture*. Chapel Hill: University of North Carolina Press, 1992.

Ruff, Allen. *"We Called Each Other Comrade": Charles H. Kerr and Company, Radical Publishers*. Urbana: University of Illinois Press, 1997.

"The Safety of Free Speech." *Chicago Commons* (November 1896), 8–9.

Salerno, Salvatore. *Red November, Black November: Culture and Community in the Industrial Workers of the World*. Albany: SUNY Press, 1989.

Salvatore, Nick. *Eugene V. Debs: Citizen and Socialist*. Urbana: University of Illinois Press, 1982.

Scanlon, Jennifer. *Inarticulate Longings: The Ladies' Home Journal, Gender, and the Promises of Consumer Culture*. New York: Routledge, 1995.

Schied, Fred M. *Learning in Social Context: Workers and Adult Education in Nineteenth-Century Chicago*. DeKalb: LEPS Press, Northern Illinois University, 1995.

Schneiderman, Rose. *All for One*. New York: Paul S. Erikson, 1967.

Schwarztrauber, Ernest E. *The University of Wisconsin School for Workers: Its First Twenty-Five Years*. Madison: University of Wisconsin School for Workers, 1950.

———. *Workers' Education: A Wisconsin Experiment*. Madison: University of Wisconsin Press, 1942.

Scott, James C. *Seeing Like a State: How Certain Schemes to Improve the Human Condition Have Failed*. New Haven, CT: Yale University Press, 1998.

Scott, Joan W. "The Evidence of Experience." *Critical Inquiry* 17, no. 4 (1991): 773–97.

Sellars, Nigel. *Oil, Wheat, and Wobblies: The Industrial Workers of the World in Oklahoma, 1905–1930*. Norman: University of Oklahoma Press, 1998.

Sennett, Richard, and Jonathan Cobb. *The Hidden Injuries of Class*. New York: Knopf, 1972.

Sewell, William H., Jr. "Refiguring the 'Social' in Social Science: An Interpretivist Manifesto." In *Logics of History: Social Theory and Social Transformation*. Chicago: University of Chicago Press, 2005.

Sheehy, Helen. *Eva Le Gallienne: A Biography*. New York: Alfred A. Knopf, 1996.

Sheffield, Alfred Dwight. *Joining in Public Discussions: A Study of Effective Speechmaking for Members of Labor Unions, Conferences, Forums, and Other Discussion Groups*. New York: George H. Doran, c.1922.

Sinclair, Upton. *The Flivver King: A Story of Ford-America*. Chicago: Charles H. Kerr, 2006. First published in 1937.

Singer, Alan. "John Brophy's 'Miners' Program': Workers' Education in UMWA District 2 during the 1920s." *Labor Studies Journal* 13 (Winter 1988): 50–64.

Skocpol, Theda. *Diminished Democracy: From Membership to Management in American Civic Life*. Norman: University of Oklahoma Press, 2003.

Smith, Erin A. *Hard-Boiled: Working-Class Readers and Pulp Magazines*. Philadelphia: Temple University Press, 2000.

Sollors, Werner. *Ethnic Modernism*. Cambridge, MA: Harvard University Press, 2008.

———, ed. *The Invention of Ethnicity*. New York: Oxford University Press, 1989.

Soltes, Mordecai. *The Yiddish Press: An Americanizing Agency*. New York: Teachers College of Columbia University, 1924.

Soo, Mary, and Cathryn Carson. "Managing the Research University: Clark Kerr and the University of California." *Minerva: A Review of Science, Learning and Policy* 42 (July 2004): 215–36.

Stansell, Christine. *American Moderns: Bohemian New York and the Creation of a New Century*. New York: Henry Holt, 2000.

Starr, Mark, and Edmund Ezra Day. "Re: 'Education in Industrial and Labor Relations.'" *Industrial and Labor Relations Review* 3 (July 1950): 575–80.

Steinmetz, George. "Reflections on the Role of Social Narrative in Working-Class Formation: Narrative Theory in the Social Sciences." *Social Science History* 16, no. 3 (1992): 489–516.

Stilwell, Kristine. "'If You Don't Slip': The Hobo Life, 1911—1916." PhD diss., University of Missouri, 2004.

Stoddard, Lothrop. *Revolt against Civilization: The Menace of the Underman*. New York: Scribner's, 1922.

Stolberg, Benjamin. *Tailor's Progress: The Story of a Famous Union and the Men Who Made It*. Garden City, NY: Doubleday, Doran, 1944.

Stone, Geoffrey R. *Perilous Times: Free Speech in Wartime*. New York: W. W. Norton, 2004.

Storch, Randi. *Red Chicago: American Communism at Its Grassroots, 1928–1935*. Urbana: University of Illinois Press, 2007.

Stromquist, Shelton. *Re-inventing "The People": The Progressive Movement, the Class Problem, and the Origins of Modern Liberalism*. Urbana: University of Illinois Press, 2006.

Studebaker, John. *Choosing Our Way: The Story of a Forum Program Sponsored by the Office of Education and the Results of a Survey of 431 Forums under Various Sponsorships*. Washington, DC: United States Department of the Interior, Office of Education, 1938.

Taylor, Charles. *Modern Social Imaginaries*. Durham, NC: Duke University Press, 2004.

Taylor, Frederick W. *The Principles of Scientific Management*. New York: Harper and Brothers, 1911.

Taylor, Graham. *Pioneering on Social Frontiers*. Chicago: University of Chicago Press, 1930.

Tibbets, Celeste. *Ernestine Rose and the Origins of the Schomburg Center*. New York: Schomburg Center for Research in Black Culture, New York Public Library, 1989.

Twarog, Emily E. LB., Jennifer Sherer, Brigid O'Farrell, and Cherly Coney. "Labor Education and Leadership Development for Union Women: Assessing the Past, Building the Future." *Labor Studies Journal* 41 (2016): 14–15.

U.S. Census Bureau. *Statistical Abstract of the United States*. Washington, DC: GPO, 2003.

Vallas, Steven P., and John P. Beck. "The Transformation of Work Revisited: The Limits of Flexibility in American Manufacturing." *Social Problems* 43 (August 1996): 345–46.

Vaughan, Mary K. *Cultural Politics in Revolution: Teachers, Peasants, and Schools in Mexico, 1930–1940*. Tucson: University of Arizona Press, 1997.

Wald, Alan M. *Exiles from a Future Time: The Forging of the Mid-Twentieth Century Literary Left*. Chapel Hill: University of North Carolina Press, 2002.

Waldinger, Roger. *The Cross-Border Connection: Immigrants, Emigrants, and Their Homelands*. Cambridge, MA: Harvard University Press, 2015.

Wallis, Keene. "A Harvest Stiff Comes Back to Town." *Workers Monthly* (November 1924): 17–18.

Waples, Douglas, and Ralph Tyler. *What People Want to Read About: A Study of Group Interests and a Survey of Problems in Adult Reading*. Chicago: University of Chicago Press, 1931.

"We Interview Mr. Televox, Mechanical Man." *Journal of Electrical Workers and Operators* 28 (January 1929): 6.

Weir, Stan. "Eric Hoffer: Far Right True Believer." In *Singlejack Solidarity*. Minneapolis: University of Minnesota Press, 2004.

Wild, Mark. *Street Meeting: Multiethnic Neighborhoods in Early Twentieth-Century Los Angeles*. Berkeley: University of California Press, 2005.

Williams, Heather A. *Self-Taught: African American Education in Slavery and Freedom*. Chapel Hill: University of North Carolina Press, 2005.

Williams, Raymond. *Problems in Materialism and Culture: Selected Essays*. London: Verso, 1980.

Williams, Whiting. *What's on the Worker's Mind, by One Who Put on Overalls to Find Out*. New York: C. Scribner's Sons, 1920.

Windham, Lane. *Knocking on Labor's Door: Union Organizing in the 1970s and the Roots of a New Economic Divide*. Chapel Hill: University of North Carolina Press, 2017.

Witte, Edwin E. "The University and Labor Education." *Industrial and Labor Relations Review* 1 (October 1947): 3–17.

Wixson, Douglas C. *Worker-Writer in America: Jack Conroy and the Tradition of Midwestern Literary Radicalism, 1898–1990*. Urbana: University of Illinois Press, 1994.

Wong, Kent, and Victor Narro. "Educating Immigrant Workers for Action." *Labor Studies Journal* 32, no. 1 (2007): 113–18.

Woodin, Tom. "Working-Class Education and Social Change in Nineteenth- and Twentieth-Century Britain." *History of Education: Journal of the History of Education Society* 36, nos. 4–5 (2007): 483–96.

Workers Education Bureau of America. *Workers Education in the United States, Report of Proceedings, First National Conference on Workers Education in the United States Held at the New School for Social Research, New York City, April 2–3, 1921*. New York: Workers Education Bureau of America, 1921.

Wright, Richard. *Black Boy (American Hunger): A Record of Childhood and Youth*. New York: Harper Perennial, 2006. First published in 1944.

Yans-McLaughlin, Virginia. "Metaphors of Self in History: Subjectivity, Oral Narrative, and Immigration Studies." In *Immigration Reconsidered: History, Sociology, and Politics*, edited by Virginia Yans-McLaughlin. New York: Oxford University Press, 1990.

Yearbook of the Eighth Annual Summer Session, Pacific Coast School for Workers. Berkeley: Pacific Coast School for Workers, 1940.

Zimmer, Kenyon. *Immigrants against the State: Yiddish and Italian Anarchism in America*. Urbana: University of Illinois Press, 2015.

Zorbaugh, Harvey Warren. *The Gold Coast and the Slum: A Sociological Study of Chicago's Near North Side*. Chicago: University of Chicago Press, 1983. First published in 1929.

Index

Page numbers in *italics* refer to illustrations.

TOBIAS HIGBIE is a professor of history at UCLA. He is the author of *Indispensable Outcasts: Hobo Workers and Community in the American Midwest, 1880–1930.*

THE WORKING CLASS IN AMERICAN HISTORY

Worker City, Company Town: Iron and Cotton-Worker Protest in Troy and Cohoes, New York, 1855–84 *Daniel J. Walkowitz*

Life, Work, and Rebellion in the Coal Fields: The Southern West Virginia Miners, 1880–1922 *David Alan Corbin*

Women and American Socialism, 1870–1920 *Mari Jo Buhle*

Lives of Their Own: Blacks, Italians, and Poles in Pittsburgh, 1900–1960 *John Bodnar, Roger Simon, and Michael P. Weber*

Working-Class America: Essays on Labor, Community, and American Society *Edited by Michael H. Frisch and Daniel J. Walkowitz*

Eugene V. Debs: Citizen and Socialist *Nick Salvatore*

American Labor and Immigration History, 1877–1920s: Recent European Research *Edited by Dirk Hoerder*

Workingmen's Democracy: The Knights of Labor and American Politics *Leon Fink*

The Electrical Workers: A History of Labor at General Electric and Westinghouse, 1923–60 *Ronald W. Schatz*

The Mechanics of Baltimore: Workers and Politics in the Age of Revolution, 1763–1812 *Charles G. Steffen*

The Practice of Solidarity: American Hat Finishers in the Nineteenth Century *David Bensman*

The Labor History Reader *Edited by Daniel J. Leab*

Solidarity and Fragmentation: Working People and Class Consciousness in Detroit, 1875–1900 *Richard Oestreicher*

Counter Cultures: Saleswomen, Managers, and Customers in American Department Stores, 1890–1940 *Susan Porter Benson*

The New England Working Class and the New Labor History *Edited by Herbert G. Gutman and Donald H. Bell*

Labor Leaders in America *Edited by Melvyn Dubofsky and Warren Van Tine*

Barons of Labor: The San Francisco Building Trades and Union Power in the Progressive Era *Michael Kazin*

Gender at Work: The Dynamics of Job Segregation by Sex during World War II *Ruth Milkman*

Once a Cigar Maker: Men, Women, and Work Culture in American Cigar Factories, 1900–1919 *Patricia A. Cooper*

A Generation of Boomers: The Pattern of Railroad Labor Conflict in Nineteenth-Century America *Shelton Stromquist*

Work and Community in the Jungle: Chicago's Packinghouse Workers, 1894–1922 *James R. Barrett*

Workers, Managers, and Welfare Capitalism: The Shoeworkers and Tanners of Endicott Johnson, 1890–1950 *Gerald Zahavi*

Men, Women, and Work: Class, Gender, and Protest in the New England Shoe Industry, 1780–1910 *Mary Blewett*

Workers on the Waterfront: Seamen, Longshoremen, and Unionism in the 1930s *Bruce Nelson*

German Workers in Chicago: A Documentary History of Working-Class Culture from 1850 to World War I *Edited by Hartmut Keil and John B. Jentz*

On the Line: Essays in the History of Auto Work *Edited by Nelson Lichtenstein and Stephen Meyer III*

Labor's Flaming Youth: Telephone Operators and Worker Militancy, 1878–1923 *Stephen H. Norwood*

Another Civil War: Labor, Capital, and the State in the Anthracite Regions of Pennsylvania, 1840–68 *Grace Palladino*

Coal, Class, and Color: Blacks in Southern West Virginia, 1915–32 *Joe William Trotter Jr.*

For Democracy, Workers, and God: Labor Song-Poems and Labor Protest, 1865–95 *Clark D. Halker*

Dishing It Out: Waitresses and Their Unions in the Twentieth Century *Dorothy Sue Cobble*

The Spirit of 1848: German Immigrants, Labor Conflict, and the Coming of the Civil War *Bruce Levine*

Working Women of Collar City: Gender, Class, and Community in Troy, New York, 1864–86 *Carole Turbin*

Southern Labor and Black Civil Rights: Organizing Memphis Workers *Michael K. Honey*

Radicals of the Worst Sort: Laboring Women in Lawrence, Massachusetts, 1860–1912 *Ardis Cameron*

Producers, Proletarians, and Politicians: Workers and Party Politics in Evansville and New Albany, Indiana, 1850–87 *Lawrence M. Lipin*

The New Left and Labor in the 1960s *Peter B. Levy*

The Making of Western Labor Radicalism: Denver's Organized Workers, 1878–1905 *David Brundage*

In Search of the Working Class: Essays in American Labor History and Political Culture *Leon Fink*

Lawyers against Labor: From Individual Rights to Corporate Liberalism *Daniel R. Ernst*

"We Are All Leaders": The Alternative Unionism of the Early 1930s *Edited by Staughton Lynd*

The Female Economy: The Millinery and Dressmaking Trades, 1860–1930 *Wendy Gamber*

"Negro and White, Unite and Fight!": A Social History of Industrial Unionism in Meatpacking, 1930–90 *Roger Horowitz*

Power at Odds: The 1922 National Railroad Shopmen's Strike *Colin J. Davis*

The Common Ground of Womanhood: Class, Gender, and Working Girls' Clubs, 1884–1928 *Priscilla Murolo*

Marching Together: Women of the Brotherhood of Sleeping Car Porters
Melinda Chateauvert

Down on the Killing Floor: Black and White Workers in Chicago's Packinghouses, 1904–54 *Rick Halpern*

Labor and Urban Politics: Class Conflict and the Origins of Modern Liberalism in Chicago, 1864–97 *Richard Schneirov*

All That Glitters: Class, Conflict, and Community in Cripple Creek *Elizabeth Jameson*

Waterfront Workers: New Perspectives on Race and Class *Edited by Calvin Winslow*

Labor Histories: Class, Politics, and the Working-Class Experience
Edited by Eric Arnesen, Julie Greene, and Bruce Laurie

The Pullman Strike and the Crisis of the 1890s: Essays on Labor and Politics
Edited by Richard Schneirov, Shelton Stromquist, and Nick Salvatore

AlabamaNorth: African-American Migrants, Community, and Working-Class Activism in Cleveland, 1914–45 *Kimberley L. Phillips*

Imagining Internationalism in American and British Labor, 1939–49 *Victor Silverman*

William Z. Foster and the Tragedy of American Radicalism *James R. Barrett*

Colliers across the Sea: A Comparative Study of Class Formation in Scotland and the American Midwest, 1830–1924 *John H. M. Laslett*

"Rights, Not Roses": Unions and the Rise of Working-Class Feminism, 1945–80
Dennis A. Deslippe

Testing the New Deal: The General Textile Strike of 1934 in the American South
Janet Irons

Hard Work: The Making of Labor History *Melvyn Dubofsky*

Southern Workers and the Search for Community: Spartanburg County, South Carolina *G. C. Waldrep III*

We Shall Be All: A History of the Industrial Workers of the World (abridged edition) *Melvyn Dubofsky, ed. Joseph A. McCartin*

Race, Class, and Power in the Alabama Coalfields, 1908–21 *Brian Kelly*

Duquesne and the Rise of Steel Unionism *James D. Rose*

Anaconda: Labor, Community, and Culture in Montana's Smelter City *Laurie Mercier*

Bridgeport's Socialist New Deal, 1915–36 *Cecelia Bucki*

Indispensable Outcasts: Hobo Workers and Community in the American Midwest, 1880–1930 *Frank Tobias Higbie*

After the Strike: A Century of Labor Struggle at Pullman *Susan Eleanor Hirsch*

Corruption and Reform in the Teamsters Union *David Witwer*

Waterfront Revolts: New York and London Dockworkers, 1946–61 *Colin J. Davis*

Black Workers' Struggle for Equality in Birmingham *Horace Huntley and David Montgomery*

The Tribe of Black Ulysses: African American Men in the Industrial South
William P. Jones

City of Clerks: Office and Sales Workers in Philadelphia, 1870–1920 *Jerome P. Bjelopera*

Reinventing "The People": The Progressive Movement, the Class Problem, and the Origins of Modern Liberalism *Shelton Stromquist*
Radical Unionism in the Midwest, 1900–1950 *Rosemary Feurer*
Gendering Labor History *Alice Kessler-Harris*
James P. Cannon and the Origins of the American Revolutionary Left, 1890–1928 *Bryan D. Palmer*
Glass Towns: Industry, Labor, and Political Economy in Appalachia, 1890–1930s *Ken Fones-Wolf*
Workers and the Wild: Conservation, Consumerism, and Labor in Oregon, 1910–30 *Lawrence M. Lipin*
Wobblies on the Waterfront: Interracial Unionism in Progressive-Era Philadelphia *Peter Cole*
Red Chicago: American Communism at Its Grassroots, 1928–35 *Randi Storch*
Labor's Cold War: Local Politics in a Global Context *Edited by Shelton Stromquist*
Bessie Abramowitz Hillman and the Making of the Amalgamated Clothing Workers of America *Karen Pastorello*
The Great Strikes of 1877 *Edited by David O. Stowell*
Union-Free America: Workers and Antiunion Culture *Lawrence Richards*
Race against Liberalism: Black Workers and the UAW in Detroit *David M. Lewis-Colman*
Teachers and Reform: Chicago Public Education, 1929–70 *John F. Lyons*
Upheaval in the Quiet Zone: 1199/SEIU and the Politics of Healthcare Unionism *Leon Fink and Brian Greenberg*
Shadow of the Racketeer: Scandal in Organized Labor *David Witwer*
Sweet Tyranny: Migrant Labor, Industrial Agriculture, and Imperial Politics *Kathleen Mapes*
Staley: The Fight for a New American Labor Movement *Steven K. Ashby and C. J. Hawking*
On the Ground: Labor Struggles in the American Airline Industry *Liesl Miller Orenic*
NAFTA and Labor in North America *Norman Caulfield*
Making Capitalism Safe: Work Safety and Health Regulation in America, 1880–1940 *Donald W. Rogers*
Good, Reliable, White Men: Railroad Brotherhoods, 1877–1917 *Paul Michel Taillon*
Spirit of Rebellion: Labor and Religion in the New Cotton South *Jarod Roll*
The Labor Question in America: Economic Democracy in the Gilded Age *Rosanne Currarino*
Banded Together: Economic Democratization in the Brass Valley *Jeremy Brecher*
The Gospel of the Working Class: Labor's Southern Prophets in New Deal America *Erik Gellman and Jarod Roll*
Guest Workers and Resistance to U.S. Corporate Despotism *Immanuel Ness*

Gleanings of Freedom: Free and Slave Labor along the Mason-Dixon Line, 1790–1860 *Max Grivno*

Chicago in the Age of Capital: Class, Politics, and Democracy during the Civil War and Reconstruction *John B. Jentz and Richard Schneirov*

Child Care in Black and White: Working Parents and the History of Orphanages *Jessie B. Ramey*

The Haymarket Conspiracy: Transatlantic Anarchist Networks *Timothy Messer-Kruse*

Detroit's Cold War: The Origins of Postwar Conservatism *Colleen Doody*

A Renegade Union: Interracial Organizing and Labor Radicalism *Lisa Phillips*

Palomino: Clinton Jencks and Mexican-American Unionism in the American Southwest *James J. Lorence*

Latin American Migrations to the U.S. Heartland: Changing Cultural Landscapes in Middle America *Edited by Linda Allegro and Andrew Grant Wood*

Man of Fire: Selected Writings *Ernesto Galarza, ed. Armando Ibarra and Rodolfo D. Torres*

A Contest of Ideas: Capital, Politics, and Labor *Nelson Lichtenstein*

Making the World Safe for Workers: Labor, the Left, and Wilsonian Internationalism *Elizabeth McKillen*

The Rise of the Chicago Police Department: Class and Conflict, 1850–1894 *Sam Mitrani*

Workers in Hard Times: A Long View of Economic Crises *Edited by Leon Fink, Joseph A. McCartin, and Joan Sangster*

Redeeming Time: Protestantism and Chicago's Eight-Hour Movement, 1866–1912 *William A. Mirola*

Struggle for the Soul of the Postwar South: White Evangelical Protestants and Operation Dixie *Elizabeth Fones-Wolf and Ken Fones-Wolf*

Free Labor: The Civil War and the Making of an American Working Class *Mark A. Lause*

Death and Dying in the Working Class, 1865–1920 *Michael K. Rosenow*

Immigrants against the State: Yiddish and Italian Anarchism in America *Kenyon Zimmer*

Fighting for Total Person Unionism: Harold Gibbons, Ernest Calloway, and Working-Class Citizenship *Robert Bussel*

Smokestacks in the Hills: Rural-Industrial Workers in West Virginia *Louis Martin*

Disaster Citizenship: Survivors, Solidarity, and Power in the Progressive Era *Jacob A. C. Remes*

The Pew and the Picket Line: Christianity and the American Working Class *Edited by Christopher D. Cantwell, Heath W. Carter, and Janine Giordano Drake*

Conservative Counterrevolution: Challenging Liberalism in 1950s Milwaukee *Tula A. Connell*

Manhood on the Line: Working-Class Masculinities in the American Heartland *Steve Meyer*

On Gender, Labor, and Inequality *Ruth Milkman*

The Making of Working-Class Religion *Matthew Pehl*
Civic Labors: Scholar Activism and Working-Class Studies *Edited by Dennis Deslippe, Eric Fure-Slocum, and John W. McKerley*
Victor Arnautoff and the Politics of Art *Robert W. Cherny*
Against Labor: How U.S. Employers Organized to Defeat Union Activism *Edited by Rosemary Feurer and Chad Pearson*
Teacher Strike! Public Education and the Making of a New American Political Order *Jon Shelton*
Hillbilly Hellraisers: Federal Power and Populist Defiance in the Ozarks *J. Blake Perkins*
Sewing the Fabric of Statehood: Garment Unions, American Labor, and the Establishment of the State of Israel *Adam Howard*
Labor and Justice across the America *Edited by Leon Fink and Juan Manuel Palacio*
Frontiers of Labor: Comparative Histories of the United States and Australia *Edited by Greg Patmore and Shelton Stromquist*
Women Have Always Worked: A Concise History, Second Edition *Alice Kessler-Harris*
Remembering Lattimer: Labor, Migration, and Race in Pennsylvania Anthracite Country *Paul A. Shackel*
Disruption in Detroit: Autoworkers and the Elusive Postwar Boom *Daniel J. Clark*
To Live Here, You Have to Fight: How Women Led Appalachian Movements for Social Justice *Jessica Wilkerson*
Dockworker Power: Race and Activism in Durban and the San Francisco Bay Area *Peter Cole*
Labor's Mind: A History of Working-Class Intellectual Life *Tobias Higbie*

The University of Illinois Press
is a founding member of the
Association of University Presses.

University of Illinois Press
1325 South Oak Street
Champaign, IL 61820-6903
www.press.uillinois.edu